THE
LEGACY
BUILDER

Five Timeless Principles for 21st Century Leaders

ENDORSEMENTS

When it comes to leadership, there are many books that discuss the "Want To" of leadership—but desire is never enough. This book will give you the much needed "How To" that is necessary to lead others, making *The Legacy Builder* a must-read for anyone involved with 21st-century leadership.

>—Clint Hurdle, Manager of the Pittsburgh Pirates MLB

The Legacy Builder is a story that illustrates the wise insights Rod Olson has gained in his work with elite coaches and leaders. The engaging story will remind you of what's really important and teach you the things you need to know if you desire to leave a powerful legacy.

>—Mark Sanborn, *New York Times* bestselling author of *The Fred Factor* and *You Don't Need a Title to be a Leader*.

This is a fantastic read with a great message for anyone in leadership. *The Legacy Builder* is one of those "buy-two give away one books." If you're looking for wisdom Rod Olson will help you find it in this book.

>—**Andy Andrews**, New York Times bestselling author of *The Noticer* and *The Traveler's Gift*

Rod Olson is one of the greatest communicators I know. He has artfully put his thoughts on these pages that will leave no man unchanged! There is more to life . . . find it here."

> —**David Cook**, Author of the bestselling book *Golf's Sacred Journey* and Executive Producer of the new major motion picture *Seven Days in Utopia* starring Robert Duvall

Why would anyone wait to buy this book? After reading only the first 39 pages, I realized it's not just another book on success . . . it's a blueprint driven by real-life examples and principles that make a difference in the way we live and the things we achieve.

> —**Jerry Moore**, Head Coach and Three-Time National Champion, Appalachian State University, Three-Time FCS & AFCA Coach of the Year

This book is what every coach and leader needs to read. *The Legacy Builder* is now a pre-requisite for every coach in our organization . . . it is a must read.

> —**Rebecca Schloegl**, President, Jeffco Youth Sports Organization

I wholeheartedly recommend this book to those that want their life to be impactful and meaningful. To those who want to make their mark on their family, friends, marketplace and community, this is a must read! The principles of true leadership illustrated in this book provide a great blueprint for leaving a legacy.

—**Augie Mendoza**, Senior Executive, YMCA

Rod's teachings have defined our organization's culture, given clarity to our leadership and positively impacted the performance of our company. The Legacy Builder is required reading for all our manager's and will undoubtedly impact their lives.

—**David B. Storm**, President & CEO, Providence Hospitality Partners

This book will change you. It will take many from mediocrity to excellence . . . whether you are a coach, business leader, or parent, *The Legacy Builder* will take you to the new levels of significance!

—**John C. Bandimere Jr.**, President, Bandimere Speedway

Coach O weaves a great story that's not preachy or pushy but powerful. It's a wakeup call for all of us who may have sidelined our will to be significant in the lives of others because we're too busy trying be successful.

—**Mitch Jelniker**, Anchor, ABC7NEWS Denver

THE
LEGACY
BUILDER

Five Timeless Principles for 21st Century Leaders

ROD OLSON

THE LEGACY BUILDER
Five Timeless Principles for 21st Century Leaders

By Rod L. Olson

Introduction by Clint Hurdle

©2011 Rod Olson

Olson, Rod L., The Legacy Builder,
Five Timeless Principles for 21st Century Leaders

ISBN: 978-0-9853833-0-5

Printed in the United States

To the late Keli McGregor,
a real-life legacy builder, mentor, and friend.

CONTENTS

INTRODUCTION
Clint Hurdle

I've been around coaches and leaders my entire life, and I'm honored to call Rod Olson my colleague, friend, and mentor. He has the heart of a teacher and the soul of a coach. He is completely dedicated to this—and the next—generation of leaders and coaches. When he asked me to take a look at this book, I did so eagerly.

This book speaks to real life challenges, the speed of life, the importance of relationships, and the need for mentors and coaches to pull us to the next level. You will find yourself feeling the power of a servant leader's heart as the pages turn quickly.

When it comes to leadership, there are many books on store shelves that discuss the "Want To" of leadership—but desire is never enough.

This book will give you the much needed "How To" that is necessary to lead others, making *The Legacy Builder* a must-read for anyone involved with 21st-century leadership.

I hope to be a simple man in a complex world while becoming a Legacy Builder in my professional and personal life. Make no mistake: Rod Olson knows what it takes to be a Legacy Builder and now you will have the tools, too.

CHAPTER 1

THE WIZARD OF OZ:
Pay No Attention to That Man Behind the Curtain

Lance Marshall slammed his hand down on his desk. "Is he serious with these numbers?" He scattered the papers in front of him and glared at the pages. "No wonder he didn't have the guts to email them!"

Standing before him, Terri winced, but stood her ground. "If you keep shooting the messenger, she may stop showing up."

Lance's gaze snapped up at her. "This isn't about you! It's about us. All of us. This company. He can't even pretend these represent acceptable growth. Get Bryan in here. Now!"

Terri hesitated and didn't move. "Lance, he's gone for the day."

"So he just dumped these on you and left? Coward."

"He thought it might be better to discuss them tomorrow. After you'd . . . considered them thoroughly."

"You mean, after I cool off."

Terri pursed her lips and remained silent.

"I want him in here, first thing. No excuses."

"Yes, sir." Terri turned to go, then paused. "Lance?"

"What? Another disaster needing to be discussed?"

She took a deep breath. "Perhaps. You did promise your wife you'd be home by seven. Something about Tony's birthday . . ."

He scowled and stared at the clock on the wall. Sleek and avant-garde, its burnished steel frame and abstract numbers reflected the rest of his office décor. Amanda had given it to him for Christmas, in hopes that he wouldn't always be late getting home. It usually failed at that task, as it did today.

Something deep in his gut tightened, hard and painful, as he thought of Amanda's face, clouded with disappointment. Again. And Tony's.

"Go home, Terri. You've got a family, too."

"Yes, sir. See you in the morning."

"I'll be here."

I'm always here.

Lance gathered the sheets of the report and stuck them into his briefcase. He'd read them tonight after everyone had gone to bed. He sent one last email, then shut down the computer. He left, his stride purposeful. He really did need to get home to Amanda and the kids, especially Tony. Sometimes he couldn't believe a dozen years had passed since they'd rushed to the hospital, more than two months before Amanda's due date, totally unprepared for how all their lives were about to change . . .

Lance tripped over a trashcan sitting next to a desk, disrupting his thoughts and his mood. He kicked it angrily. It toppled, flinging the trash over the floor, and hit the closest desk with a solid thud.

Lance mumbled under his breath and started to leave,, then remembered that the cleaning crew only came in two days a week now, a cost-cutting measure. Snarling at himself, he squatted to pick up the litter.

Cost-cutting measures. He felt swamped by them. As a company, they were doing OK, but the pressures from the board to improve the profits dramatically, not just keep a track of steady growth, pulled at him like dogs over a carcass. After all, the profits last year had been truly spectacular. They'd moved into this new space, improved equipment, took on new clients . . .

Lance paused, looking at the cubicles around him, silent here at the end of the day. A far cry from the rented, open warehouse space that had housed the original company he'd started with three friends. That company had launched like a bottle rocket, in part because they'd laughed a lot and worked even more.

His mouth twisted in a half-smile as he thought of those guys, teammates from his high school football team.

They'd been raw, naïve, and enthusiastic. He'd been their quarterback, always the quarterback, calling the plays.

C'mon, guys, just one more hour. We can get this shipment out and sleep in late tomorrow.

Right, Lance, like you ever sleep in. We're starved!

I'll go get take out.

Chinese. Extra eggrolls.

"Why does EVERYONE want something from me?"

And he'd do it. He would bring over the food on the old bicycle, passing out bags as he rode by. They'd finish the order, then run a couple of the Coach's old plays to let go of the day and laugh. The guys were gone now, moving on to new companies of their own.

They'd made a dream fly. Now all he had was the bottom line.

Lance's phone buzzed in his pocket and he took it out. Amanda.

He silenced it. "Why does EVERYONE want something from me!"

* * *

As the garage door slid shut behind his car, Lance let himself in through the kitchen. He braced for a fight, but met only silence. The kitchen and dining room lay buried beneath the remnants of a joyous celebration. Streamers hung from the chandelier over the dining table, and balloons bounced merrily around on the ceiling, lifted by helium and tossed about by the air from the floor vents. The cake sat in front of the only place at the table that didn't have a straight-back chair near it, and the chocolate delight looked as if it had been shredded instead of cut. Tony's name had been smeared, and Lance guessed that Amanda had let him play in the cake, once pieces had been distributed to Connie and Robert.

Where are they?

Lance listened. The house, an open construction laid out with Tony's wheelchair in mind, conducted sound like an echo chamber. After a moment, he heard muted voices, which told him they were on the patio. He left his briefcase on the couch and paused at the door, watching his family have fun without him.

They clustered around a fire pit, roasting marshmallows in the glowing embers of the wood fire. Robert, his lanky frame bulked up from last year's football season, perched on a bench next to his mom. He'd received early admission to Stanford. Lance beamed with pride when he'd heard, then realized what it would cost.

Coach could have gotten him a scholarship. Maybe we should never have left Minnesota.

Connie laughed, jerking Lance to the present again. His only daughter was barely three when Tony was born, so she took having a disabled brother as a natural, as if every family had one. She helped Tony thread the marshmallow onto the straightened hanger, both of them wrestling with the effort. She positioned it in the embers, since Tony couldn't see the fire.

Amanda's hand rested on Robert's shoulder, although she watched Connie and Tony, her eyes caring and cautious.

High school sweethearts. That's how everyone introduced Amanda and Lance. True, and he'd been amazed watching her grow and mature. Working with Tony had kept her lithe and toned, and he was awed by her strength and courage, her intelligence, in raising all her children.

Lance slid open the glass door and put on his best Robert DeNiro imitation. "Toh-NY! Happy, happy birthday, Toh-NY!"

Tony burst into laughter and jerked spastically, sending the hanger and marshmallow soaring.

Connie lunged and caught it, glaring at her father. "Little late for the party, Dad."

Amanda stood, admonishing Connie. "Show some respect, young lady."

"But he missed—"

"He's well aware of what he missed."

Robert watched his marshmallow burst into flames and melt off the hanger, dropping into the smoldering embers.

"Sorry I'm late," Lance said evenly, as he bent and whispered again to Tony. "Happy birthday, Tony."

Tony jumped and grinned, and his hand searched across the soundboard on his wheelchair until he found what he sought, a button that spoke the word, *Yes!* in a mechanical tone.

"Did you have a good time at the party?"

Yes! Yes!

"As a matter of fact, we all did." Connie grabbed Tony's chair and pulled it away from Lance. "Now it's Tony's bedtime. Too bad you couldn't have stopped by earlier."

"Connie." Amanda's tone sounded the warning.

"Don't worry, Mom. I'll get him started. You can finish up whenever you get done here." With that, she turned the chair and headed both of them back into the house.

Lance watched them go for a moment, then turned to Robert, only to find that his older son had disappeared. Puzzled, Lance looked around the yard, but saw no movement among the shadows.

"He does that sometimes." Amanda sighed. "He's gotten very good at just disappearing. Kinda like his father." She turned and started gathering up the bags of marshmallows.

That tight, hard pain in Lance's gut deepened. "Amanda . . ."

"What was it this time? Vendor reports? New client proposals?"

A bitter taste formed in the back of Lance's mouth. "End-of-the-month reviews."

"Oh, and those are always such a surprise! Since they only occur, oh, let's see . . . twelve times a year, they really can't be planned for, can they? Sort of like an annual event like a birthday. Just sneaks up on you, doesn't it?"

"They're important!"

"So is this family!"

Lance exploded. "You have no idea how hard I work for this family!"

Amanda stood her ground. "In fact, I do know how hard you work! I see it every day! You've always worked hard for this family. You've always worked your dream and made our life great. But when did it change, Lance? When did it stop being the dream? When did enough stop being enough for you?"

Lance felt as if he'd been slapped. "What did you say?"

Amanda let out a long deep breath and picked up the remaining hangers; two still had burnt marshmallows dangling from them. "You heard me. And you may not like it, but you need to think long and hard about what happens next. Because while I still love the man I married, the one I live with now is coming apart at the seams."

Then Amanda walked away, too, her words echoing in his head: *When did it stop being the dream? When did enough stop being enough?*

CHAPTER 2

THE DECISION:
Going Back to Move Forward

Lance spent more time twisting around in the sheets than sleeping that night. His mind, captured by Amanda's words and the unending cycle of work, kept buzzing. But, more importantly, Amanda never came to bed.

He missed her, missed feeling her presence beside him. Lance didn't travel much these days, and it had been a long time since they'd last slept apart. Just another sign of how far his life had spun out of orbit.

Finally, he got up around 2 a.m. and found Amanda asleep on the sofa in their office. The tear streaks in her make-up made his chest ache, but she looked so peaceful, he didn't awaken her. Instead, he covered her with a throw and turned out all the lights.

Back in bed, Lance vowed he'd fix this. He might not be able to do anything about work, but *this* he could fix. Any promises he made today, he *would* keep.

He awoke to the smell of bacon and the sound of silence. As he got up, Lance realized he'd missed the kids; they had left for school. He could catch them later. First, he knew he needed to set things right with Amanda.

Standing in the door of the kitchen, Lance paused, watching his wife work her magic with an omelet. Too often, he'd taken for granted how easy she made his life. Not only did she make running the house look effortless, but she oversaw all of Tony's therapy and doctors, as well as running a small business out of their home.

"Have I mentioned how remarkable I think you are?"

Amanda's eyebrows arched as she slid the omelet onto a plate. "Is that the beginning of an apology?"

"As a matter of fact, it is."

She set the plate in front of him. "Please don't."

"But—"

"Not yet." She handed him a fork . . . then slid a manila folder over to him. "Wait until you see this. Do you remember how you always said that you could always talk to Coach, any time and any place. No matter what the problem is, no matter how hard?"

Lance nodded. "I was just thinking about Coach last night."

Amanda nudged the folder. Curious, Lance opened it . . . and stared. "What is this?"

"It's a round-trip ticket to Minneapolis. Then there's a car rental so you can head west out Highway 12. I reserved a room at a new inn just around the corner from the old high school, and I called Coach last night. He's expecting you, said he'd meet with you the minute you got in."

"Amanda . . ."

She held up a finger. "Last night, I kinda told you I wanted you to be the man I married. That's not entirely true, and I'm sorry for yelling it at you. The man I married was loving, kind, dedicated, and full of dreams. The foundation was there, and I think Coach had a lot to do with that."

"But you were also immature, naïve, and lacking wisdom in a lot of ways. You've gained all that and more. I love that about you and wouldn't go back for the world. But I watch you struggling, and it hurts. Hurts in part because I'm not the one who can help you. You have not been happy, or even content, with anything in a long time.

> **"I think you've lost your foundation. I think Coach can help you rebuild it."**

Not with work. Not with us." She paused. "Not with me. I think you've lost your foundation. I think Coach can help you rebuild it. Please try. For us. For yourself."

Lance stared at the ticket, a glimmer of hope starting to flicker in his mind. "Let me think about it."

"Lance . . ."

This time he held up a finger. "I really do have to handle the month-end today, but I'll think about this. I promise."

* * *

Lance felt more relaxed on the drive to his office than he had in a long time. The idea of going to see Coach lingered in his mind, growing in strength, and the fact that Amanda would take the steps to call Coach and make the reservations emphasized how much she still cared for her husband. It relieved one fear that had nagged at him over the past few weeks, as she'd grown more distant.

Lance rolled his shoulders, then reached for the coffee cup on the console. Weariness still consumed him, and he still had the month-end to complete. He tried to put Coach and Amanda out of his mind. Time for him to kick into work mode.

Lance strode into the office, back straight and shoulders set. He nodded a good morning at Terri, then set his briefcase on the desk and booted up the computer. As he waited for the computer, he opened the briefcase and pulled out Bryan's report and the folder with the ticket. He spread his palm over the folder, the idea of the trip truly taking hold in his mind.

Pushing it aside for the moment, he turned to Bryan's report, glancing through it again. It annoyed him just as much today as it had the evening before. Lance flipped through the pages, mumbling, "Weak, weak, weaker." He dropped it as a beep from the computer told him he had mail waiting. He sat, opening the latest, which was from the chairman of his board. As he read through the demands, the veiled threats, his face grew hot and he clinched his fist on the desk.

"Terri!"

She appeared in the doorframe, waiting.

"Get Bryan in here. We have to take care of this now."

She hesitated, her lips pursing as if she fought back what she needed to say. She crossed her arms across her chest.

Lance stared, impatient. "What?"

She took a deep breath. "He called in sick. He sounded horrible."

A growl of rage exploded from Lance as he slammed one fist on the desk. Terri jumped, wincing, and took a step back, glancing over her shoulder as if she were about to bolt.

Lance pointed at her. "Call him. Tell him if he's not in here by noon, don't bother coming back. At all. Ever."

Her eyes widened. "He's your best rep! You can't fire him for being sick!"

He grabbed the papers and flung them around the office. "I can for being incompetent!"

Terri backed away, then disappeared.

"Unbelievable!" Lance turned to his window and placed his palms against the glass, leaning heavily against it. His shoulders tightened, and he closed his eyes, wishing he could push away the pressure that had settled across his neck.

He's your best rep.

Lance let out a long breath, took another in and opened his eyes, looking out across the parking lot. His entire world felt as if it had been jarred from its axis.

You haven't been happy, or even content, with anything for a long time. Amanda's words.

He's your best rep. Terri's words.

Lance turned back to his desk, his gaze falling on the folder. He stared at it a few moments, then bellowed, "Terri!"

She appeared instantly in the door. "Yes, sir?"

> **His entire world felt as if it had been jarred from its axis.**

"Don't call Bryan."

Her face brightened. "I was hoping—"

"Do call all my appointments for the next week and cancel them."

"Sir?"

"I'm going out of town for a few days."

"But the month-end—"

"Can wait."

Terri stared at him, then her eyes narrowed in suspicion. "Are you OK?"

Lance looked at his watch. Amanda would be at a school meeting with Tony, but that was fine. He'd leave her a note.

"No," he said. "But, I will be." He slipped the trip folder back in his briefcase. "There's a note from the chairman in my inbox. Would you please respond that I've been called out of town? Then shut everything down and lock my door."

"You will . . . you will be back?"

He picked up the case. "Yes." He headed for the door, pausing to touch her arm. "Promise."

* * *

Lance packed, fixed a bit of lunch, then wandered about the house, waiting to see if Amanda would return. He stopped in each of the kid's rooms, startled at how much had changed since he'd been in them last. In Connie's room, posters of skinny young pop singers had been replaced by images of stocky rock and country artists. A magazine page featuring a model in a purple formal had the words PURRFECT PROM!! scribbled across the top. Tony still loved Stevie Wonder and Disney movies. Robert apparently admired Peyton Manning, Tim Tebow, and Drew Brees, although a poster of the top ten quarterbacks of all time took center place over his desk.

"Never forget the classics," Lance murmured with a grin.

He finally left Amanda a short note of love and thanks. The drive to the airport ran right by the high school, and Lance stopped at the football field. Stepping up into the bleachers, he sat, watching the team work, listening to the coaches calling out to the players. The sights and sounds felt so familiar Lance wondered if he could still play. The game called to him like nothing else.

Robert exchanged passes with one of the assistant coaches, warming up, backing up a little with each throw. The team had done well this year, and a twinge of regret made Lance shift uneasily. He'd only been to one game. They only had three left in the regular season, but they might go to the playoffs.

"I want this back," Lance whispered. "Show me how."

He has a good arm, he can spin it. The ball traveled sure and true, even as the two increased the distance between them. Regret slipped into a sense of pride.

"I want this back," Lance whispered. "Show me how."

Robert paused for a drink of water. Turning, he spotted his father in the stands and froze. After a moment, he took off his helmet and shaded his eyes against the afternoon sun.

He probably thinks I'm a mirage. Lance raised his arm in greeting. Robert held still a few moments, just staring, until the coach called to him. Then he raised his arm in return, quickly, before turning his focus back to practice.

Lance headed back to the car and sat, overwhelmed by how hollow and empty he felt, at how consumed he was by an unnamed anger at the world. Then he picked up the phone and dialed a number he'd never forgotten, even after twenty-seven years.

"If you're still sure, I'm on my way."

CHAPTER 3

"COACH":
The Legacy Builder

Driving Highway 12 west out of Minneapolis, a route he'd not taken in almost twenty years, Lance felt as if he were rolling back time. When he first left the airport, he searched through the satellite radio stations until he found some classic rock, and with the tunes he slipped farther into the past. As the city fell away, he examined the passing landscape, amazed at how much had changed—yet how much had stayed the same, especially as the route took him into his hometown.

The speed limit dropped to 45, then 30, and he turned off the radio and lowered the windows, despite the brisk air of autumn in Minnesota. It refreshed his spirit.

He found the inn Amanda mentioned quickly, checked in, then put his luggage in the room. He could see the high school from his second story window, so he decided to walk the short distance over. School had let out earlier and kids cluttered the streets, running back and forth, tossing or kicking balls about, their shouts and squeals like music. *Small-town America,* he thought. *Gotta love it.*

Football practice had ended, and he passed a few of the players as they drifted away from the school, their bodies still flushed red from the exertion, sweat plastering their hair to their scalps. A few walked with girls, who seemed to have a love-hate relationship with the way their boyfriends looked and smelled. They'd walk by their sides for a bit, then wrinkle their noses and walked a step or two farther away. Lance laughed under his breath, remembering Amanda doing the same.

Ew, why don't you shower in the locker room?

It's easier at home. I can just shower and fall into bed. You don't love me when I smell?

I love you all the time, silly. I just don't like you when you're smelly and clammy. Don't you touch me!

They'd grown up together, started dating when they were sixteen. Lance had never wanted to be with anyone else. *You've got too much to lose to keep messing it up.*

Lance pulled open the front door of the school and spotted his own face staring back at him. Framed photos from the glory days of the 70s and 80s ranged across the back wall of the lobby. Photos from the 50s and 60s covered a wall to the left, and those of the 90s and 2000s were on the right and down the main hall.

He paused and stared at the photo of the much younger Lance, his straight, thin body in mid-air, stretched across the goal line. He remembered that moment, a post-season playoff bid and an ill-advised choice that had almost cost them the game. He had dropped back to pass, then decided, probably too quickly to pull the ball down and run. As he approached the end zone, he was forced to go airborne as a defensive lineman dove at his legs and just as he reached for the goal line, the meanest linebacker in the league hit him from the side, spinning him in midair like John Elway in Super Bowl XXXII versus the Packers.

But they'd won.

Lance grinned. He'd always done anything possible to win.

He headed on down toward the locker room, wandering through a strange maze of hallways. Coach always said that their high school hadn't been planned so much as grown. Wings built to accommodate the growing town branched off in odd directions. Only the gym and locker room areas had remained unchanged. As he neared them, Lance's steps slowed as he looked over the trophy cases lined up outside the gym. The gold and dark wood of the trophies sparkled, even though they were crammed into every nook and corner of the cases.

Most of the prizes had come to the school because of Coach. He'd started there just out of college, back in the 50s, and he'd trained thousands of young athletes. When

> **He'd always done anything possible to win.**

Lance attended, the Coach's emphasis had been football and baseball. But he'd branched out into girl's soccer, track, and basketball in later years.

> **"Oh, the talent is his. I'm just building the foundation to grow it."**

The sport, in the long run, didn't really matter as much as the coaching the kids themselves. Lance paused and looked at the slowly tarnishing award that represented his first state championship. The first of three. Starting quarterback as a sophomore, almost unheard of, but Coach believed in him, and had given him the tools to win.

When a reporter once questioned the youth of his quarterback, Coach had just replied, "Oh, the talent is his. I'm just building the foundation to grow it. You think he's good now. Wait two years."

Two years. Lance grinned. His senior year, they'd gone 11-0 for the regular season. Then all the way to State Champions. The next year, he headed to an out-of-state college with a full scholarship, and Coach was well on his way to becoming a Minnesota sports legend.

"Lance?"

Lance turned.

"Lance Marshall, it IS you! Coach Moore said you might drop by, but I didn't know whether to believe it. After all, it's been what? Twenty-five years?"

"Twenty-seven." Lance grinned and held out his hand to Coach Doug Dawson, who'd been Coach's assistant for at least thirty years. "Good to see you, Coach Dawson."

"You, too! I didn't know if I'd recognize you, but you haven't changed all that much."

"A little grayer. Not as thin as I was then." Lance jerked a thumb over his shoulder at the trophies.

"Who is?" Coach Dawson asked, patting his stomach. Then they both laughed since Coach Dawson, if anything, was thinner than he'd been thirty years before. Back then, he'd been lanky. Now he was downright pole-like.

"Come on back to the offices. Coach and I were just finishing up a review of today's practice, but we're mostly done. I know he's anxious to speak with you."

"I appreciate him taking the time, believe me."

Coach Dawson pushed open a door leading into a long hallway. "Oh, he does it all the time. You wouldn't believe the kids that come back to talk to him. You know he and Gail never could have any of their own."

Lance followed, the smell of the locker room hitting him immediately. "Yeah, I heard."

"But you'd think they had adopted several hundred the way they keep coming back here, showing off the kids, grandkids. Sometimes just to tell him what they've accomplished lately. And a lot of the kids he's coaching now belong to the ones he coached fifteen, twenty years ago."

"Life in a small town." The scent in the hall sparked even more memories, and they rushed over Lance like a flood.

"You got that right. You have kids?"

"Three. Two boys and a girl."

A memory returned to him of Amanda at his side during the pre-game homecoming celebration.

Don't stand too close.

I have to escort you out. Besides, I'm not sweaty yet.

No, but you smell like the locker room.

I like the locker room.

I know. Curse of a girl who loves a football player.

"Any of them play sports?" Coach Dawson paused halfway down the hall and pushed through another door into the coaches' office suite.

"My oldest, Robert, plays football."

Coach Dawson grinned. "Quarterback?"

"Of course."

"Coach! Look who I found wandering the halls."

The coaches' suite consisted of a small anteroom, three offices, and a meeting room. The anteroom and the offices of the two assistant coaches were in good shape and relatively neat, especially considering they'd been the home of the football team for more than fifty years.

"Come in, Lance! Come in!"

The office of the man who'd been their coach for most of those fifty years, was cluttered and appeared disorganized. The man who stood as a legend in Minnesota sports, however, told a different story. Coach Moore stood up and stepped over two stacks of paper in order to come from behind his desk and greet Lance. Behind Coach's desk chair, a bookshelf overflowed with playbooks, film canisters, videotapes, and DVD cases. On the far wall, a haphazard stack of files sat atop an ancient filing cabinet. Nothing was labeled, marked, or titled. But Lance remembered that if you asked Coach for something, he'd go to the right stack and pull it out for you.

"Lance Marshall!" Coach pulled Lance into a bear hug, then held him at arm's length to look him up and down. "You've aged well!" He released Lance and stepped back. "Physically, anyway," he added, a slight gleam in his dark eyes. "Not surprised about that part. And we haven't had a QB as good as you were since you graduated. You are one of a kind." He turned and moved a stack of papers from a chair to the floor. "Welcome back to my organized chaos. Have a seat!"

"Thanks." Lance sat as Coach moved back behind the desk. Nearing eighty, Coach was thicker and slower than Lance remembered, but he stood ramrod straight and had a clear, aware expression on his face.

"I have to admit surprise that you're still coaching."

Coach chuckled. "Lots of folks think I should retire, but, to be honest, son, I don't know what else I'd do. Don't like golf. Not fond of card games."

"Is Gail still teaching?"

Coach waved his hand dismissively in the way old men do. "Been out of the classroom more than twenty years. She's a master gardener now. And she SURE doesn't want me around all the time."

"That can't be true."

"You just ask her. She wants you to come to dinner before you leave."

"I'd love to."

Then, small talk finished, both men fell silent. Coach leaned back in his chair, watching Lance. Lance leaned forward, resting his elbows on his knees, and stared down at his hands.

Finally, Coach cleared his throat. "So. Amanda phoned."

Lance nodded.

"Son, why don't you start with why your wife called me instead of you."

CHAPTER 4

COACHED UP:
Five Non-Negotiables and One Rule

L ance covered the basic issues, then leaned back in his chair. "It took me a long time to see it, but I feel like I've been shoved out of the game. I can't see downfield anymore, like I'm acting—or reacting, actually—blindly."

Coach nodded. "Amanda said you acted like a stranger in your own home."

Lance grimaced. "I'm a stranger in my own skin."

Reaching for a baseball in an open desk drawer, the older man turned it in his hands, examining it as if he were seeing the well-worn ball for the first time. "Angry a lot?"

"All the time. My own employees are afraid of me."

"This may have happened because things came so easily to you?"

Eyebrows arched, Lance sat forward, a flash of anger running through him. "What?"

Coach put the ball down. "You don't think that because you worked so hard. But, Lance, you worked hard *perfecting* your skills, your technique in the game. You had a deep-set talent, so you never worked hard *learning* the basics elements. So when you stopped practicing, they went away." He paused. "Ever think you could just step into a game and run the plays, even today?"

> "... the five non-negotiable principles of sports. You listened, but you didn't learn them."

"Of course. What player doesn't?"

"A smart one."

Lance froze, working hard to press down his expanding anger.

"And . . . now you're angry with me, when all I've done is point out the obvious. Age changes a man. That's basic fact. Believe me, I know that all too well. Learned it the hard way. You're older, heavier. Your joints are stiffer, reactions times slower, memory duller. But because it came so easily to you as a kid, you think it still should."

Coach stood, moved some books, and perched one hip on the edge of his desk. "I always taught my players, of whatever sport, the five non-negotiable principles of sports. You listened, but you didn't learn them. You walked through them on instinct, never getting out of line because that was your nature." He paused. "Think of it this way. Many times, talented, gifted students absorb facts and figures like a sponge. They have great memories, good reasoning. They get all A's because they *get* the material without studying. But, eventually, usually in high school or college, they hit a wall, as if their brains reach a saturation point. Now to continue, they have to actually study.

"But most of them don't know how. They didn't have to study, so they never developed good study habits. They don't know how to plan, how to work ahead. They wind up writing papers the night before they're due and cramming for exams. This will be the pattern for the rest of their lives if they don't change it. That's why a lot of gifted students are brilliant . . . but they never reach their full potential.

"You were like that in sports. You didn't see that those non-negotiables weren't just about football. They were about life."

"And now I've hit a wall."

Coach stood and returned to his chair, nodding. "Now, you've hit a wall. When you four boys started that company, it was like a continuation of high school and college. You drove it, remaining in control, the quarterback who could see far enough downfield to guide the team. Now, you're not. Life has forced a harsh reality on you, and you don't have the foundation to deal with it. Fortunately, you have a wise wife . . . and you've instinctually realized something's seriously askew."

The anger had eased in Lance, and he sat straighter, suddenly understanding why: Coach was giving him a game plan. "I need to start over."

Coach nodded. He stood and motioned for Lance to follow him. They went into the locker room, where Coach thumped one of the lockers without pausing. "You need to suit up and decide what kind of leader you want to be."

> **"You need to suit up and decide what kind of leader you want to be."**

At the end of the room, they pushed through a door that led into the tunnel to the stadium. They emerged, and Lance felt the last warmth of the afternoon sun on his face. They turned on to the track circling the field, their shoes crunching roughly on the surface. In the far end zone, a young man, wearing only sweats, bounced on his toes, took aim, and fired the ball off into a practice net.

"He's pretty good," Lance murmured.

"He works hard. He does this every afternoon except right before a game."

"Like I used to do."

Coach coughed. "No. You never worked this hard. You didn't have to. But it's also why you never went beyond college."

Lance stopped, staring at him. "Are you kidding me?"

Coach shook his head. "No. Pro scouts look for drive and ambition as well as talent. Dedication as well as love of the game. Football had been a relatively easy path for you, and they saw that."

"I'm not lazy."

Coach turned. "I'm not saying you were . . . or are. You've hit a wall." He crossed his arms. "Look, we're describing you, but most people hit a wall sooner or later. The only people who don't are the ones who stop trying, stop achieving. They settle for something less than extraordinary. Our friend out there with the ball will eventually hit that wall as well, but his path will be different. It happens when you're overworked, make a wrong choice, find yourself under too much pressure. You lose your vision for life, feel too many people pulling at you, always wanting something, and you just want to quit and stare at the stars for awhile."

"I need to start over."

"You need to rebuild your foundation. It won't be easy, just necessary. But you're not alone."

Lance let out a long breath. "I have no idea where to begin."

Coach uncrossed his arms and walked again, their steps releasing the pungent scent of the track. "After I talked to Amanda, I took the liberty of setting up five appointments for you."

"With whom?"

Coach waved his hand. "We'll get to that later. Each one is highly successful in his field. They're smart and grounded. Each is going to share one of the five non-negotiables with you, talk about how it's worked in his life, and give you a task. The goal in this is to have you learn the principle this time, and reinforce it by doing."

He stopped, his face somber. "Lance, I'm serious about this part, which is why I'm not telling you who you'll meet with until it's time to show up. You will have twenty-four hours to put each principle into action and tell me the results. If you don't, we'll stop the journey, the meetings, right then and there. Understand?"

> "The goal in this is to have you learn the principle this time, and reinforce it by doing."

Deep inside, Lance wrestled hard with the idea of turning the next few days over to Coach, no matter how much he trusted him. But he also realized that if he didn't do this, he'd be putting everything he cared about at risk. Ego warred with common sense.

"Yes, sir, I understand?"

"So you're game? You agree."

Lance paused, but common sense won. "I agree."

"Good!" Coach grinned and slapped him on the shoulder. "Go back to your room. Get some rest. I'll call you early in the morning with your first instructions. Oh, and I recommend Dottie's Café over on Main for most of your meals. Almost like home cooking, and she makes a mean omelet."

Back in his room, Lance undressed and showered, Dottie's meatloaf settling nicely in his stomach. Just as he was about to turn on the evening news, Lance's cell phone buzzed and he checked the caller ID.

Amanda.

Lance answered it, suddenly realizing that for the first time in years, he was eager to tell his wife about his day.

CHAPTER 5

KELI:
SPECIFY THE WIN
One Thing at a Time;
One Day at a Time

THE 1ST NON-NEGOTIABLE

Dottie's omelet, in fact, exceeded Coach's description, and Lance felt energized afterwards, eager to dive into the day. He'd just returned to his room when a text arrived with Coach's instructions. Lance stared at the phone a moment, not really believing the name of today's contact. But the appointment was set for 10:30, so he hit the road quickly.

Keli. Lance remembered him . . . or rather the boy he used to be. Keli had been a couple of years behind Lance in high school, and hadn't reached his full potential by the time Lance graduated. But under Coach's tutelage, that had changed in great measures. Keli had been an All-State tight end, played for one of the top colleges in the country, then enjoyed a short career in the NFL.

Lance stared up at the building as he approached it, feeling slightly intimidated by the name of the major league franchise emblazoned across the top. When he gave his name to the security guard at the front desk, the guard nodded and made a quick call. Moments later, a lovely woman in her mid-50s stepped of the elevator and motioned for Lance to follow her.

"He's expecting you," she said simply. "Coach called him yesterday."

When the doors opened on the executive floor, Lance stepped out onto carpet so plush it cushioned each step and helped mute the sounds of an active office environment. The woman nodded and smiled as she passed people in the hallway. They turned a corner and headed toward two large mahogany doors. She opened both at once and led him inside.

Lance bit his tongue to keep from exclaiming, "Wow!" Scents of rich wood, luxurious leather, and fine cigars greeted him in a room of masculine elegance. The deep tones of mahogany and cherry wood held tastefully placed accents of brass. Despite the dark furnishings, the room glowed with light from the tall windows, which overlooked a carefully landscaped lake circled by a walking track.

"Mr. Marshall," the woman announced.

Keli rose from behind an expansive desk that matched his six-foot, eight-inch frame. "Lance!"

With that acceptance, Lance's escort nodded and left. Keli came from behind the desk, looking as fit and trim as he had been in college. He embraced Lance with a bear hug, then backed off to look at him. "Yep, Coach was right. But he always is." He motioned at the two leather sofas in front of tall bookcases. "Let's sit here. I hate talking to people from behind a desk."

Lance sat. "Coach was right about what?"

Keli grinned. "Life has been good to you, but you're looking a little worn down. When was the last time you worked out?"

"It's been awhile," Lance admitted.

"Since the buy-out?"

Lance's eyes widened and Keli chuckled. "Coach keeps up with all his kids, especially the ones who had the greatest potential. We still have lunch about once a month. He told me when that overseas conglomerate made you an offer you couldn't refuse. You're still in charge, but . . ."

Lance's mouth twisted. "Not as much as you might imagine."

Keli spread his arms wide. "Trust me, all this luxury comes with a lot of accountability. Being the president of a franchise like this means answering to a lot of different folks, far beyond the players and ticket holders. I know about having someone, or a few someones, breathing down your neck. That's why I asked you when you'd last worked out." He leaned back and crossed his legs. "For a guy like you, that tells me you're out of balance."

Lance's eyebrows arched. "Balance?"

"It's one of Coach's principles. In order to reach your greatest potential, your life must be in balance. When it's not, you lose sight of what's really important. The end, the results, the bottom line becomes your goal and your priority, especially when someone's shoving you from behind."

"But those are the priorities in business."

Keli shook his head. "The bottom line is only one of the *goals*. It shouldn't be a priority." He leaned forward. "Look at it this way. One of my goals here is to win games. But if that's all I focus on, I forget that winning is a destination with many paths. To win games, I need to build a sustainable organization, one that makes sure everyone in the organization feels safe, secure and significant. I have to be sure all our employees and players are in balance professionally and personally. That means hiring the best coaches I can find, with philosophies of coaching and life that dovetail with each other. By focusing on the care of the individuals in the club, by focusing on the process instead of just the results, I control the pace here, instead of letting it control me. When I provide the tools, the incentive, and the care, the team wins games. The desired end comes out of the process that is executed one day at a time."

"That's not exactly what we were taught in business school."

Keli laughed. "No. They'll teach you the 'devil is in the details' and to write another business plan. Which is true, but it's just the beginning. True leadership is about inspiration and encouragement, as well as coaching . . . and balance. Balance goes hand-in-hand with maturity, and it crosses all aspects of your life, mental, spiritual, emotional. And being in balance as a man and a leader means providing yourself with the same tools that you should provide for those around you."

Keli stood. "Coffee?"

Lance nodded and Keli slid open a door in one of the shelves, where a coffee service waited. He poured two cups, then returned to the couch, handing one to Lance.

> "Balance goes hand-in-hand with maturity, and it crosses all aspects of your life, mental, spiritual, emotional."

Keli took a deep breath and continued. "Coach taught me that one way to maintain your balance in life is to 'specify the win' for each day. Decide what I want to achieve each and every day. And just for that day. One thing at a time, one day at a time. It is my job, as the leader to always work with the end in mind, but I can't let myself, or my people, get distracted by the future. We teach our people to focus on what a 'win' is for them personally, each day at work. However, it's not just for work. To keep your life in balance, you need a 'win' for work and a 'win' for home. If you can do that and just take one thing at a time, one day at a time, then you can control the pace instead of the pace controlling you."

Keli paused and sipped his coffee. "You can't imagine how important this is, Lance. We get so focused on what's out there, those envisioned 'results,' that we forget how to get there. We become so results-driven, we forget about how important the process of getting there is. When was the last time you lost your temper with an employee?"

Lance started. "Yesterday."

"Why?"

"His month-end reports were inadequate and sloppy."

"Why? Has he performed this way before?"

"Not until a couple of months ago?"

"Why did his work change?"

Lance hesitated. "I don't know."

"Why not?"

Lance felt slightly chagrined. "I haven't asked."

Keli put down his cup. "Lance, one of my best employees was fired from a previous job because he was going through a divorce. His boss had told him to keep his personal life out of the office. But, we're all human. It's not healthy to be compartmentalized. Hasn't your work sometimes interfered with your personal life and vice versa?"

Lance couldn't help but think about Tony's birthday party . . . and the work he'd missed when Tony was born. "Of course."

"This is why having a sense of balance with your priorities, an understanding of how important the process is, will keep you moving forward. If you stay results-driven, moments of crises will only give you a sense of failure because they interfere with the bottom line. If you see them in balance, as part of the process, then you can work through hard times with a different view of success."

Keli stood suddenly and walked to his desk. Opening a drawer, he pulled out a baseball, so new and polished that its leather reflected the light from the windows. He tossed it at Lance, who caught it easily. "What's this?"

"Another thing Coach taught me." Keli sat in front of Lance again. "He has one of these in his desk, too."

Lance thought about the baseball he'd seen Coach turn over and over in his hands yesterday. "What's it for?"

"On one side, you write your daily 'win' for your work. On the other, for your home. Don't think of them

> **"If you stay results-driven, moments of crises will only give you a sense of failure because they interfere with the bottom line."**

as personal and professional aspects. And they're not tasks. They're your life. Completely."

Lance stared at the baseball in his hand, suddenly feeling even more out of balance. "My life is all about performing tasks and getting results."

"No wonder Amanda called Coach."

Lance looked up, a sharp retort on his lips, then saw that Keli grinned at him.

"I guess my 'team' didn't end with high school."

Keli stood. "Now you're talking. Oh, and one last thing. Remember things that are built to last, are not built fast. God bless ya brother, and call me if you have any questions about any of this."

"I will."

Lance drove back to the inn, the baseball perched on one of the drink holders. "What am I going to do with you?" Remembering Coach's admonition to put each newly learned principle into effect within twenty-four hours, he knew he'd have to decide something soon.

Back in his room, he turned the ball over and over in his hands, thinking about the last few weeks at home and the office. The disappointment in his children's faces. In Amanda's. The way Terri jumped when he called her, how she'd defended Bryan.

> **"Remember things that are built to last, are not built fast."**

KELI: SPECIFY THE WIN

A sudden realization hit him like a hard slap. *She knew.*
Terri knew what was going on with Bryan. She knew . . .
and he didn't. Why hadn't they told him?

Because they believe you don't care. The thought stung.
Of course, he cared.

But how long had it been since you've shown it?

Pulling a pen from his pocket, Lance wrote on one side
of the ball: *That they know I care more about them than the
bottom line.*

He sighed, looking at the words. *Now. How do I put
that into practice?*

Before he could think of an answer, his phone vibrated
on his belt. He checked the caller ID and grinned.
Amanda. Eager to share his day's visit with her, he
answered, expecting a pleasant greeting from his wife.

Instead, he heard the words he dreaded most.

"Lance, I'm at the hospital with Tony."

CHAPTER 6

TONY:
A Wake-up Call

Lance called Coach as he headed for the airport. "His shunt failed. Amanda sounded terrified." Lance had a hard time keeping the fear from his own voice. "It's bad this time."

"Gail and I will be praying," Coach responded. "Others will be, too."

Lance knew that Coach was a man of great faith, but the simple declaration caught him off guard. He hesitated, unsure of what to say. Finally, he said simply, "Thank you."

Coach's voice strengthened. "He'll get you through it, son. No matter what."

Lance hung up, the words echoing in his mind. *No matter what.* He didn't want to think about that part, about how often malfunctioning shunts turned fatal. He thought about Amanda, alone with Tony, and Lance had to fight a sense of deep-seated panic. They'd worked so long and hard with Tony. Born more than ten weeks early, Tony arrived weighing barely two pounds and fighting a boatload of problems. The doctors had given him less than a 20 percent chance of surviving. His son had started life hooked up to a plethora of cords and tubes, and even a preemie diaper dwarfed his little body. Then the surgeries started.

But Tony did survive. And he'd grown into one of the strongest members of the family. Blindness had sharpened his hearing, and music kept his world hopping. Cerebral palsy kept him from walking and talking, but his mind had an unexpected sharpness that charmed anyone who met him. He and Connie were best friends, and he listened to all her teenage angst, then made her laugh. She fed his music habit, and last year, she'd bought him a audio dramatization of the Bible, and they'd spent hours listening to it.

Tears blurred Lance's vision. He blinked them away and kept driving, trying not to think about how he'd pushed all three of them away. Instead he called Amanda, who could barely talk. "It's completely failed," she whispered. "The build-up of fluid and the infection is worse than they thought, Lance. They've taken him to surgery, but they're not hopeful."

A spike of fear shot through Lance again, and he tensed every muscle to keep from screaming. Instead, he tightened his grip on the wheel and forced the words out. "I'll be there as soon as I can."

Far too many nightmarish hours later, Lance opened the door to Tony's hospital room. Only one soft, reflective light illuminated his son, who was back from surgery, and his wife, whose head was bowed. Her hands clutched a Bible, and her lips moved silently. Tubes and wires stretched out from Tony's body, monitoring every aspect of his life, reminding Lance of those tense, harsh moments following his birth.

"Amanda," he whispered softly.

She was up and in his arms before he could take a breath. He held her tightly as she pressed her cheek against his chest, clutching his suit coat with both hands. "I'm so scared!"

"Me, too." Lance stroked her hair. "What are they saying now?"

Amanda looked up at him. "Same as always. The surgery went well, but the next few hours will tell." She shook her head. "I've been watching the nurses, watching their faces. They don't have a lot of hope."

"He has to make it. He has to."

She touched his cheek. "I know." Amanda stepped away and tugged at his arm. "Come, sit with me. You've got to be exhausted." She gave him a soft smile. "I know how much you love flying."

They sat, and Lance wrapped an arm around her, pulling her close. "Yeah, right." His eyes focused on Tony. "I'll be OK. Where are the kids?"

"When they took Tony to surgery, I made them go get something to eat, then go home and take care of the house and pack bags for me and Tony." Her arm bumped the lump in his jacket pocket. "What's that?"

In the high emotion of the moment, Lance almost laughed. He pulled out the baseball Keli had given him, which he'd stuck in his pocket at the last moment. "Part of Coach's re-education of me." He summarized Keli's lesson on balance.

> "Coach not only understands, he's praying for us."

Amanda turned the ball around in her hands, pausing when she saw what he'd written about work. One eyebrow lifted, but she said nothing. Finally, she handed it back to him. "I'm sorry I took you away from that."

Lance stared at her. "Are you kidding? This . . ." he glanced at Tony, "is more important than anything. Coach not only understands, he's praying for us." He pulled her to him, and she leaned heavily against him, closing her eyes with a long sigh.

"I'm glad you came. Sometimes I wish I didn't need you so much."

Lance stilled, her words bothering him in a way he couldn't quite grasp. "Why?"

"Because you have so much on you with the company, especially since the buy-out. I feel like we just add to that load."

Lance felt as if his heart had stopped. He gripped her, and Amanda's eyes opened in surprise.

"No," he said forcefully. "Don't say that. Don't even think it. The only reason I can deal with all that is because I have you to come home to. You and the kids." He stroked her face. "I know it's been hard, and I've not been there. But that will be different. It's why I went to Coach, why you wanted me to go."

Slowly, she nodded. "We'll get through it."

They sat, silently holding each other, until two of the nurses came in and began to check Tony. One of them smiled gently at Amanda and Lance. "We'll be here awhile, if you want to take a break, get something to eat."

"I ate awhile ago," Amanda said, nudging Lance toward the door. "You need to eat."

"I'm OK."

"Your stomach is growling. We've been here before. You know it'll be awhile. Go eat."

The nurse nodded. "Seriously, this is going to take awhile. Go. We'll find you if something changes."

Lance recognized the wisdom of it, even though he didn't want to leave, and he headed for the cafeteria. He felt numb, not hungry, but he knew all too well how exhausting hospital stays can be. He ate without tasting the food, his mind locked on his family.

How far off track have I gotten that she'd see herself and the kids as a burden? Do I really make them feel as if they're in my way?

Obviously, yes.

Lance left the cafeteria, the numbness spreading, his feeling of isolation from his family, even his co-workers, sinking into his bones. He'd been so focused on making his company a success, of proving to his new board that they'd been right to take a chance on him and his company, that he'd lost vision of anything else. Anything important.

Gail and I will be praying . . .

Coach was praying for them. So was Amanda. But he couldn't.

I have pushed God away, too.

Back on the medical floor, Lance passed the family waiting room, paused, and went in. Empty at this late hour, the room's chill matched his own. A television flickered in a silent pantomime. On one corner table, a Gideon-placed Bible offered comfort to anxious families.

Lance sank into one of the chairs and picked up the Bible, rubbing one hand over the cover. His wife knew hers inside and out. His daughter and son listened to it regularly on CD.

But he didn't even know where to begin.

Grief washed over him, and Lance slid from the chair to his knees. Simple, plaintive words poured out of him.

"Lord, please help us. Heal Tony. Please don't take him from us. We need him. *I* need him. I need them. Help me to find my way home, into their hearts. Guide me. Guide us." He took a ragged breath. "Heal us."

He could say nothing else. As eloquent as he could be in the boardroom, now . . . nothing. But Amanda always said God could hear your heart. He hoped that was true, now more than ever.

"Daddy?"

His head snapped up. Connie and Robert stood in the doorway, eyes filled with tears as they stared at their dad on his knees. Their faces pinched with concern. "Mama said you'd gone to eat . . ."

> **"We forgive you Daddy, but don't do it again."**

He struggled to stand. "I'm sorry," was all Lance could manage.

But it was enough. His children rushed him, and he wrapped both of them in his arms, pulling them close. "I'm sorry," he said again, as he kissed the top of Connie's head and clutched Robert's shoulder. "I've been an idiot."

"Yes, you have," Connie whispered. Then she looked up at him and grinned. "We forgive you Daddy, but don't do it again."

"I won't. Promise." He looked at Robert, abruptly realizing that his son was now at least an inch taller than he was. "You looked good out there at practice."

Robert's face flushed, "Thanks, Dad."

"Mr. Marshall?"

They all three turned to the nurse standing in the doorway. "Is it Tony?"

She motioned for them to follow. "He's awake."

* * *

The next two days blurred pass Lance. Tony, despite the doctor's worries, awoke with few complications. He remained woozy and a bit nauseous, but they knew that would fade soon. Amanda and Lance slept at the hospital, ever watchful, but 48 hours after his surgery, Tony awoke them, begging for his soundboard . . . and breakfast.

> "I want you to go back and finish what you started with Coach."

The doctors wanted to keep Tony a couple more days, but as Lance and Amanda shared lunch in the cafeteria, she told her husband that she wanted him to go back to Minnesota.

"I want you to go back and finish what you started with Coach." He started to protest, but she reached for his hand, squeezing it tightly. "Tony's going to be OK. We know that now. The rest of this stay will be routine. We've been through this before. Yes, I'd love to have you here, but I can't tell you how much the change I already see in you means to me. I love you, and I admit I can't wait to see where else this takes you . . . us."

Lance had to agree, and later that afternoon, he found himself back on a plane. Sitting next to the window, he turned the baseball over in his hands, looking at the phrase he'd written for work. Now he also understood exactly what a "win" would be for his family. He pulled out a pen and wrote, "Family: That they know they are more important to me than anything. That we will be walking through life together, always."

CHAPTER 7

CLINT:
Simplicity

THE 2ᴺᴰ NON-NEGOTIABLE

Despite his exhaustion from the hospital stay, Lance woke early the next morning, his mind churning with ideas for putting his daily "wins" into action. He started by emailing each member of his leadership team, expressing how valuable they were to him as well as the company. He spent extra time carefully crafting Bryan's. Lance had pushed Bryan hard because of his value to the team as well as his potential.

That done, Lance took a quick shower, and headed for a nourishing breakfast at the café. By 8am, he sat in Coach's office, watching the older man search for a clean place to set a tall cup of coffee.

Coach finally sat his computer keyboard on top of the monitor and sat the mug in its place. He nodded. "The emails were a great start. Tell me more about your family."

Lance detailed the hospital visit, especially his promises to Amanda and his reconciliation with his children.

Coach grinned. "Connie sounds like she has you pegged."

"I think they both do. They're old enough to remember the old Dad, before I went off my rocker."

Coach chuckled. "Children are far more resilient than we sometimes give them credit for. And smarter." He shifted in his chair and focused on Lance. "Ready for the next visit."

Lance took a deep breath and held it a few seconds. "Yes."

Coach turned and braced a stack of papers with one hand, sliding one sheet out, like a magician pulling a tablecloth from beneath a stack of dishes. He handed it to Lance, who stared at the stack of papers in astonishment.

"Remember Clint?"

Lance nodded, looking from the stack to the paper in his hand. "Absolutely. He was a year ahead of me, but the best receiver I ever had. Good catcher, too. He went on to play pro ball in the minor leagues."

"Stayed there. He's a manager now." He pointed at the paper. "That's the directions to his park. He's expecting you."

"So am I the only player who hasn't stayed in touch."

Coach simply motioned at the paper. "Go. And in the morning, let's meet at Dottie's for coffee instead of here.

Be there at 5:30. Tomorrow's a longer drive for you, so you'll need start early."

Lance left, reading the driving directions as he walked. The park was only a couple of hours away, and he pulled up to a park silent and cautiously winterized. Parts of the parking lot had been cordoned off for repaving, and the boarded-up concession stands reminded him of a house fortified for a storm. In the offices, however, activity buzzed efficiently, and an assistant showed Lance into Clint's office.

Clint stood and greeted Lance with the fierce hug of an old friend. At 46, Clint's buzz-cut hair showed only light touches of gray, and his wiry, muscled physique reminded Lance of the quick-moving receiver and catcher who'd helped the high school win several championships.

"You're still in good shape," Lance said as he sat in a comfortable chair in front of Clint's desk. "Like you could still stretch a double into a triple."

Clint beamed. "As a matter of fact, I still do. Only now I do it when no one can see how slow I've gotten. One advantage of being a manager."

"Congrats on that, by the way. Not all of us managed to stay in sports."

"True. Although Coach's teaching remained seared into most of us."

Lance grimaced. "Except me."

Clint waved his hand dismissively. "Nonsense. It's there. You've just forgotten."

Glancing around the office, Lance noted how vastly different Clint's décor was from Keli's plush, luxurious office. This office spoke of a man focused on efficiency. The spare furnishings were practical and strong, as if they'd last a lifetime. Just as Keli's office showed signs of his personal life, the shelves behind Clint's office were lined with Little League trophies, finger paintings, and snapshots of his family. One larger portrait caught his attention, and Lance pointed. "Is that your family?"

Clint reached behind him and grabbed the photo. He handed it to Lance. "Sure is. Pride of my life."

Four children clustered around Clint and his wife, a simply dressed woman of gentle beauty. Lance squinted, noticing the almond-shaped eyes and round face of their younger daughter. "Is she . . . ?"

Clint nodded. "Down syndrome."

Lance resisted the urge to apologize. He knew how that response to Tony—"I'm sorry about your son"—irritated Amanda. She'd remain polite, but explain that there was no need for regrets.

"How's her heart?"

Clint looked surprised for a second. "Good. She missed that complication."

Lance nodded and handed the picture back. "My son Tony arrived almost two months early." He summarized the medical issues they'd been through with Tony, including the shunt failure.

Clint replaced the photo on the shelf. "Coach mentioned a health issue, but not the details. No regrets?"

"None. Except for all the times I hear about a father who's left a marriage and family who has a special needs kid."

Clint let out a long breath. "Tell me about it. They don't understand how much you can learn about yourself, and about being a man from these kids. I have learned so much from Maddie. She's even helped me be a better coach."

Curiosity made Lance sit a little straighter. "How so?"

"She's a walking, talking example of Coach's non-negotiable of simplicity."

"Tell me more."

"That's what we're here to talk about. Simplicity. Trying to remain a simple man in a complex world. Not easy. But by focusing on the basics, sticking to them, you can have a clarity in your vision and your process.

"When I watch Maddie, I see a child who has few distractions in her world. She sets her mind on one thing, and little else interferes until she's done. Same way with coaching."

He stood up and walked to a window overlooking the ball field, motioning for Lance to follow. They watched as players and coaches wandered out onto the deck, many of them still stretching and warming up muscles.

"*. . . I require players and coaches to be FAT.*"

"Wrong time of year for spring training, isn't it?"

Clint laughed. "True. Many of these guys only stay indoors this time of year. But we have a long season, and not all the games are played in summer weather. So anytime the temps rise high enough, we head outdoors. That's just one way I require players and coaches to be FAT."

"Say what? FAT?"

Clint nodded in amusement. "Sorry. We're used to the term around here. It's an acronym. Stands for Faithful, Available, and Teachable. Before we sign any player to a contract or hire a coach, he must have those characteristics." He turned. "Let's go down there."

"*Stands for Faithful, Available, and Teachable.*"

Clint led Lance through the building, into the locker room, and out onto the field, explaining as they walked. "For a player—and our coaches—to be Faithful, they must fully trust the organization, understanding that we have their best interests at heart, not only as a player, but as people. And, they need to give as well as receive. They will need to be Available, be willing to make time to be the best they can for the team as well as for their families and communities.

"To achieve these two, they'll need to have a Teachable spirit or they have no shot. They can't think they know everything there is to know about baseball. Too many players show up on our doorstep thinking they learned all they need to know in high school or college. Too many coaches and players think that whatever they learned earlier in their careers is sufficient. John Wooden, the legendary UCLA basketball coach, once said that what separates the great coaches from the average ones are the ones who don't think they know it all.

"You see, Lance, coaches make that mistake, after they win a couple of titles or have some success, they think they have it all figured out. This isn't just about results or winning, it's about life. It's about getting back to the basics, simple principles that most of us forget over time. Mature coaches aren't distracted by the tyranny of the urgent. They understand what they can control and what they can't. We call that 'controlling the controllables.' Great coaches and athletes understand what they can control and what they can't and they simply let go of the things they can't. They stay focused on the simplicity of who they are and that they are there to help people get to the next level."

Clint paused for a second and went on, "I can't say that enough. *A coach's job is to help an individual, or a team, get to a level that they cannot get to by themselves.* When that job is done properly the wins come as a result."

> "A coach's job is to help an individual, or a team, get to a level that they cannot get to by themselves."

Clint and Lance wandered up into the bleachers and sat, watching as the drills became more intense. Clint gestured at the first base coach. "That is a remarkable man. After his playing career ended, he began coaching. He had many opportunities to coach with other major league clubs, but he was looking for something special. He wanted to be a part of an organization that was about more than winning. When he heard about our philosophy of coaching and development, he called me. Took a huge pay cut to come here, and let go of all the unhealthy things the culture of pro baseball was selling in regard to winning."

"Letting go is not my specialty."

Clint chuckled. "Yeah, I remember when you tried to tell Coach what plays to run."

Lance replied, "Coach had a few things to say about that."

"We were all surprised he let you play that week!" He paused, his voice softening. "Coach said you had some issues at work."

"Yeah, you could say that."

"My guess is that your team sees you as their control freak boss. They're scared of you and for their jobs. No one maximizes their potential or performance in a state of fear, and you can't FORCE anyone to do something they don't want to. Not your employees, not your new owners. You need to let go of the non-essentials and focus on the controlling variables. Focus on the only two things you really can control. Your Attitude and your Effort." He glanced again at the team.

"You make it sound so simple."

Clint stood and slapped Lance on the shoulder. "It is, my friend. You're the one making it complicated. Just remember. Attitude and Effort. Over the years, we've found that 90 to 99 percent of the problems we had with employees in the organization, including the players, boiled down to those two things. Lance, I have

> "Focus on the only two things you really can control. Your Attitude and your Effort."

always told my assistant coaches that I will never come in and take over their position and start coaching their people. That is their job. But if I ever see a bad attitude or a poor effort, I will coach that immediately. Those two things are a non-negotiable in regard to the simplicity of our ball club, and that simplicity is what our success hinges upon."

An assistant beckoned Clint to the press room. "I'm sorry it looks as though the media is calling. Feel free to hang around as long as you like. Remember, Lance, you can't give away what you don't possess yourself. Strive to be a simple man in a complex world. Attitude and Effort."

On the drive back, Lance kept repeating those two words over and over, applying them in his mind to the events of the last month. Right after the buyout, everyone had worked hard, but lately getting his people to go above and beyond had become a trial. Understanding finally, Lance pulled over to the side of the road, took out his pen and wrote "Attitude" and "Effort" on the baseball. Then picked up the phone and called Terri. He told his incredulous assistant to shut down the office on Friday and send everyone home, then set up a company-wide meeting for Monday morning.

He pulled back onto the highway, energized, and brainstorming even more about how he could emphasize Attitude and Effort in every facet of his life. He knew his world was about to change significantly.

CHAPTER 8

DR. KESS:
The Three-Dimensional Leader

THE 3RD NON-NEGOTIABLE

Like in most small towns, the work day started early. Dottie's opened at five, and the smell of hot biscuits and bacon filled the air. A table reserved for local farmers buzzed with early morning gossip, The talk ranged from crop futures and weather conditions to the latest episode of *American Idol*. A coffee station just inside the door invited customers to grab a cup and take a seat.

Lance had snagged a booth early, downing his first cup and a hot biscuit before the sun rose. As Coach entered and settled in, Lance got up to pour his mentor a cup and refill his own. As he set the pot down, his phone buzzed three times in quick succession, signaling the arrival of three new emails. Lance stopped, setting the cups on the stand. He clicked through the emails, his chest tightening at the news they brought.

Three of his managers were all struggling with the same client, the same problem. One of the emails contained the entire exchange with the client, and Lance could read the anger between the lines of each message. The client wanted to end the negotiations; his managers wanted to let him walk.

A surge of anger shot through Lance, as if nothing in the last few days had changed. How dare they tear down the rapport he'd built! Did they not realize how important this was, how desperately they needed to grow in that territory? This should have been a coup, not a disaster!

Without looking up from the phone, Lance swung back toward the coffee stand. He stopped abruptly, thudding into someone. Hot coffee showered over Lance's left arm and hand, soaking his sleeve and cell phone.

He jumped back with an enraged growl, shaking his arm and staring down at the phone. "Why don't you watch where you're going, you stupid—"

He stopped, looking up into the eyes of a woman who could have been his grandmother. White curls looped around the frames of her glasses, and her cheeks flushed with embarrassment as she looked from him to her spilled coffee on the floor.

"I'm sorry," she muttered.

Every ounce of rage drained from Lance. *What have I done?* "No, ma'am. You've done nothing. I'm sorry. I wasn't looking up." He bent and scooped her cup up, tossing it into the trash. "Let me get you another cup."

"No," she mumbled, her expression still a bit stunned. "I don't think I could drink it now."

"Let me help you . . ."

Her eyes finally focused on him. "I'm old, young man. Not helpless. And you need to learn some respect."

"Yes, ma'am." He watched her leave, then looked over at Coach, who'd observed the incident with a wry grin.

"One step forward and two steps back, Lance?"

Now Lance's cheeks heated with embarrassment. "Seems like it."

Coach sipped his coffee. "Right. So did you throw a touchdown the first time you threw a pass?"

Lance leaned back. "Of course not."

"Then give yourself a break. Changing direction in your life is not like driving a car or sailing a boat. You can't just move the gibe from one side to the other and stay the course. You're going to slip. You're going to fail. The objective is to get back up and continue the process. How did it go with Clint?"

Lance paused as the waitress appeared and they ordered breakfast. Then Lance summarized his meeting with Clint, and his plans for implementing new strategies at work that

> **"You're going to slip. You're going to fail. The objective is to get back up and continue the process."**

would focus more on attitude and effort. He pointed at his phone, sharing the messages. "I realized after I tried to run over that lady that I need to change to the point where I can respond to situations like that properly, without thinking about it."

"And your managers?"

"Same thing. I ran into her because I was so angry at them. Without realizing it, I lashed out. Unfortunately, she was in the way."

Coach nodded. "Like your family is in the way."

Lance stared, astonished.

> ". . . remember there are only three things you can do when you make a mistake: Admit it, Fix it, and Don't repeat it."

Coach sipped his coffee. "Well, that's a better reaction that I think I would have gotten a few days ago. Surprise is better than rage."

"You think my family is in my way?"

"Not me. Them."

Lance took a deep breath, Amanda's words echoing in his head: *I feel like we just add to that load.*

"I'm working on that."

"Just don't stop, and remember there are only three things you can do when you make a mistake: Admit it, Fix it, and Don't repeat it."

Lance grinned. "I won't. And I'm going to email my managers after breakfast, talk to them about Attitude and

Effort, encourage them to focus on the solution, not the screaming match."

"What would you have done before this trip?"

"Stepped in. Taken over. Fixed everything."

"To what effect?"

Lance sniffed not wanting to say it. "It would have demoralized them and made the client disrespect them."

"You're not their father, Lance. You're their leader. Their coach. If you want them to trust you and be loyal to you, you have to capture their hearts and earn their trust. Lance, consistency in your behavior will breed trust and trust will breed loyalty. This is key, as well as focusing on process."

They paused as the waitress brought food and more coffee. As she left, Coach bowed his head in silent grace over his meal. Lance sat still, watching, once again struck by Coach's quiet, steady faith.

"Speaking of being a heart capturer," Coach announced, even before he looked up, "today I'm sending you to see a really good friend of mine. Dr. Kess has been coaching coaches for more than 20 years. He's a professor at the university, and you're going to attend one of his classes this morning. A master's level course on reaching the 21st century athlete." He reached for his coffee cup. "Trust me, it's not the same game it used to be."

Lance returned to his room before he headed out, to change clothes and freshen up. He also made a few notes about his client, then called Terri. She linked the four of them in a conference call, and Lance spoke calmly about the account and the client, encouraging them to brainstorm solutions, leaving the blame in the closet. "I hired you because you're capable of dealing with situations like this. Show me what you can do."

The call made him run late, but he felt an unexpected sense of pleasure and pride at the eager brainstorming they'd shared, and he'd hung up feeling they would rectify the problem.

An hour later, Lance drove onto the university campus and found the building and room number Coach had given him. Class had been in session for more than 10 minutes when he peered through the door, but Dr. Kess motioned him to come inside. Lance felt awkward as he found a seat, and he noticed some of the students shifting uncomfortably as well.

Dr. Kess appeared thin, but his clear voice was firm, and his energetic actions made him seem to bounce about in front of the room. *Wiry,* Lance thought, *not frail.*

"Ladies and gentlemen, this is Lance Marshall. He's auditing our class today. He is not an official of the university and therefore has no affect on your grades or my pay. So no need to be nervous at his presence."

Most of the students grinned or snickered, and the tension in the room eased. A couple of them even gave him reassuring glances of welcome. Coach had told Lance the class was a master's level, but he still found it startling to see how many of the students were older, some in their forties and fifties.

"Today's athlete is quite different from they way we were as children. Even children raised in the turbulent 70s and 80s still offered up trust to coaches and teachers simply because of the positions they held. They extended loyalty to coach and team without question. But with the advent of the Internet and more betrayals by authority figures than we can count, our students have been raised in a jaded world. The time of blind obedience has passed. They don't trust without reason, and while motivation by fear will work, it'll only last for short periods of time. This is because the 21st century athlete is not as mentally tough as we would hope them to be. Remember, when I refer to mental toughness, I am referring to a person's ability to be comfortable with being uncomfortable. For a variety of reasons we will discuss another day, they have been conditioned to respond to difficult situations with a flight response or to blame someone else. In other words, the 21st century athlete has been conditioned to change lanes when things get tough rather than stay the course and work through it. Lastly, we all need to feel

"Remember, when I refer to mental toughness, I am referring to a person's ability to be comfortable with being uncomfortable."

safe, secure, and significant every day or we will begin to lose hope and our motivational levels will decrease. People today don't care what you know until they know how much you care about them."

Dr. Kess pointed to an image projected on the front wall of the classroom, a pyramid divided into three sections. A similar pyramid sat on his desk, not much bigger than a paperweight. "Today's coaches must be three-dimensional. You must go beyond being able to teach the fundamentals of the game. Today you must reach them body, mind, and spirit. Let's look at this closer."

He reached for the pyramid on his desk and separated the three pieces. "This bottom piece here, this is the largest section. This represents the fundamentals of the game. You must be intimately familiar with the basic principles and forms of your sport as well as have an up-to-date knowledge of truths and facts about the sport you are coaching. You'll need a technical competency yourself and be able to cast a vision for your team, develop that vision, and take it through to implementation. And, truthfully, with the vast amount of knowledge available to us today, there's no excuse not to be competent in the fundamentals. But all this is just the foundation."

He set that piece on the desk and picked up the next one. "Here . . . this is the second dimension of being a three-dimensional coach, the athlete's mind. You will need to understand the psychology of this young person and how he or she relates to the rest of the world. More than ever before, motivating a young athlete requires developing an understanding of the person inside the uniform. Current research shows that more than 90 percent of motivation today depends on the relationship between coach and player."

Dr. Kess picked up a remote control and clicked it. A page from Facebook reflected from the back wall. "One of my students told me he has 759 'friends' on Facebook, but only five real relationships. He goes home to his parents almost every weekend because he shares little with the people in his dorm and on his team. As always, people crave connection, real relationships with others. They know how powerful relationships can be, and how shallow their world can be."

Dr. Kess continued, "Don't get me wrong; they won't be looking to you to be their 'buddy.' You're their coach. They want you to be someone they can trust and believe in who will challenge them to new levels. They will expect you to lead them and know how to provide feedback and discipline when they screw up. So if you want to motivate your team members, you need to develop a relationship with them. Only then, can you inspire them to persist and

> **"They want you to be someone they can trust and believe in who will challenge them to new levels."**

pursue when they want to quit. Only then, can you help them achieve what they don't think possible."

Setting the second section aside, Dr. Kess picked up the smaller top. "This, my friends, is the smallest but most important dimension. This is their heart."

He turned it around in his hands. "Fragile yet infinitely strong. Easy to break, but if captured in the right way, in a process that's built on trust and daily care, the heart bond between a coach and his or her athletes can inspire both to greater heights than either imagined.

> **"Great coaches are easy to please, but hard to satisfy."**

"Great coaches are easy to please, but hard to satisfy. If you've earned the right to speak into your player's lives, then they will absorb everything you can offer and they will not resent you when you give them feedback on their progress. They will embrace the core principles you teach them so intensely that they'll become second nature. If you can capture their heart, you will have no trouble with motivation or performance execution. Not to mention, team chemistry will go through the roof! They'll have fun and they'll win, and they won't even realize that you've led them to skills that will serve them the rest of their lives."

Dr. Kess set the pyramid top down. "Take out a piece of paper, please."

The students rustled through notebooks to pull out paper, and a young man next to Lance handed him a fresh sheet. He pulled a pen from his pocket and waited.

Dr. Kess switched back to the slide of the pyramid. "Draw this on your paper. Then I want you to put an X on the pyramid, representing where you think you are as a coach." He waited as they drew, then continued. "Now place a check mark where you think your TEAM or athletes would put you."

A few groans echoed around the room. Lance stared at his pyramid, well aware of where his employees, his "team," would probably place him. He knew most respected his skills and his goals. But as a motivator, a coach . . . a heart capturer?

Not so much.

Dr. Kess cleared his throat. "This next part may be hard on some of you. If you're married or involved with someone . . . where would he or she put you? Draw a circle where you think your significant other would put you."

Lance desperately wanted to put the circle representing his wife in the top portion of the pyramid. She loved him, of course, but was he capturing her heart?

I wish I didn't need you so much. And, Amanda's response to Connie's accusation: *He knows what he missed.*

Lance looked up at Dr. Kess's pyramid. *They want you to be someone they can trust and believe in.*

Motionless, Lance realized that Amanda didn't believe she could rely on him. He'd lost her trust in him to be there when she needed him.

Dr. Kess continued, "Now if you have children at home, put a plus sign where they would say you are on the pyramid if we asked them."

All of a sudden, Dr. Kess's class couldn't end soon enough.

CHAPTER 9

COACH O QUARTERBACK SCHOOL:
The Power of Speaking Greatness

THE 4ᵀᴴ NON-NEGOTIABLE

The next morning, Lance arrived at Coach Moore's office before anyone else did, pacing impatiently on the sidewalk in front of the school. Coach got out of his ancient pick-up with a tall cup of coffee in one hand, and his eyebrows arched when he saw Lance. Then he merely grinned and motioned Lance inside.

"How did it go with Amanda?"

"Sometimes I wonder if I knew back when I was 16 how amazing she really is."

Coach moved a stack of papers and sat the cup down. "No. You were 16. You had no idea how astonishing and strong a grown woman could be. He shrugged. Of course, she wasn't exactly all that mature yet either."

"I told her about the pyramid and Dr. Kess's ideas. The self-test. And I apologized for taking her and the kids for granted, especially her work with Tony. She's so strong and efficient with him, completely accepting that he'll never leave home and mature the way Connie and Robert will."

"He'll be 18 soon and out of the special needs education system. Have you talked about transition services for him?"

Lance closed his eyes a moment. "I haven't. Amanda has. She keeps trying to talk to me, but I can't deal with it."

Coach looked at him silently.

Lance sighed. "I know. I can't let her do this alone."

"I don't remember you having a hard time talking to people. Even when you said some pretty strong things, you said them without a lot of hesitation."

"Yeah, well, this time I'm trying to say the RIGHT things. Maybe that's why I'm wondering off into left field."

Coach grinned. "I think today's visit will help you with that. Do you know where Coyote Ridge Park is? It was built some time after you left."

Lance nodded. "I've passed it a few times since I got back."

"Go in the front entrance and circle around to the back. You'll see an open field at the back where a guy will be working with a young boy, tossing the football back and forth."

"OK."

"That's Coach O. Jed Olson. One of the best collegiate coaches I've ever met. He does something else for a living these days, but he still gives private quarterback lessons to a few kids throughout the year. He can take a good player and turn him into a great one. Even NFL coaches and players have hired him."

"What's his secret?"

"That's what you're about to find out. Don't interrupt if he's in the middle of a lesson. He knows you're coming, and he'll get to you as soon as he can."

"This will help me with Amanda?"

"And Robert and Connie, and every employee you've ever hired. And come back here when you're finished. Gail wants to see you tonight. I'll lead you over to the house."

Lance headed out, pulling into the park about 15 minutes later. He followed the drive past a picnic shelter and an expansive playground. A lake sparkled in the sun, and a family with four children fed eager, noisy ducks and geese. Tennis courts gave way to a broad field bordered by giant oaks. Two cars sat in the narrow lot, and behind them two men casually tossed a football back and forth as a young boy listened closely to one of them.

Lance parked and got out, and the man next to the boy nodded at him.

"Be with you in a bit," he called out.

Lance waved back an agreement and leaned against the hood of his car. Even at this distance, Lance could see that the kid paid seriously close attention to Coach O's words, nodding occasionally. Coach O would show him something, explain it, model it, and then he would have the young boy throw the ball back to his dad.

Finally, Coach O called to his pupil's father, "Take a break, John. Josh is going to show me what he can do."

John nodded, then walked over to Lance as the boy ran out a distance, the ball tucked in at his side. John stuck out his hand. "I'm John. You must be Lance."

A little surprised, Lance nodded.

"Jed told me you were coming. He talked to Coach Moore this morning. He's the one who convinced Jed to work with Josh."

"Why didn't he want to work with your son?"

John crossed his arms and focused on his son. "Josh is good, but I know he can be better. But at ten, he's younger than most of the athletes Jed works with."

"Ten is pretty young. My son plays quarterback, but at ten it was still all about going to Dairy Queen after games."

John paused. "Let me back up a bit. A few years ago, a Fortune 500 company I'd helped start was poised to turn global. A shake-up at the executive level left me less than thrilled, so I knew I needed to move on, take some time, and figure out what came next. In the meantime, I began coaching my ten-year-old son's football team and became fascinated by what these ten-year-olds could accomplish. We had a group of solid, enthusiastic youngsters, even though only one had exceptional athletic ability. Nonetheless, we were able to compile a 12-1 record, including pre-season and post-season. We went on to win our version of the 'Super Bowl,' not because I'm that great a coach, but because these young players have an astonishing will to work hard and have fun, while executing well. I mean, we only lost one fumble the entire season."

"Impressive!"

"The success of this team started me wondering what a kid could accomplish if he had coaches who really knew the details and intricacies of a particular position, like Jed does with quarterbacks. My youngest son, Joshua, was one of the quarterbacks on our team. I wanted to see how he would develop under the tutelage of a true quarterback coach. I began to ask around in coaching circles and multiple recommendations led me to Jed. In fact, they told me you probably can't get this guy but if you can, he is the best around at developing kids."

"He does this for a living?"

John shook his head. "Not at all, although he could if he wanted to. He only works with a few quarterbacks a year, says it fills the football void in his life. Jed had held multiple positions as quarterback coach, offensive coordinator, and head coach at the collegiate level. I had to make a lot of calls to convince him to work with Josh. He usually only works with young men at the high school or college level. In fact, the youngest he had worked with previously was thirteen. I finally convinced him to meet with Josh under the agreement that we would meet just once and see how things went.

"I went to our first meeting expecting Jed to work with Josh on three step drops and correct his throwing mechanics. Instead, we spent the first thirty minutes on the proper stance under center and the last fifteen minutes talking about leadership and the type of leader Josh should aspire to be."

Lance stared at John. "The kind of leader he wanted to be? He's ten."

John ran one hand through his hair. "I think part of Jed's success is that he does teach to their level, but he isn't afraid to challenge them to higher levels. In retrospect, I think he was testing Josh, seeing if he had the maturity, patience, and aptitude to learn the details. And that's the way it went for a while. In fact, we met half a dozen times before Josh was allowed to throw the ball more than ten yards. I expected Josh to get bored, but he continues to be excited about these lessons. He ALWAYS leaves energized."

"So how does he look as a player? Has he improved since you started these?"

"Honestly, I didn't think it would happen this quickly, but yes. Josh's progress has been significant. Not only does the ball look as if it jumps off Josh's hand without effort, but his manner changed significantly. He's matured and he possesses a quiet confidence and calm that was never there before."

John shifted, pulled a pair of sunglasses out of his pocket, and slid them into place. "I couldn't quite put my finger on it at first, but there's something significantly different about the way Jed coaches. After about a dozen sessions the difference became apparent . . . it's the way he *spoke* to Josh. Not just what he said, but the tone and, just as important, the sequence of the instructions, criticisms, and encouragement. This technique transformed my son. I had to learn more about it. When I discussed what I had noticed with Jed over a cup of coffee, he told me he was using an approach he called 'Speaking Greatness,' and that through this process you could capture the heart of the athlete."

> "'Speaking Greatness,' and that through this process you could capture the heart of the athlete."

John gave a slight shrug, "I didn't know what he meant. He explained that once you captured the heart, the desired physical response and performance would follow. As we continued our discussion, I was overcome with the mixed emotions of regret and excitement. Regret, that I had not been exposed to this approach or used it more broadly in my entire life! My business career, my children, my wife. But I also felt excitement that I, hopefully, have another forty plus years to 'Speak Greatness' into those I encounter."

John waved at Josh, who returned the gesture. "You know what's even better?"

"Tell me."

"I've discovered that while 'Speaking Greatness' is great for the recipient, the true benefit comes in how God works in the heart of the person who is doing the speaking. When you 'Speak Greatness' to others, you benefit as well, in ways you can't imagine. My wife says once you start speaking greatness at home, you will never stop. You will never go back to how you used to speak to people. It's amazing."

> **"My wife says once you start speaking greatness at home, you will never stop."**

"A reflective effect."

John grinned as he pushed away from the car. "More than you can dream." He stepped forward to greet his son, who glowed from the morning's effort.

"Did you see, Dad?"

"Every second." John put his arm around Josh's shoulder. "You ready to show your mom?"

"You bet!" He scrambled for the car, as much a ten-year-old boy as a quarterback.

John shook Jed's hand. "Thanks, again. Next week?"

"Absolutely."

Jed stood next to Lance as they watched father and son drive away, the football tucked under one arm. Jed pulled a towel out of his car and draped it around his neck. "Let's stand in the shade."

They left the parking lot and headed for the ring of trees at the field's edge. "John been talking your ear off?"

Lance chuckled. "He's definitely impressed with the work you've done with Josh."

"Josh is a good kid. He's got a deep, natural talent, but he mostly needed encouragement. A reminder—lots of reminders—that he has greatness inside him. And it is my job to help him discover it."

"He IS ten."

"Oh, yeah. But I think John has learned almost as much about being a coach and leader as Josh has about being quarterback."

Lance turned to face Coach O, who was at least two inches taller. "I suspect he'd agree with you on that."

"He just needed to learn to do less pushing and do more leading, more encouraging."

"How so?"

Coach O paused, peering at Lance intently. "Coach Moore said you'd already visited Dr. Kess."

"Yes."

"So you understand the three-dimensional pyramid. Fundamentals, understanding the psychology of motivation, and capturing the heart?"

"Intellectually, yes. In practice, I haven't exactly hit the end zone."

Coach O snorted a laugh. "Coach Moore also said you could laugh at yourself."

> "People forget that there's life and death in the power of the tongue."

"More in the last few days than the last few months, though. My sense of humor took a hit like everything else good in my life. I've not been a great guy to hang out with lately."

"Said some harsh things to important folks?"

"Just about everyone."

Coach O nodded. "People forget that there's life and death in the power of the tongue. It's absolutely *not* true that words don't hurt. They *can* hurt, and they can change a life. You know, that the basic definition of a coach is. 'someone who helps an individual or a team get to a level they couldn't get to by themselves.'"

"I've heard that a couple of times this week."

"And it's true, but it goes even a step farther— that's not only a coach's job, it is a leader's job, and also a parent's job, to find out what their athletes, their employees, and their children are gifted at and help them flourish. Fan the flames."

"How?"

"For one thing, don't focus on what they can't do, focus on what they can do."

"People do make mistakes."

"Sure they do. We all do. The kids I coach do, and when they make them, I critique them and teach them how to correct them. I tell them, OK, you made a mistake, good, mistakes are how we learn. Then, I tell them there are only three things they can do when they make a mistake: Admit it, Fix it, and Learn from it. When they hear that, all of a sudden they're more motivated because they don't worry about failing. They know it's OK, part of the learning process. So we correct, but we focus on excellence and process. When we give feedback, we focus on the process not results. Any idiot can state what the kid did wrong. We call these types of coaches 'Coach Obvious.' They simply restate the results of what the kid did. For example, a kid misses a tackle, and the coach runs over and screams, "make the tackle" at the kid. Lance, today's athlete may not be as mentally tough as we used to be, but they are smart, and they want their coach to help them fix what they did wrong, not just restate results. When I give feedback to people, I practice a 3:1 ratio when critiquing performance. This means for every correction that you wish to make, you must tell them three specific things they're doing right first."

"That can't always be easy."

"No, it's not. Some kids need more work than others. But when you're correcting their mistakes AND praising their successes, it has an amazing effect."

"Such as?"

> "*. . . the ability to motivate someone to do something is about 90 percent trust."*

"One, they know you are the real deal, that you're not just telling them what they want to hear. You have to remember most of these kids have been getting trophies for just showing up. They yearn for authentic coaching and feedback. You fix as well as praise; you're not just telling them how good they are. They know it's not an empty compliment just to make them feel better. So they start to trust you."

Lance nodded, taking it in.

"Two, the more they trust you, the more they want to please you and not disappoint you. Remember, great coaches are easy to please and hard to satisfy."

Coach O moved the football from one hand to the other, absently twirling it. "Lance, the ability to motivate someone to do something is about 90 percent trust. If you want me to do something, I need to be able to trust that you've got my back. You'll stand behind me when I do great, as well as when I don't do so great. With your wife and your employees, if they've lost faith in your willingness to support them, then you've lost their trust. You can yell at them all day long, but that won't make them more inclined to work harder. Constant criticism and sarcasm tears down their spirit. It creates an environment of fear and again, when people are in a state of fear all they care about is survival not performing at a high level."

Lance thought for a second about how criticism flows so easily out of his mouth, at work and at home.

"One of the things I learned working with these kids is that I need to have a transformational vocabulary. I need to use words that take them to another level. Here's an example. Say Josh is throwing out routes to receivers and I say, 'Josh that was a great pass, *but* . . .' What happens to everything I said before the word 'but'?"

"It's gone, forgotten, almost like you never said it."

"Correct. But what if, I simply replace the word 'but' with the word 'now'? For example, 'Josh that was a great pass, *now* I want you to try this!' You see, Lance, the word *now* is a transformational word. It inspires people to go to the next level in their performance. You still get the message across, you still critique and correct them, and you also challenge them to another level."

"It's all about the process."

"Exactly. And this works with everyone, not just athletes. I know this sounds radical because it's so far away from the way we've been taught to manage or to coach. But if you will 'Speak Greatness' at least five times a day— to your employees, your colleagues, your superiors—you'll see a difference immediately."

"John said it had a bit of a 'reflective' effect."

Coach O nodded. "Without a doubt. It's an intentional behavior that'll change you as much as the people you're speaking to."

"You make it sound really simple."

"Yep. Because the concept *is* simple. It's living it every day, stopping to think every time before you speak, that's harder. But definitely worth it."

> **"I challenge you to THINK before you speak."**

Coach O pulled a marker from his pocket and wrote the letters **T H I N K** across the side of the football. "Here. I want you to take this and put it in your office. You don't have to explain it if you don't want to. But you'll know that this isn't just the word "think." The letters stand for 'True. Helpful. Inspiring. Necessary. Kind.' I challenge you to THINK before you speak." He handed Lance the football.

"Thanks. I just hope I can put all this into practice as well as you do."

Coach O slapped Lance on the shoulder. "I think you already have."

CHAPTER 10

THE ASSISTANT COACH:
Value People over Productivity

THE 5ᵀᴴ NON-NEGOTIABLE

The advice from Coach O's session swirled in Lance's mind as he headed back to the gym. He felt both overwhelmed and uplifted, and he couldn't quite believe that his time with Coach Moore had come to an end. Coach had been right—Lance had heard all this before, mostly when he'd been in high school. Everything felt familiar and right, like renewing an acquaintance with an old friend. Still, Lance was chagrined to realize that so little of it had "stuck."

He entered the school, his footsteps echoing off the walls as he turned down the hallway to the gym. Lance realized that his reluctance to leave ran deeper than mere nostalgia for his high school days, and he thought about Dr. Kess's words about safety and security. Here, he felt

both of those things. Here, he felt cherished, and he knew
he needed to rebuild those feelings for his own children.

Lance entered the coaches' anteroom
and immediately saw that Coach Moore's
office was dark and silent. He stopped,
wondering if he'd misheard the time of
their meeting.

"Lance?"

He turned, and Coach Doug Dawson
waved from behind his desk, then motioned
for Lance to join him. He entered an office
much neater than that of the head coach and sat.

"Do you value people over productivity?"

Coach Dawson opened a small refrigerator behind
his desk and handed Lance a bottle of water, which he
accepted gratefully. "Coach Moore got a call from the
principal for some sort of conference. He'll be back in a
bit. Have you learned a lot?"

Lance twisted off the lid. "More like re-learned it. I
can't believe how much I've forgotten."

Coach Dawson opened his own bottle. "Because you
haven't been living it."

Lance looked closer at him. "How do you mean?"

"Do you value people over productivity?"

Lance now puzzled. "I don't understand."

"Has Coach ever mentioned how we came to work
together?"

Lance shook his head.

"Not surprised. That's like him. He respects everyone's privacy. Lets them tell their own stories."

"I thought he hired you here."

"Yes . . . and no." Coach Dawson shrugged one shoulder. "We've been at this school more than 35 years. Before that, Coach was briefly at a really small school south of here, near the state line. He convinced them to hire me to coach and teach a couple of math courses. I was still a kid, barely out of school, and thought I knew everything there was to know about winning."

Lance grinned. "Winning."

"Yeah, you hear it coming, don't you?"

"After these few days, yeah."

"Yep, I'd been on the job only a few months. One evening after practice, Coach pulled me aside and took out a pad and pencil. He said, 'All right, I want his name.' I stared at him. 'Whose name?' He licked the end of the pencil and prepared to write. 'The guy who told you that winning games is what this is all about. That winning, no matter what the cost to your players and you, would make you a better coach. I want his name because I'm going to hunt that sucker down.'"

They both laughed. "That was the first time I'd ever heard anything about motivating kids through relationship, by reaching their hearts and minds. I'd been taught that coaching was about technical skills and motivating players through fear." He paused. "That night he told me how much of his coaching philosophy wasn't new, just older principles he'd put back into place. He told me how he had hurt so many along the way, just for the sake of winning, and how he vowed he would never do that again. He got me on my feet as a coach, but also as a man."

"I can see why you'd be loyal."

Coach Dawson peered at Lance a moment. "Actually, I'm loyal more because he almost fired me the week of the state championship game."

Lance's eyes widened. "Say that again."

Setting his water aside, Coach Dawson pulled his chair closer and braced his elbows on the desk. "My father had been ill for six months. I'd made a dozen trips home to help my mom. It had been a rough season, but we'd made it to championship game, in part, because we never stopped encouraging our team on what they were doing right and fixing what they were doing wrong. Our team was loading the bus to the game when I got the call about my dad. They didn't think he'd last through the night.

"But I wasn't going to walk away from the team. I wasn't about to leave Coach. We all had worked so hard and deserved every reward. Finally, Coach said, 'Doug, there will be other championship games. I promise you that. But you will not have another father. This man taught you to throw a ball and be a man. He gave you a safe and secure place to grow up. He brought you into the world. You need to be there when he leaves it.'"

"You went?"

"No, not at first. I told Coach I could catch a red-eye flight after the game. He told me that if I didn't leave immediately, he would fire me and then hunt me down. So I left immediately. Incredibly, I made it home on time. I was there when he lost consciousness, and I was still there when my dad passed away. I wouldn't have been if I'd waited for that red-eye flight. And there *were* other championship games. Enough that folks now call Coach a legend. Y'see, Lance, we can talk coaching philosophies all day long, but Coach lived it out that night. He valued me, and my family, over the program and a game. I am loyal to Coach because he lives these principles out every day. When Coach says, 'Value people over productivity,' he means it. To me, that's what makes Coach a legend. Not the winning. If you'll put what you have learned into action every day, you'll see exactly what I mean."

> **"He brought you into the world. You need to be there when he leaves it."**

Lance started to respond, but Coach Dawson's gaze shifted up and behind him, and he knew Coach Moore had returned. He stood and turned.

"Hiding out?"

"Hardly," Coach Dawson said. "I was just picking his brain a bit about coaching philosophies and what he's learned this week. Thought I might have missed something."

Coach Moore nodded at his assistant as if sharing a private joke, then motioned for Lance to follow him. "Come on, champ. My wife has already let me know that she's tired of holding dinner on us. Lock up, would you, Doug?"

"I'll take care of it."

Lance and Coach Moore headed for the parking lot. "Why don't you follow me in your car? Gail's dinner always makes me so sleepy, I don't want to leave the house after we eat."

"No problem."

"Don't get lost."

"Never again."

Coach grinned at him as he opened the door on his old pick-up and got in, slamming it behind him.

As he followed Coach toward his home, Lance couldn't get Doug Dawson's story out of his head, nor the obvious connection to his own life. Pulling out his cell phone, he dialed Terri's personal number. When she answered, he said simply, "Tell me what's going on with Bryan. The whole story."

CHAPTER 11

ENDGAME:
Leaving a Legacy

Coach Moore and his wife Gail lived in the same renovated farm house they'd purchased thirty-five years ago. The broad backyard had been a practice field for thousands of young players over the years, and Gail still loved to entertain on the deck behind the house. The men could smell the food when they got out of the car, and Coach had just started explaining Gail's new recipe for grilled vegetables when Amanda rounded the corner of the house.

Lance stopped, eyes wide and disbelieving, as she trotted toward him. "Surprise!" she whispered as she pulled him into a hug. Lance returned the hug, holding her as if she might float away when he let go.

"Wow!" she said, when he finally released her. "I need to send you out of town more often."

"Never," he said, his voice teasing. "You're never getting rid of me, never ever again."

She laughed, slipping her arm in his as they walked around to the back of the house. "Gail called me, invited me up. She said you'd changed a lot over the last few days. According to Coach."

"I think I have. I know I have a lot to work on. Everyday stuff."

Coach, who had walked on ahead of them, now offered up cups of hot chocolate as Gail began forking steaks from the large brick grill, plopping them on to a large platter. "I wasn't about to wait for you boys to do the grilling tonight. I'm starved!"

"Let me get that." Lance grabbed the hefty platter and carried to the picnic table, setting it near a large Dutch oven brimming full of grilled vegetables. The heat from the open fire of the grill wafted over them as they settled down on the wooden benches, pushing away the chill of the autumn night.

"Lance, would you say grace?" Coach asked.

Lance stared at him a moment. He'd not said grace in a long time. In fact, the only prayers he'd muttered recently had been ones of desperation at the hospital. He glanced at Amanda, who nodded her encouragement.

Gail's soft voice made it unanimous. "Just speak from your heart, dear."

They bowed their heads, and Lance cleared his throat. "Lord, thank you for this food and for the people you put in our lives. May we never take them for granted. Amen."

"Amen," Coach said. "That didn't sound like you'd wandered *that* far from Him."

"I guess not."

Gail passed him a bowl of salad. "What did you learn from your session with Coach O?"

Lance glanced from her to Coach Moore. "Tag teaming me?" he teased.

"Tandem teaching," his mentor responded with a smile. "Although we do make a good team."

"So do you and Amanda," Gail said.

> "Lord, thank you for . . . the people you put in our lives."

"I agree." Lance brushed his wife's arm. "And, I know I'd rather not ever repeat the past year again."

"Amen!" Amanda agreed.

Lance filled them in on the high points from the day's session, ending with the somber news he'd gotten from Terri. "Bryan's always been my best man. But he's really failed a lot lately. Terri told me his wife has multiple sclerosis."

"Oh, no," Amanda whispered.

"Obviously, things are tough emotionally and financially. She's receiving treatments, but she has a lot of bad days. She had to quit her job, and there are times she can't even take care of their kids."

"They have three little ones," Amanda said to Gail and Coach.

"I have to find a way to help. I told Terri to find a nanny service that can fill in when they need it. We'll pick up the tab. And we'll set up Bryan so he can work from home as a satellite employee when he needs to. I hope that'll ease some of their stress."

Coach exchanged a knowing look with Gail. "So you think you can follow the path of a three-dimensional leader?"

Lance nodded. "I do. It's a challenge, but I know I can turn things around."

"Just keep that pyramid in front of you."

"I definitely have that in mind."

"That's a start, but I meant that in a more concrete way."

"How so?"

"Test yourself, just like you did in Dr. Kess's class. Draw the pyramid on a piece of paper and put your X on there, then the circle for Amanda and the kids, then a check for your employees. I encourage my coaches as well as my players to do that on a regular basis. Once a week even. Or a month. It's a simple thing that can keep you on track, and help you apply Coach O's advice of 'Speaking Greatness' into people in every direction. Even if you do nothing else, those will keep you focused on the process and on your own attitude and effort."

"I could ask you about them," Amanda offered.

Gail shook her head. "No. Don't push him to do it. Has to be from his heart." She glanced lovingly at her husband. "Besides, you'll know when he's not doing it, just like you did this time." She turned back to Lance. "Do you have a pen on you?"

Lance nodded and pulled one from his shirt pocket. Gail handed him one of the paper napkins.

"I want you to write the name of someone who's made a major impact on your life—in a positive way."

Lance scribbled the name.

"Now, tell me one or two things this person did so consistently that it captured your heart and made this person an important part of your life."

> **"It's now time for you to decide what your legacy will be, and how you'll pass it on."**

Lance hesitated, then took a deep breath. "He was so calm and even keeled. His teaching never varied. He challenged me and cared about me as a person, not just as a player."

Gail nodded. "Then you need to realize that you are that person's legacy. His lessons will live on in you, then they'll be passed from this generation to the next. It's now time for you to decide what your legacy will be, and how you'll pass it on."

Lance looked down at the napkin, silently reading the name of the man across the table from him."

Gail's soft voice continued. "You can write your legacy, dear, starting today. By taking all this in and changing the way you lead, the way you behave toward others, you can control what people will say about you ten minutes from now and hundred years from now. I encourage you to start the process of building your legacy right now. And start with your beautiful wife and children at home."

> "You can write your legacy, dear, starting today."

Lance looked from Gail to Coach, who nodded his encouragement. Silent, Lance reached over and slipped his hand into Amanda's.

* * *

Two days later, Lance stood on the front porch of a modest ranch house, nervously shifting his weight from one foot to the other. He looked around, noticing that while the home could use some work, it was obviously well cared for and loved. He glanced down at his briefcase again, as if something about it might have changed in the last five seconds. Inside were the details on setting up a satellite office and the package from the nanny service. He prayed again that this went well.

He rang the doorbell again. This time the door opened, and Bryan stared at his boss, a wary expression turning to fear in his eyes.

Lance cleared his throat. "Bryan, I'm here because I care about you, and our company would not be where it is today without your personal commitment to excellence, your loyalty, and your integrity. I have a plan to offer you, which I hope will be a win-win situation for all of us. We need to talk."

Bryan stared at him a moment, not quite believing him. Finally, he stepped back and invited Lance in.

Lance turned just before the door shut, to look at the baseball resting on the dash of his car. Since returning from his visit with Coach, he'd carried it everywhere. For now, it represented more than his need to specify the "win." It reminded him how much he'd changed. He would never speak—or lead—the same way again.

With a genuine sigh of relief, Lance shut the door to his past. Time to start a whole new way of life.

Time to start becoming a Legacy Builder.

THE 5 NON-NEGOTIABLES

1. Specify the Win
2. Simplicity in a Complex World
3. Be a 3-Dimensional Leader^{SM}
4. The Power of Speaking Greatness^{SM}
5. Value People over Productivity

THE 5 NON-NEGOTIABLES OF THE LEGACY BUILDER

1. Specify the Win

- Maturity and balance go hand in hand.
- Specify daily what a "Win" is for you at work and especially at home
- Be Process Driven: Things that are built to last are not built fast.
- You control the pace of leadership, don't let the pace control you.
- Focus on One thing at a time . . . one day at a time.

2. Simplicity

- Are you a F.A.T. leader?
  The Criteria for an uncomplicated and qualified leader:

  F—aithful: You fully trust the organization, you believe without seeing.

  A—vailable: You make time to help yourself, others, & your community.

  T—eachable: You possess a teachable and coachable spirit.

- "Control the Controllables". . . Great Coaches and Leaders can discern what they can control and what they cannot.
- A Coach or a Leader's Job is to take an individual or a team and get them to a level they cannot get to themselves.
- You can't give away what you do not possess yourself as a leader.
- Focus on Attitude and Effort daily, these 2 things control everything else.

© 2007 COE Institute

3. Be a 3-Dimensional Leader ᴿᴹ

▸ The 3 Dimensions of Leadership

Level 1—You are fundamentally sound and you maintain high competency levels.

Level 2—You know and practice the secrets of motivating the 21st century team member.

Level 3—You are a master relationship builder that is focused on capturing people's hearts while holding them accountable.

▸ Be Mentally Tough: The ability to be comfortable with being uncomfortable.

▸ Everyone needs to feel Safe, Secure and Significant every day.

▸ Remember 90% of motivation lies in relationship, people today want a leader that authentically cares about them both professionally and personally.

▸ Great leaders and coaches are easy to please and hard to satisfy.

▸ Earn the right to speak into your people by capturing their heart.

4. The Power of Speaking Greatness^{SM}

‣ Realize that "life and death lie in the power of the tongue."

‣ Speaking Greatnes^{SM} is a style of communication that allows a coach or a leader to motivate others by giving feedback in such a way that the individual listens to the instruction and or criticisms and is not motivated by fear but by the desire to reach new levels and not disappoint the coach.

‣ Focus on the process or performance rather than just results.

‣ Practice a 3:1 Ratio when giving feedback or critiquing your people.

‣ Utilize a transformational vocabulary and work on helping others discover what the 'greatness' is that is inside of them and fan that flame!

‣ There are only 3 things we all should do when we make a mistake:

1) Admit it   2) Fix it   3) Don't repeat it or learn from it

‣ **T. H. I. N. K.** before you speak and ask these questions:

T—rue: Is what I am about to say True? If not, do not speak.

H—elpful: Is what I am about to say Helpful or will it escalate things?

I—nspiring: Is what I am about to say going to inspire them to the next level in their performance?

N—ecessary: Is what I am about to say truly necessary or am I just wanting to hear myself talk?

K—ind: Is what I am about to say going to be received as a kind, professional comment? If not bite your tongue and re-phrase.

5. Value People over Productivity

- ▸ True Legacy Builders live out these principles daily.

- ▸ Emphasizing people always enhances performance.

- ▸ Don't buy the lie that winning or success will cure all your problems . . . Legacy Builders want to win, but that is secondary to winning in life.

- ▸ Keep your antennas up for opportunities to demonstrate to your family or team members that they are more valuable to you than what they can do for you.

- ▸ Remember consistent behavior breeds trust and trust breeds loyalty.

BUILDING YOUR LEGACY NOW

I encourage you to do as Lance Marshall, and on the line below write down the name of someone that has had a positive, profound impact on your life. In fact, if it wasn't for them you may not be in the position you find yourself at this very moment.

The Greatest Leader I have ever known personally is

_____

The One Thing that they consistently did to capture my heart was

_____

One day perhaps someone will read this book and write your name down as the leader that impacted them profoundly . . . that would be nice. However, the true measure of a Legacy Builder is what people learned from you and what they carry on from your life. What will people write and say that you did for them? I challenge you to start writing your legacy today by being a 3-Dimensional Leader^{SM} that Speaks Greatness^{SM} into others!

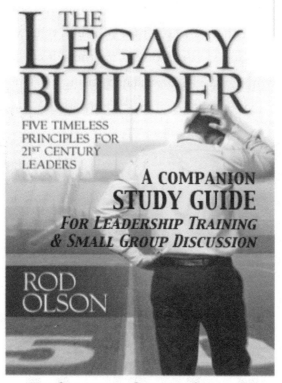

TO ORDER A STUDY GUIDE(S)
GO TO: WWW.LEGACYBUILDERBOOK.COM

ACKNOWLEDGMENTS

First, I wish to thank all the teachers and coaches that I have had over the years, who are holding this book in disbelief. Please remember to keep teaching the bad kids, too.

Truly many have contributed to the production of this book, and I have been humbled by the encouragement, support, and selfless help that so many have given to me. I would like to thank my parents, who long ago passed on, for the foundation of faith and values they instilled in me. Next, I wish to thank my wife Marla for bringing me back to those values and for her steadfast support of me as I dragged her all across this wonderful country. To my children, Colt, Connie, and Lance, for giving me the time to write and for putting up with a dad in process. I love you guys.

To those in my inner circle (which are many): I will not name names as it would take too long, and I don't want to risk leaving someone out. I wish to thank you all for being legacy builders for me as we journey through life together. Iron does sharpen iron as one man sharpens another, this wouldn't have happened without you.

To my good friend Scotty Kessler, who showed me another way to lead and coach: thank you for taking the time to disciple me and for the freedom to share these principles with the world.

To Derek Fullmer for giving me a model of what a true leader can be. Thank you for being a mentor who loves me, holds me accountable, and challenges me. What a blessing you are to me and my family.

To Ramona Richards and the MT6 Media team who made this story come alive: you are truly gifted. Thank you for putting up with an impatient ball coach.

To John Seiple, Doug Dawson, and Roy Dobie: thank you for your encouragement and help in allowing me to have the time to make this to happen.

To Jerry Moore and all the coaches that I have worked for and with over the years: you are the inspiration for the characters in this book.

To all the players that have called me 'Coach' over the years and have put into practice all the words in this book. For those that I coached without these principles, I apologize and ask for your forgiveness, and for those who experienced these principles firsthand and had their lives transformed with me, thank you.

Finally, I wish to thank God for the principles and His Son who lived them out. The good in this book comes from Him and whatever may be wrong with this book is on me . . . as it should be.

ABOUT THE AUTHOR

ROD OLSON, or "Coach O," is the founder and CEO of the Coaches of Excellence Institute and the Coach O Consulting Group. Rod is a globally sought-after speaker, author, and advisor on 21st-century coaching, leadership, and parenting.

Following a twenty-year college coaching career, Rod has taught leadership at Quantico for the U.S. DEA Leadership Academy, motivation at the USA Olympic Coaching Schools, and peak performance to the Pittsburgh Pirates major league baseball club. He has also mentored numerous CEOs of Fortune 500 companies, as well as many head coaches at all levels of sport.

Coach O resides with his wife and children near the beautiful Rocky Mountains in Denver, Colorado.

More information about Coach O can be found at www.coach-o.com and www.coachesofexcellence.com.

NEW YORK

THE ADIRONDACKS

THE MOHAWK VALLEY

THE SOUTHERN TIER

THE LAKESHORE

EAST OF THE HUDSON

THE CATSKILLS

NEW YORK CITY
AND LONG ISLAND

CONTENTS

To Sally—always there for us,
always ready to go

New York

OFF <u>THE</u>

BEATEN

PATH™

THIRD EDITION

WILLIAM G.
AND KAY SCHELLER

A Voyager Book

The Globe Pequot Press

Old Saybrook, Connecticut

ABOUT THE AUTHORS

William G. Scheller, contributing editor of National Geographic Traveler, is also the author of *New Jersey: Off the Beaten Path* and the Appalachian Mountain Club's *Country Walks Near New York.* His articles have appeared in the *Washington Post* Magazine, the *Christian Science Monitor,* and *Canoe.* Kay Scheller is also co-author of *New Jersey: Off the Beaten Path* (third edition) and a contributor to National Geographic's *Crossing America,* Fodor's *Boston,* and Fodor's *New England.*

Text illustrations by Carole Drong
Cover map copyright © DeLorme Mapping

Library of Congress Cataloging-in-Publication Data

Scheller, William.
  New York : off the beaten path / by William G. and Kay Scheller. — 3rd ed.
    p. cm. — (A Voyager book.)
  Includes index.
  ISBN 1-56440-473-0
  1. New York (State)—Guidebooks. I. Scheller, Kay. II. Title.
III. Series.
F117.3.S35 1994   94-9293
917.4704'43—dc20   CIP

Manufactured in the United States of America
Third Edition/Third Printing

INTRODUCTION

At first glance, there would appear to be one overriding problem with fitting a state like New York into the Off the Beaten Path series of travel books: The paths that run between Montauk and Niagara, between Binghamton and Massena, are among the most heavily beaten in the United States. The Dutch were in lower Manhattan before the Pilgrims landed at Plymouth; the population of New York State was eclipsed by that of California only within the past thirty years. Could there by any stones left unturned in such a place, any byways not trod so often as to become commonplace?

Yes, there are—precisely because of the long history of New York and the many millions of people who have lived and worked there. New York occupies a unique position in American history, a position between that of the small, densely settled New England states and the western expanses left untamed well into the nineteenth century. With the exception of the Dutch settlements at New Amsterdam and along the Hudson Valley, New York remained a virtual frontier until the late 1700s. When it was settled the newcomers were not colonists from abroad but in many cases migrating New Englanders, men and women setting the pattern for the next hundred years of westward expansion. New York thus became a transitional place between old, coastal America and the horizons of the West.

More than that, the future "Empire State" became a staging area for the people, ideas, and physical changes that would transform the United States in the nineteenth century. Its position between the harbors of the Atlantic coast and the Great Lakes assured early prominence in the development of canals and later railroads. Its vast resources made it an industrial power, while its size and fertility guaranteed its importance as a farm state. It began its growth early enough to create an infrastructure of small towns connected by back roads, rivers, and canals and remained vigorous in a modern era conducive to the rise of great cities along busy trunk-line railroads. All the while, the state's geographical diversity allowed its different regions to assume varied and distinct personalities.

The spiritual and intellectual atmosphere in New York was no less responsive to change. This is where the quietist Shakers played out much of their experiment in plain living. It's also where a young man named Joseph Smith announced that he had been shown lost books of the Bible proclaiming God's mission in the New World and founded Mormonism. The nineteenth-century fascination with spiritualism flourished in New York State, as did the early pop-culture phenomenon known as Chautauqua. Washington Irving proclaimed a native American literature here, and the artists of the Hudson River School painted American nature as it had never been painted before. When the English Arts and Crafts movement arrived in the United States at the end of the last century, one of its principal beachheads was at the studios of Elbert Hubbard in East Aurora, New York.

This book is about the rich legacy of tangible associations that all of this activity has left behind. New York is crammed as are few other states with the homes, libraries, and workshops of famous individuals, with battlefields and the remnants of historic canals, with museums chronicling pursuits as divergent as horse racing, glassblowing, gunsmithing, and winemaking. In a place where people have done just about everything, here are reminders of just about everything they've ever done. And while some of the destinations listed here regularly find their way into conventional guidebooks, most are hidden among the placid backwaters of the state. New York has no shortage of small and middle-size towns easily overlooked by superhighway travelers, and unlike many of the pretty villages of nearby New England, they have remained uncommercialized and very unself-conscious. An exploration of the New York State countryside will reveal dozens upon dozens of these communities and their attractions, along with miles of lush farmland and undisturbed natural surroundings.

The sheer size of New York State makes a system of geographic subdivision necessary in a book with upward of 150 individual listings. We have thus drawn a new set of boundaries within New York (see map), defining seven distinct territories: East of the Hudson, the Adirondacks, the Mohawk Valley, the Finger Lakes, the Niagara-Allegany Region, the Catskills, and New York City and Long Island. As much as possible, these boundaries have been drawn to reflect the natural distinctions that divide one area from another; however, a small number of arbitrary decisions were unavoidable. If you occasionally disagree, and would rather see Saratoga clustered with the Mohawk Valley than with the Adirondacks, just ignore our designation. You won't need a visa to hop from one chapter to another.

Within each chapter, the order of individual listings has been determined geographically, as explained in the chapter introductions. Few readers will be proceeding dutifully from site to site, so no attempt has been made to provide detailed linking directions. Still, it's nice to know what's near what if a slightly longer drive would make visits to several destinations possible.

And so, off to New York State. An especially enlightening journey is promised to all those New Englanders who thought the world ended at Lake Champlain; to Manhattanites for whom "Upstate" is terra incognita; to Midwesterners, Westerners, and Southerners who feel they hold the patents on small towns and open country; and to travelers from abroad who would like to learn a little more about how America came to be what it is.

The rest of you are from New York State, and you know what you've been hiding.

Note to Readers: In the course of writing this book, we were careful to obtain the most recent available information regarding schedules and admission fees at each attraction described. All of these details were accurate at the time the book went to press; however, hours of operation and prices are always subject to change. Just to be sure, use the telephone numbers provided to check these details before each visit.

The prices and rates listed in this guidebook were confirmed at press time. We recommend, however, that you call establishments before traveling to obtain current information.

EAST OF THE HUDSON

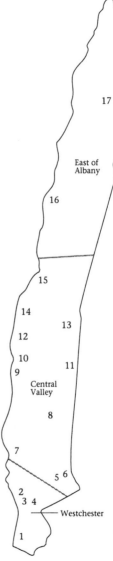

1. Hudson River Museum of
   Westchester
2. Kykuit (Rockefeller Estate)
3. Lyndhurst
4. Sunnyside
5. Caramoor
6. Le Chateau
7. Boscobel
8. Harrolds
9. Culinary Institute of America
10. Mills Mansion
11. Troutbeck
12. Old Rhinebeck Aerodrome
13. Crailo Gardens
14. Clermont
15. Olana
16. Crailo
17. New Skete Communities

EAST OF THE HUDSON

The first of our seven New York State regions begins in the crowded bedroom communities of Westchester County and extends northward into the western foothills of the Berkshires and the Green Mountains. Hilly itself throughout, it encompasses the eastern slopes of one of the most beautiful river valleys in the world. Anyone in need of convincing should drive north along the length of the Taconic State Parkway, which runs through the high country midway between the Hudson and the Connecticut and Massachusetts borders. Along with the more easterly and meandering State Route 22, the Taconic makes for a nice back-door entry into New England and an even more scenic trip than the more heavily traveled New York State Thruway on the other side of the river. Most of the attractions described in this chapter, however, are clustered along the river itself and are mainly accessible via U.S. Route 9, once the carriage road that connected the feudal estates of Old Dutch New York. Franklin D. Roosevelt's Hyde Park and the sumptuous Vanderbilt estate are two of the valley's best-known latter-day country seats; in this chapter, though, we'll concentrate on less publicized homesteads and other points of interest. The orientation is from south to north.

WESTCHESTER COUNTY

Just beyond the New York City limits, in Yonkers, ◆ **The Hudson River Museum of Westchester** occupies the magnificent 1876 Glenview Mansion, enhanced by a recent addition designed to provide exhibition space. As the preeminent cultural institution of Westchester County and the lower Hudson Valley, the museum's resources reflect the natural, social, and artistic history of the area.

A visit to The Hudson River Museum includes a walk through the four meticulously restored rooms on the first floor of the mansion itself. You'll hardly find a better introduction to the short-lived but influential phase of Victorian taste known as the Eastlake style, marked by precise geometric carving and ornamentation—the traceries in the Persian carpets almost seem to be echoed in the furniture and ceiling details.

Aside from the furnishings and personal objects that relate to the period when the Trevor family lived in the main building, the museum's collections have grown to include impressive holdings of Hudson River landscape paintings, including work by Jasper Cropsey and Albert Bierstadt.

In contrast to the period settings and historical emphases of the older parts of the museum, the state-of-the-art Andrus Planetarium features the Zeiss M1015 planetarium instrument, the only one of its kind in the Northeast. A contemporary orientation is also furthered by as many as thirty special art, science, and history exhibitions each year, centered on the work of American artists of the nineteenth and twentieth centuries. There are a Summer Jazz Series in July and August and a Victorian Holiday celebration each December.

The Hudson River Museum of Westchester, 511 Warburton Avenue, Yonkers 10701, (914) 963–4550, is open Wednesday, Thursday, and Saturday, 10:00 A.M. to 5:00 P.M.; Sunday, noon to 5:00 P.M.; and Friday, 10:00 A.M. to 9:00 P.M. Admission to the museum galleries is $3 for adults; $1.50 for senior citizens and children under 12. Admission to the planetarium is $4 for adults, $2 for senior citizens, and $2 for children under 12.

Hundreds of years before Glenview Mansion was built, the Philipse family assembled a Westchester estate that makes the Glenview's 27 acres seem puny by comparison. Frederick Philipse I came to what was then New Amsterdam in the 1650s and began using his sharp trader's instincts. By the 1690s his lands encompassed the southern third of what is now Westchester County.

In 1716 Philipse's grandson, Frederick Philipse II, assumed the title of Lord of the Manor of Philipsborough. It was he who started construction of **Philipse Manor Hall,** now a state historic site housing a museum of eighteenth-century life among the Hudson Valley gentry. Following the inheritance of the estate in 1751 by Col. Frederick Philipse (III), the Georgian manor house was rebuilt and enlarged to become the family's year-round seat. Philipse planted elaborate gardens and imported the finest of furnishings for the hall. His tenure as Lord of the Manor, however, ended when he decided to side with the Tory cause at the beginning of the American Revolution. He stayed for a while with his family in British-occupied New York City but evacuated to England along with His Majesty's troops at the end of the war.

3

Having been confiscated along with the rest of its Tory owner's properties after the revolution, Philipse Manor Hall was auctioned by the state of New York and passed to a succession of private owners during the century that followed. The state purchased its former property in 1908 and has since maintained the mansion as a museum of the history, art, architecture, and upper-class lifestyle of prerevolutionary New York. Inside and out it remains one of the most perfectly preserved examples of Georgian style in the Northeast.

Philipse Manor Hall Historic Site, Warburton Avenue and Dock Street, Yonkers 10702, (914) 965–4027, is open from late May through late October on Wednesdays and Thursdays from 11:00 A.M. to 2:00 P.M. and on Sundays from 2:00 to 5:00 P.M. Call for winter schedule. Visitors are encouraged to call the site before their visit, especially when planning to stop by on a holiday. Admission is free. Group tours are available by appointment.

The one-time owner of the house at our next stop would not have gotten along with Frederick Philipse III at all. He was Thomas Paine, arch-patriot, who wrote of "the times that try men's souls." In 1784, one year after the formal end of the American Revolution that Paine had so vociferously fueled with his pamphlets, the state of New York granted him 300 acres, the site of what is now called the **Thomas Paine Cottage and Museum,** in reward for his services to the newly founded nation. The house originally stood atop the hill overlooking the later Paine Avenue but was relocated to its present site after being donated by its last private owner to the New Rochelle Huguenot Association in 1908. The Huguenot connection is not with Paine but with the town of New Rochelle, where the house stands. New Rochelle was founded by refugee members of the French Protestant sect in the late seventeenth century.

Although the author of *Common Sense* lived in this little house until his death in 1809, he didn't leave behind enough possessions to enable modern curators to maintain it entirely as a Paine memorial. Most of the actual Paine associations are concentrated in the rear room on the first floor, the "Paine Room."

The other rooms in the cottage contain artifacts relating to the colonial history of the New Rochelle area and its Huguenot settlers. Of particular interest is the revolutionary-period bedroom.

4

The Thomas Paine Cottage and Museum, 20 Sicard Avenue and (around the corner at) 983 North Avenue, New Rochelle 10804, (914) 632–5376, is open from 2:00 to 5:00 P.M. Friday through Sunday in spring, summer, and fall and by appointment the rest of the year. The suggested donation is $3 for adults; $1 for children under 12.

Up in the Pocantico Hills, overlooking the Hudson River and the Palisades in New Jersey, the Rockefeller family has a magnificent estate. Before he died, Nelson A. Rockefeller bequeathed the mansion and 87 acres of land to the National Trust for Historic Preservation. It is scheduled to open to the public for tours in May 1994.

The forty-room Colonial Revival mansion is named ❖**Kykuit** (pronounced KYE-cut), Dutch for "lookout"—aptly named for its location. Furnishings include eighteenth- and nineteenth-century antiques and fine porcelains from the collection of John D., Jr., as well as Nelson's early Chinese ceramics and twentieth-century paintings, tapestries, and prints. Terraces and sculpture gardens, which include the works of noted modern artists such as Picasso and Calder, surround the house.

More than 200 acres of the estate remain in the hands of the Rockefeller family and will not be included in the tour. The public will get to see the entire first floor of the mansion, the five-chamber art gallery housing Nelson's modern art collection, the orangerie—a large greenhouse—and the coach barn, with its collection of antique horse-drawn carriages and automobiles.

Kykuit, Pocantico Hills, North Tarrytown 10591, (914) 631–8200, is open for tours from early May through October. Tours last two and a half hours and are available by advance reservation only. The tours begin at Philipse Manor, where visitors are shown a video and then transported by van to Kykuit. Tickets are $18 for adults; $16 for students and senior citizens. Visitors can also take a boat from Manhattan to Kykuit. Call (800) 533–3779 for information.

In 1838 the great Gothic Revival architect Alexander Jackson Davis designed ❖**Lyndhurst.** Overlooking the broad expanse of the Tappan Zee from the east, this beautiful stone mansion and its landscaped grounds are the property of the National Trust for Historic Preservation.

Lyndhurst

Lyndhurst, built for former New York City mayor William Paulding and originally called Paulding Manor, or the Knoll, represented the full American flowering of the neo-Gothic aesthetic that had been sweeping England since the closing years of the eighteenth century. Davis and his fellow American Gothic architects and landscapists were striving for a quirkier, more romantic effect than that represented by the classical styles of the preceding century or the more recent Greek Revival, just as the Hudson River painters would soon show their disdain for the strictures of academic art.

Lyndhurst is unusual among American properties of its size and grandeur in having remained under private ownership for nearly a century and a quarter. Paulding and his son owned the estate until 1864, when it was purchased by a wealthy New York merchant named George Merritt. Merritt employed Davis to enlarge the house and to add its landmark tower; he also constructed a large greenhouse and several outbuildings. The greatest legacy of his stewardship, however, was the commencement of an ambitious program to develop an English-inspired romantic landscape to complement the Gothic architecture of the main house.

One of the most notorious of America's railroad robber barons, Jay Gould, acquired Lyndhurst in 1880 and maintained it as a country estate. Upon his death in 1892, Lyndhurst became the property of his oldest daughter, Helen, who left it in turn to her younger sister Anna, duchess of Talleyrand-Perigord, in 1938. The duchess died in 1961, with instructions that the estate become the property of the National Trust.

There are several annual events, such as a Rose Day, Sunset Serenades (a summer music series), a dog show, and Christmas festivities, including candlelight tours during the first three weekends in December.

Lyndhurst, Route 9 just south of the Tappan Zee Bridge (635 South Broadway), Tarrytown 10591, (914) 631–0046, is open May through October, Tuesday through Sunday, 10:00 A.M. to 5:00 P.M., and November through April, Saturday and Sunday, 10:00 A.M. to 5:00 P.M. Open on Monday holidays. Closed Thanksgiving, Christmas, and New Year's Day. Admission is $6 for adults, $5 for senior citizens, and $3 for children 6 to 16.

Far less imposing than Lyndhurst but a good deal homier, ◆ **Sunnyside** stands just to the south in Tarrytown and offers a fascinating glimpse of the life of active retirement enjoyed there by its owner, Washington Irving. Irving described his country retreat as "a little old-fashioned stone mansion, all made up of gable ends, and as full of angles and corners as an old cocked hat." Not surprising for the man who wrote *The Legend of Sleepy Hollow, Rip Van Winkle,* and *Diedrich Knickerbocker's History of New York,* Sunnyside is a steep-gabled, Dutch Colonial affair, ivied with time and possessed of more than a little whimsy.

Washington Irving spent two periods of retirement at Sunnyside—the years 1836–42 and the last thirteen years of his life, 1846–59. It was here that he wrote *Astoria,* his account of the Pacific Northwest, as well as *The Crayon Miscellany, Wolfert's Roost,* and *The Life of George Washington.* Here too the author entertained such visitors as Oliver Wendell Holmes, William

7

Makepeace Thackeray, and Louis Napoleon. In the time not taken up with work and hospitality, he planned his own orchards, flower gardens, and arborways. These survive to this day, as do favorite Irving possessions such as the writing desk and piano on view in the house.

Sunnyside, West Sunnyside Lane (1 mile south of the Tappan Zee Bridge on Route 9), Tarrytown 10591, (914) 631–8200, is open daily 10:00 A.M. to 5:00 P.M.; closed Thanksgiving, Christmas, and New Year's Day; and closed Tuesdays from December through March. Admission is $6 for adults, $5 for senior citizens, and $3 for children ages 6 to 17. A grounds pass is available for $3.

Another important figure of the early Republic, political rather than literary, made his country home to the northeast at Katonah. This was John Jay, whom George Washington appointed to be the first chief justice of the United States and who, with Alexander Hamilton and James Madison, was an author of the *Federalist Papers*. Jay retired to the farmhouse now known as the **John Jay Homestead** in 1801, after nearly three decades of public service, and lived here until his death in 1829. His political career began in 1774, when he was elected to the Continental Congress, of which he was later president. He also served as minister to Spain, was coauthor (with Benjamin Franklin and John Adams) of the Treaty of Paris ending the revolution, was secretary for foreign affairs during the Articles of Confederation, and later became a chief justice of the Supreme Court and a negotiator of the Jay Treaty with Great Britain in 1794. Afterward he was elected to two terms as governor of New York under the provisions of the state constitution he had helped write in 1777.

Finally, retired to his Westchester farmhouse, Jay busied himself with farming and horticulture and with monitoring the early stirrings of the abolitionist movement, with which he was sympathetic. His son William and his grandson John Jay II lived at the old family homestead, as did John II's son, Col. William Jay II, a Civil War officer of the Union Army. The last Jay to live at the Katonah estate was Eleanor Jay Iselin, the colonel's daughter. After her death in 1953, the property was purchased by Westchester County and turned over to the state of New York as a state historic site.

Having survived so long in the Jay family, the John Jay Homestead is still well stocked with furnishings and associated items

8

that date back to the days when the great patriot lived here. Sixty acres of John Jay's original 900-acre farm are part of the state historic site.

The John Jay Homestead State Historic Site, Route 22, Katonah 10536, (914) 232–5651, is open May through December. From Memorial Day to Labor Day the hours are Wednesday through Saturday, 10:00 A.M. to 5:00 P.M.; Sunday, noon to 5:00 P.M. Call for off-season hours. The last tour enters the mansion at 4:00 P.M. Group tours are by advance reservation. There is a suggested donation of $4 for adults and $2 for children and senior citizens.

Not far from the John Jay Homestead is another Katonah landmark, ◆ **Caramoor.** Perhaps the last of the truly grand private homes to have been built in the Hudson River Valley, Caramoor was constructed between 1929 and 1939 by Walter Tower Rosen, a Berlin-born lawyer and investment banker, as a country retreat and showplace for his growing collection of European paintings, sculpture, furnishings, and objets d'art. Rosen built his mansion in the Mediterranean style, incorporating into the building entire rooms removed from European chateaus and reassembled on the site.

Caramoor survives today not only as a house museum but also as the home of an important summer music festival. Unlike many such programs, the Caramoor festival was not merely grafted onto a beautiful location but is a direct outgrowth of the interests and intentions of Walter Rosen and his wife, Lucie Bigelow Dodge Rosen: Both were accomplished amateur musicians. A series of three concerts in the music room in 1946 was the genesis of today's Caramoor Music Festival. In 1958 the addition of the Venetian Theater to the estate's complex of buildings made possible both larger audiences and more ambitious performances, including opera and ballet.

Caramoor was opened as a museum in 1968. The entire lower floor of the house is open to the public, including the galleries containing the Rosens' collections of handpainted Chinese wallcoverings, fifth-century B.C. Greek vases, English and Italian lacquer furniture, and Renaissance art. Each of the thirteen "period" rooms is a treasure in itself.

Caramoor, Girdle Ridge Road, Katonah 10536, (914) 232–5035, is open year-round Tuesday through Saturday from 11:00 A.M. to 4:00 P.M. and Sunday from 1:00 to 4:00 P.M. Groups are welcome by appointment. Admission to the house and grounds is $5; $3

9

for the grounds only. There is no extra charge for concerts or lectures. Festival performances in the Venetian Theater and Spanish courtyard take place throughout June, July, and August; for ticket information call the above number or write Caramoor, Box R, Katonah 10536.

CENTRAL VALLEY

It takes an interesting region to supply the wherewithal for an interesting regional museum, and the town of Brewster in southern Putnam County has done a good job of filling the bill for the **Southeast Museum.** Brewster has been the center of a diverse number of enterprises, including mining, railroading, circuses, and even the manufacture of condensed milk. Reminders of all these phases of local development are on exhibit at the museum, which is housed in the 1896 former town hall of what is actually the town of Southeast but referred to locally as Brewster.

Southeast was settled long before the Brewster family rose to prominence in the 1840s and 1850s, lending their name to the community that grew up around the railroad depot. The first settlers came about 1725. For more than one hundred years, their main pursuits were agriculture and modest local trade. In the middle-nineteenth century, though, Brewster's economic horizons expanded through the arrival of the Harlem Railroad, later part of Commodore Vanderbilt's vast New York Central system. Railroad days in Brewster are represented at the museum by the artifacts in the David McLane collection.

Brewster was also winter quarters for a number of circuses in the past century. Many of these small local enterprises were later consolidated by P. T. Barnum, who hailed from just across the state line in Connecticut. This most colorful aspect of Brewster's past is recalled in the museum's collection of early American circus memorabilia.

The Southeast Museum, Main Street, Brewster 10509, (914) 279–7500, is open Tuesday through Thursday from noon to 4:00 P.M.; Saturday and Sunday from 2:00 to 4:00 P.M. Admission is free.

In 1907 financier J. P. Morgan built a stone-and-brick Tudor mansion on a hillside overlooking the Hudson River Valley for his friend and minister, William S. Rainsford. The mansion was privately owned until 1973, when it was restored and reborn as a French restaurant called ❖ **Le Chateau.** Today, with its dogwood-lined approach, patio and gardens, richly paneled rooms, and elegantly set tables, the restaurant affords patrons the opportunity to enjoy a rapidly diminishing phenomenon—a true dining experience. At Le Chateau, classic French food is prepared and presented in a grand style that matches the atmosphere in which it is served.

Among the house specialties at Le Chateau: *Huîtres vivarois,* small baked oysters on the half shell in a spinach and curry mousseline sauce; *Foie gras des landes en terrine,* goose liver baked in a terrine with port, Madeira, and cognac; roasted baby quail; filet of salmon baked in parchment paper; roast venison; Paris Brest, chocolate cake with mocha filling; and cheesecake dotted with clouds of whipped cream. A fixed-price menu is available for $45; a three-course, a la carte dinner averages $43.

Le Chateau, Route 35 at the junction of Route 123, South Salem 10590, (914) 533–6631, serves dinner Tuesday, Wednesday, and Thursday from 6:00 to 9:00 P.M.; Friday and Saturday from 6:00 to 10:00 P.M.; and Sunday from 2:00 to 9:00 P.M. Reservations are a must, and jackets are required.

There was something about the Hudson River Valley that brought out the feudal lord in people with the means to do something about it—a natural invitation, as it were, to create surroundings commensurate with the stately grandeur of the river itself. The wealthy landowner States Morris Dyckman answered the call in 1804. He built a country seat, called ❖ **Boscobel,** that was and is one of the glories of Federal architecture in the United States.

Boscobel was also one of the great triumphs of historic preservation in an era, the 1950s, notorious for its disregard and wanton destruction of fine old buildings. Threatened with being leveled to make way for new construction, Boscobel was rescued largely through the efforts of Benjamin W. Frazier and the generosity of *Reader's Digest* cofounder Lila Acheson Wallace. The building was dismantled and reassembled, piece by piece, on its present site in Garrison-on-Hudson, 15 miles north of its old foundations.

Boscobel today looks inside and out much as it did in Dyckman's day. The Federal-period furnishings include work by New York's own Duncan Phyfe, and some of Dyckman's own collections of porcelain, silver, and finely bound books have been

11

Boscobel

returned. Outside, formal rose gardens and an apple orchard suggest the landscaping of a country estate of the early nineteenth century.

Boscobel Restoration, Inc., the nonprofit organization that maintains the house, also schedules a program of special seasonal events for which Dyckman's related mansion makes a perfect backdrop. These include a summer concert series, Christmas candlelight tours, and workshops and lectures.

Boscobel, Route 9D, Garrison-on-Hudson 10524, (914) 265–3638, is open daily except Tuesdays and the months of January and February; it's also closed on Thanksgiving and Christmas. April through October the hours are 9:30 A.M. to 5:00 P.M. (last tour at 4:15); November, December, and March the hours are 9:30 A.M. to 4:00 P.M. (last tour at 3:15). Admission is $5 for adults, $4 for senior citizens, and $2.50 for children 6 to 14.

Your six-course meal at ◆ **Harrolds,** in Stormville, might begin with veal galantine served with cassis sauce, followed by onion soup with Emmenthaler cheese. You might then move on to salad with country herb dressing, an entrée of roasted duck with blackberry sauce on a bed of wild rice pilaf, and a basket of fruit with a glass of port, and then crown your meal with an ethereal linzer torte. Or you may opt for one of the other choices on the nightly menu, which is wheeled on a blackboard to your table. As you would expect of a restaurant that has earned *Mobil Travel Guide*'s five-star rating for the seventeenth consecutive year, everything will be deliciously prepared, artfully presented, and graciously served. Harrolds is housed in a large, timbered cabin with a big stone hearth and brass chandeliers. Harrold Boerger is general manager of the twenty-two-year-old restaurant; his wife, Eva Durrschmidt, is presiding chef. They work together to ensure diners a splendid gastronomic experience.

Harrolds, Route 25, Stormville 12582, (914) 878–6595, serves dinner Wednesday to Friday from 6:00 to 9:00 P.M. There are two seatings on Saturday, 5:30 P.M. and 9:30 P.M. Reservations are a must, jackets are required, and credit cards are not accepted. The six-course, fixed-price meal is $60 per person, not including wine. Harrolds has a superb wine list.

Not all of the Hudson Valley landowners were as well-to-do as States Dyckman; most were burghers of a far more modest stamp. The legacy of the life led by one such family is preserved in the

Van Wyck Homestead, east of the river in Fishkill. The house was begun in 1732 by Cornelius Van Wyck, who had purchased his nearly 1,000 acres of land from an earlier 85,000-acre Dutchess County estate, and was completed in the 1750s with the construction of the West Wing. For all the land its owners possessed, the homestead is nevertheless a modest affair, a typical Dutch country farmhouse.

Like so many other farmhouses, the Van Wyck Homestead might have been forgotten by history had it not played a part in the revolutionary war. Located as it was along the strategic route between New York City and the Champlain Valley, the house was requisitioned by the Continental Army to serve as headquarters for Gen. Israel Putnam. Fishkill served as an important supply depot for General Washington's northern forces from 1776 to 1783. Military trials were held at the house; one such event was reputedly the source used by James Fenimore Cooper for an incident in his novel *The Spy*.

Another factor leading to the homestead's preservation was its having reverted back to the Van Wyck family after the revolution ended. Descendants of its builder lived here for more than 150 years. Today it is operated by the Fishkill Historical Society as a museum of colonial life in the Hudson Valley. The house features a working colonial kitchen fireplace with a beehive oven, which is used during special events. An interesting sidelight is the exhibit of revolutionary war artifacts unearthed in the vicinity during archaeological digs sponsored by the society.

The Van Wyck Homestead, Snook Road (near the intersection of Routes 9 and 84), Fishkill 12524, (914) 896–9560, is open May through October on Sundays from 1:00 to 5:00 P.M. and by appointment. There is an admission charge of $2. Bus tours are welcome, and a group rate is offered. Special events include September and holiday craft fairs, a June midsummer festival, and a St. Nicholas Day holiday tour.

You're now in ◆**Culinary Institute** country. Founded in 1946, it's the oldest culinary college in the United States and the only residential college in the world devoted entirely to culinary education. And the public is invited to sample the fare from any or all of its four award-winning, student-staffed restaurants on the 150-acre Hyde Park campus.

St. Andrew's Cafe features casual, well-balanced dining, attractively presented, with dishes ranging from wood-fired pizza to beef tenderloin to apple strudel. The restaurant is open Monday through Friday. Lunch is served from 11:30 A.M. to 1:00 P.M., and dinner from 6:00 to 8:00 P.M.

The **Caterina de Medici Dining Room** offers fixed-price menus and features contemporary and traditional regional Italian specialties. The restaurant is open Monday through Friday. There is one seating for lunch at 11:30 A.M., and one seating for dinner at 6:30 P.M.

The **Escoffier Restaurant** highlights classic French cuisine in an elegant setting and features table-side presentations. It's open Tuesday through Saturday. Lunch is served from noon to 1:00 P.M., dinner from 6:30 to 8:30 P.M.

The **American Bounty Restaurant** serves a variety of regional American dishes as well as poultry from the Julia Child Rotisserie kitchen. The restaurant is open Tuesday through Saturday. Lunch is served from 11:30 A.M. to 1:00 P.M., and dinner from 6:30 to 8:30 P.M.

The Culinary Institute of America is at 433 Albany Post Road, Hyde Park 12538, (914) 452–9600. Reservations are recommended at all of the restaurants and can be made by calling (914) 471–6608 Monday through Friday, 8:30 A.M. to 5:00 P.M. Jackets are required at The Escoffier Restaurant. Enter through the main gate and follow signs for the restaurants.

Those who love cooking—or eating—will enjoy poking through the **Culinary Institute's Conrad N. Hilton Library,** which opened in September 1993. The $7.5 million, 45,000-square-foot facility houses one of the largest collections of culinary works in the country. In addition to almost 50,000 books, the library has a video viewing center and a video theater. Visitors may see the collections of food writer Craig Claiborne, gastronome George Lang, and acclaimed chef August Guyet.

The Culinary Institute's Conrad N. Hilton Library is open Monday through Thursday, 8:00 A.M. to 11:00 P.M.; Friday, 8:00 A.M. to 10:00 P.M.; Saturday, 9:00 A.M. to 5:00 P.M.; and Sunday, noon to 8:00 P.M. The research staff is available Monday through Friday from 8:30 A.M. to 5:00 P.M. The library is immediately on your left after you pass through the main gate.

Lewis Country Farms, a 16-acre farm with restored 1861 barns (complete with silo, original post-and-beam ceiling supports and fieldstone walls) is an all-season kids' stop and shopping mecca.

There are live farm animals for petting, a life-size animated band, antique wagons and sleighs, and special weekend events. There's a flower shop, a gift shop, a farmers' market selling locally grown produce, an old-fashioned country butcher, freshly baked goods and homemade fudge, a greenhouse and garden center, and a year-round Christmas shop. And when you get hungry, the folks at Lewis Country Farms will serve up homemade soups and chili, sandwiches, and a heaping salad bar.

Lewis Country Farms, Overlook and DeGarmo roads, Poughkeepsie 12603, (914) 452–7650, is open daily.

Heading north past Poughkeepsie, we're back in mansion territory—but with a difference. Homes such as Philipse Manor Hall and Boscobel were built by men whose fortunes were founded in vast landholdings, but palaces such as the ◆**Mills Mansion** in Staatsburg represent the glory days of industrial and financial captains—the so-called Gilded Age of the late nineteenth century. The idea behind this sort of house building was to live not like a country squire but like a Renaissance doge.

Ogden Mills's neoclassical mansion was finished in 1896, but its story begins more than a hundred years before. In 1792 the property on which it stands was purchased by Morgan Lewis, great-grandfather of Mills's wife, Ruth Livingston Mills. Lewis, an officer in the revolution and the third postindependence governor of New York State, built two houses here. The first burned in 1832, at which time it was replaced by an up-to-date Greek Revival structure. This was the home that stood on the property when it was inherited by Ruth Livingston Mills in 1888.

But Ogden Mills had something far grander in mind for his wife's legacy. He hired a firm with a solid reputation in mansion building to enlarge the home and embellish its interiors—a popular firm among wealthy clients, one that went by the name of McKim, Mead, and White.

The architects added two spacious wings and decked out both the new and the old portions of the exterior with balustrades and pilasters more reminiscent of Blenheim Palace than anything previously seen in the Hudson Valley. The interior was (and is) French, in Louis XV and XVI period styles—lots of carving and gilding on furniture and wall and ceiling surfaces, along with oak paneling and monumental tapestries.

The last of the clan to live here was Ogden L. Mills, at one time U.S. secretary of the treasury, who died in 1937. One of his surviving sisters donated the home to the state of New York, which opened it to the public as a state historic site.

The Mills Mansion, off Old Post Road, Staatsburg 12580, (914) 889–8851, is open from mid-April through Labor Day on Wednesday through Saturday, 10:00 A.M. to 5:00 P.M., and on Sunday, noon to 5:00 P.M. From Labor Day through the last Sunday in October, the mansion is open on Wednesday through Sunday, noon to 5:00 P.M. It is also open during the Christmas season. Call for hours. Admission is free.

◆ **Troutbeck,** on the banks of the trout-filled Webatuck River in Amenia, is an English-style country estate that functions as a corporate conference center during the week and as a country inn on weekends. The 422-acre retreat, with its slate-roofed mansion with leaded windows, is a perfect place for couples who are looking for a true "inn" experience. There are fireplaced rooms with canopy beds, an oak-paneled library, gardens—even a pool and tennis courts. And, of course, gourmet dining.

The former home of poet-naturalist Myron B. Benton, Troutbeck was a gathering place for the literati and liberals of the 1920s. Ernest Hemingway and Sinclair Lewis are among those said to have stayed in the Tudor mansion built in 1918.

Including rooms in two outbuildings, a 240-year-old renovated farmhouse and a garden house, Troutbeck has a total of thirty-six rooms. But on weekends, when it functions as a country inn, it books a maximum of twenty-five.

Each weekend, Troutbeck's award-winning chef prepares menu selections such as smoked duck pâté with onion-lingonberry marmalade, grilled sushi tuna mignon over black olive-and-garlic orzo, and rainbow mousse cake.

Troutbeck, Leedsville Road, Amenia 12501, (914) 373–9681, is open year-round. Rates, which include all meals and spirits, begin at $595 per couple.

No more mansions for a while. Continuing north along the Hudson, the next point of interest is the ◆ **Old Rhinebeck Aerodrome,** 3 miles upriver from the town of Rhinebeck. Proprietor and curator Cole Palen has made the aerodrome more than just a museum—many of the pre-1930s planes exhibited here actually take to the air each weekend.

The three main buildings at the aerodrome house a collection of aircraft, automobiles, and other vehicles from the period 1900–37 and are open throughout the week. On Saturdays and Sundays, though, you can combine a tour of the exhibits on the ground with attendance at an air show featuring both original aircraft and accurate reproductions. Saturdays are reserved for flights of planes from the Pioneer (pre–World War I) and Lindbergh eras. On Sundays the show is a period-piece melodrama in which intrepid Allied fliers do battle with the "Black Baron." Where else can you watch a live dogfight?

All that's left at this point is to go up there yourself, and you can do just that. The aerodrome has on hand a 1929 New Standard D-25—which carries four passengers wearing helmets and goggles—for open-cockpit flights of fifteen minutes' duration . The cost is $25 per person.

Old Rhinebeck Aerodrome, 42 Stone Church Road, Rhinebeck 12572, (914) 758–8610, is open daily, May 15 through the end of October, from 10:00 A.M. to 5:00 P.M. Air shows, from June 15 through October 15, are on Saturdays and Sundays at 2:30 P.M. The fashion show, in which ladies from the audience dress up in vintage clothing, begins at 2:00 P.M. Biplane rides are available before and after the shows. Weekday admission is $4 for adults, $2 for children ages 6 to 10, and free for children under 6. Admission for weekend air shows is $9 for adults and $4 for children ages 6 to 10. The plane rides cost extra, as mentioned above.

◆ **Crailo Gardens,** in the small town of Ancram, near the spot where the borders of New York, Massachusetts, and Connecticut meet, is a place to contemplate earthbound delights rather than aerial excitement. The Crailo Gardens and Nurseries represent more than a quarter-century of devotion on the part of founder Edwin R. Thomson to the cultivation of dwarf and rare conifers. Thomson's collection now exceeds 400 cultivars of *Chamaecyparis, Juniperus, Picea, Pinus, Thuja,* and others; he has some 3,000 plants for sale and starts about 1,000 each year. All of the plants that are available for sale are in containers, with the exception of those in a permanent exhibit area, which is open to the public after 2:00 P.M. on Sunday afternoons. Crailo Gardens is open daylight hours from May through September and during other months, weather permitting. An appointment is advised during off season.

Crailo Gardens, Route 82, Ancram 12502, (518) 329–0601, is open to visitors during the above-mentioned summer hours. Admission is free.

There was a time when every schoolchild worthy of a gold star on his or her reports knew the name *Clermont.* Of course—it was the first successful steamboat, built by Robert Fulton and tested on the Hudson River. Less commonly known, however, is that the boat formally registered by its owners as *The North River Steamboat of Clermont* took its name from the estate of Robert Livingston, chancellor of New York and a backer of Fulton's experiments. ❖**Clermont,** one of the great family seats of the valley, overlooks the Hudson River in Germantown.

The story of Clermont begins with the royal charter granted to Robert Livingston in 1686, which made the Scottish-born trader Lord of the Manor of Livingston, a 162,000-acre tract that would evolve into the entire southern third of modern-day Columbia County. When Livingston died in 1728, he broke with the English custom of strict adherence to primogeniture by giving 13,000 acres of his land to his third son. This was Clermont, the Lower Manor, on which Robert of Clermont, as he was known, built his home in 1730.

Two more Robert Livingstons figure in the tale after this point: Robert of Clermont's son, a New York judge, and *his* son, a member of the Second Continental Congress who filled the now-obsolete office of state chancellor. It was the chancellor's mother, Margaret Beekman Livingston, who rebuilt the house after it was burned in 1777 by the British (parts of the original walls are incorporated into the present structure).

The Livingston family lived at Clermont until 1962, making various enlargements and modifications to their home over time. In that year the house, its furnishings, and the 500 remaining acres of the Clermont estate became the property of the state of New York.

The mansion at Clermont State Historic Site (also a National Historic Landmark) has been restored to its circa 1930 appearance; however, the collections are primarily half eighteenth- and half nineteenth-century French and Early American. Tours of Clermont include the first and second floors. An orientation

Olana

exhibit and a short film are given at the gift shop. There are formal gardens, woodsy hiking trails, and spacious landscapes (perfect for picnics) on bluffs overlooking the Hudson.

Clermont, off Route 9G, Clermont 12526, (518) 537–4240, is open from April 15 through Labor Day weekend, Wednesday through Saturday, 10:00 A.M. to 5:00 P.M.; Sunday, 12:00 to 5:00 P.M.; also 10:00 A.M. to 5:00 P.M. on Memorial Day, Independence Day, and Labor Day. From the Tuesday after Labor Day through October 31, the hours are noon to 5:00 P.M. Wednesday through Saturday, 1:00 to 5:00 P.M. Sunday, and 10:00 A.M. to 5:00 P.M. on Columbus Day. The grounds are open daily year-round from 8:30 A.M. to sunset.

History generally conditions us to expect the great houses of the world to belong to industrialists and landholders, while artists—so the cliché has it—starve in garrets. One artist who built many fanciful garrets and starved in none of them was the

Hudson River School master Frederic Edwin Church, whose Persian Gothic castle, ◆ **Olana,** commands a magnificent view of the river south of the town of Hudson. What the popular landscape painter did here was nothing less than sculpt the perfect embodiment of his tastes and then live in it for the rest of his life.

Church had been a commercial and critical success for more than a decade when he decided to build his castle on the Hudson property he and his wife had purchased in 1860. In 1867 and 1868 the Churches had traveled throughout Europe and the Middle East, and the trip made quite an impression on their sensibilities, as reflected in the thirty-seven-room mansion they began building in 1870. Olana, which was completed two years later, draws heavily upon Islamic and Byzantine motifs. Persian arches abound, as do Oriental carpets, brasswork, and inlaid furniture. The overall setting is typically Victorian, with no space left empty that could possibly be filled with things. What makes Olana untypical, of course, is the quality of the things.

Although Church employed as a consultant Calvert Vaux, who had collaborated with Frederick Law Olmstead on the design of New York's Central Park, the artist was the architect of his own house. When scholars describe Olana as a major work of art by Church, they are not speaking figuratively; the paints for the interior were mixed on his own palette.

Olana, Route 9G, Hudson 12534, (518) 828–0135, is open *by guided tour only* from April 15 to Labor Day, Wednesday through Sunday. The first tour begins at 10:00 A.M. weekdays and Saturdays and noon on Sundays; the last tour starts at 4:00 P.M. Also open on Memorial Day, Independence Day, and Labor Day. Call for September and October hours. Tours are limited to twelve people, so call for reservations. An admission fee is charged. The grounds are open year-round from 8:00 A.M. until sunset.

EAST OF ALBANY

As fascinating as Olana is, by the time you leave you may be humming the old Shaker tune "It's a Gift to Be Simple." So head north and east to the **Shaker Museum** in Old Chatham. The museum is housed in a collection of buildings located just 12 miles from Mt. Lebanon, New York, where the Shakers established their first community.

21

The Shakers, formally known as the United Society of Believers in Christ's Second Appearing, were a sect founded in Britain and transplanted to America just prior to the revolution. A quietist, monastic order dedicated to equality between the sexes, sharing of community property, temperance in its broad sense, and the practice of celibacy, the sect peaked in the middle nineteenth century with about 6,000 members. Today there are fewer than a dozen Shakers living in a community at Sabbathday Lake, Maine.

Ironically, it is the secular aspects of Shaker life that are most often recalled today. The members of the communities were almost obsessive regarding simplicity and purity of form in the articles they designed and crafted for daily life; "Shaker furniture" has become a generic term for the elegantly uncluttered designs they employed. In their pursuit of the perfect form dictated by function, they even invented now-ubiquitous objects such as the flat broom.

The Shaker Museum has amassed a collection of more than 18,000 objects, half of which are on display. The main building contains an orientation gallery that surveys Shaker history and provides highlights of the rest of the collection. The museum's library contains one of the two most extensive collections of Shaker material in the world. The Summer Kitchen serves light lunches and beverages.

The Shaker Museum, Shaker Museum Road (off County Route 13), Old Chatham 12136, (518) 794–9100, is open daily May 1 through October 31, from 10:00 A.M. to 5:00 P.M. Admission is $6 for adults, $5 for senior citizens, $3 for children ages 8 to 17, and free for children 8 or under. Family admission is $14.

When we think of the Dutch in America, we generally recall only the settlement of New Amsterdam, later New York, at the mouth of the Hudson River. But the colony of "New Netherland" actually extended as far north along the valley as Albany—or rather, Fort Orange, which is what the Dutch called their northern outpost in the seventeenth century. Just across the river from Albany, in Rensselaer, stands ◆ **Crailo,** an early eighteenth-century house that recalls a time when the Dutch were still the predominant cultural presence in this area, despite their loss of political control to the British.

When Crailo was the center of preparations for the French and Indian Wars, the Dutch had already been in the vicinity of

Albany for more than a century. Present-day Rensselaer and environs were colonized in the 1630s; the town name itself was that of the family who held the "patroonship," virtually a feudal proprietorship, of this vast area on the east bank of the Hudson. Crailo itself was occupied by Hendrick Van Rensselaer, heir to a substantial portion of the estate.

Crailo changed with time and tastes. It received the Georgian treatment, complete with a new east wing, in 1762; at the beginning of the 1800s, another Van Rensselaer added Federal touches. The house passed out of family hands and suffered through a variety of uses, only to be purchased by descendant Susan DeLancey Van Rensselaer Strong in 1899 and donated to the state twenty-five years later. Since 1933 the house has been maintained as a museum.

The house has been fitted up as a museum of the Dutch roots of Albany and the Hudson Valley. Displays include artifacts from Fort Orange, furs, paintings, Dutch furniture, and household objects unique to the Hudson Valley. On special occasions visitors can even watch demonstrations of eighteenth-century cooking. There are also outdoor concerts and an annual Twelfth Night celebration. The museum has extensive school programs, including a cooking class, by appointment.

Crailo, 9½ Riverside Avenue, Rensselaer 12144, (518) 463–8738, is open April 15 through October 31, Wednesday through Saturday from 10:00 A.M. to 5:00 P.M. and Sunday from 1:00 to 5:00 P.M. Tours are given on the hour and half-hour; the last tour is at 4:00 P.M. Also open Memorial Day, Independence Day, and Labor Day. Call for off-season hours. Admission is free.

Natural and social history are the focus of a Troy institution geared specifically to young people. This is **The Junior Museum,** a hands-on learning center that has everything from a reproduction of a circa 1850 log cabin to constellation shows in the planetarium.

The main gallery of the museum features annually changing art, history, and science exhibits. Upstairs, in addition to the cabin, is a gallery of physical and natural science exhibits that include honeybees in an observation hive, a red-tailed hawk, live reptiles, and both salt- and freshwater aquariums. Downstairs the major exhibit is entitled "Balanced on the Back of a Turtle," with a longhouse, Iroquois stories, hunting, harvesting, and lots of hands-on fun.

23

The Junior Museum, 282 Fifth Avenue, Troy 12182, (518) 235–2120, is open Wednesday, Thursday, and Friday from 1:00 to 5:00 P.M. and Saturday and Sunday from 11:00 A.M. to 4:30 P.M. During spring and winter school vacations, hours are extended. Admission is $3.50 for adults, $2.50 for children, and free for children under 2. It includes shows in the planetarium and shows with live animals.

HOOSIC VALLEY

Most of us know that the Battle of Bunker Hill was not actually fought on Bunker Hill (it took place on Breed's Hill, also in Charlestown, Massachusetts), but how many can identify another military misnomer of the revolution?

We're talking about the 1777 Battle of Bennington, an American victory that laid the groundwork for the defeat and surrender of General Burgoyne at Saratoga that October. The battle, in which American militiamen defended their ammunition and supplies from an attacking party made up of British troops, Tory sympathizers, mercenaries, and Indians, took place not in Bennington, Vermont, but in Walloomsac, New York. True, the stores that the British were after were stashed in the Vermont town, but the actual fighting took place on New York soil.

The state of New York today maintains the site of the battle as an official state historic site. It's on a lovely hilltop in eastern Rensselaer County, studded with bronze and granite markers that explain the movements of the troops on the American militia's triumphal day. The spot is located on the north side of Route 67 and is open throughout the year during daylight hours, weather permitting. Visitors can check road conditions by calling ◆**Bennington Battlefield** at (518) 686–7109. On a clear day visitors can enjoy fine views of the Green Mountain foothills, prominent among which is Bennington's obelisk monument. Drive over to visit the monument and give the Vermonters their due—but really, doesn't "Battle of Walloomsac" have a nice ring to it?

The last stop on this ramble up the east shore of the Hudson offers proof that in this part of the world, the monastic spirit did not pass into history with the Shakers. Cambridge is the home of the ◆**New Skete Communities,** a group of monks, nuns, and laypeople organized around a life of prayer, contemplation, and physical work. Founded in 1966 within the Byzantine Rite of the Roman Catholic church, the New Skete Communities have been a part of the Orthodox church in America since 1979.

Visitors to New Skete are welcome at two of the community's houses of worship. The small Church of the Transfiguration of Christ, open at all times, contains a number of icons painted by the monks and nuns, while the larger Church of Christ the Wisdom of God—open to visitors only during services—has, imbedded in its marble floor, original pieces of mosaic that were brought from the A.D. 576 Church of Sancta Sophia (Holy Wisdom) in Constantinople.

As with many monastic communities, the monks and the nuns of New Skete help support themselves through secular pursuits. At New Skete their business is the breeding of German shepherds and the boarding and training of all breeds. The monks have even written two successful books, *How to Be Your Dog's Best Friend* and *The Art of Raising a Puppy*. They also operate a gift shop, where they sell their own cheeses, smoked meats, fruitcake, and the famous New Skete cheesecakes made by the nuns.

The New Skete Communities, New Skete Road, Cambridge 12816 is accessible from Cambridge Center via East Main Street and Chestnut Hill Road. For information call (518) 677–3928.

THE ADIRONDACKS

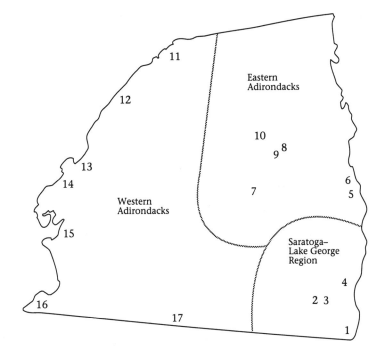

1. Saratoga National Historical Park
2. Saratoga Spa State Park
3. National Museum of Racing and Thoroughbred Hall of Fame
4. Hyde Collection
5. Fort Ticonderoga
6. Crown Point State Historic Site
7. Adirondack Museum
8. Mt. Van Hoevenburg Recreational Area
9. John Brown Farm State Historic Site
10. Six Nations Indian Museum
11. St. Lawrence Seaway
12. Frederic Remington Art Museum
13. Boldt Castle
14. The Antique Boat Museum
15. Sackets Harbor Battlefield
16. Fort Ontario
17. Steuben Memorial State Historic Site

THE ADIRONDACKS

North of the Mohawk Valley, spread between Lake Champlain and the St. Lawrence River, New York's Adirondack Mountains compose one of the nation's great expanses of near-wilderness and surely the largest slice of backcountry in the northeastern states. The state-protected Adirondack Forest Preserve alone accounts for more than 2 million acres of mountains, woodlands, and lakes, and this is only part of the 6-million-acre Adirondack State Park. For sheer vastness and emptiness, the Adirondack region is rivaled in this part of the country only by the northern interior of Maine; but while inland Maine—except for the Katahdin massif—is generally flat or gently rolling, the northern counties of New York contain forty-two peaks more than 4,000 feet in height. (The highest is Mt. Marcy, near Lake Placid, at 5,344 feet.) As in northern Maine, parts of the Adirondacks are still logged, although many areas have returned to a near-approximation of what they looked like when white men first saw them.

Ironically, the Adirondacks have benefited from being left on the sidelines during the "discovery" of nearby Vermont and New Hampshire in the years following World War II. The two New England states have acquired a certain cachet, and they have been more heavily developed and populated as a result. The equally beautiful Adirondacks, meanwhile, have drifted along in the public consciousness largely as the place where the famous summer chairs come from (it seems they really did originate here) and as the locale for Gilded Age "camps" on estates running into the tens of thousands of acres. Throw in the Thousand Islands, Saranac Lake, and Lakes Placid and George, and the perception is complete.

But there's so much more. In addition to being a "hidden" wilderness recreation land of such vast proportions, the Adirondacks have numerous historical connections, particularly in the form of battlefields that saw clashes between British and American forces when the region was a frontier buffer between Canada and the new Republic to the south. Today's border is marked by the engineering marvel of the St. Lawrence Seaway and by the binational resort area that has sprung up around the Thousand Islands. The southeastern gateway to the Adirondacks, Saratoga, is one of the horse-racing capitals of America.

Farther north are museums that chronicle the life of the Iroquois, the art of Frederic Remington, and Adirondacks craftsmanship, boat building, and pioneer life.

Head north beyond Saratoga, then, for the real "upstate" New York, a domain that rivals the expansiveness of the West yet is rooted in the traditions of the East.

(*Note:* The overall place-to-place direction followed in this chapter is counterclockwise—north, then west and south.)

SARATOGA–LAKE GEORGE REGION

North of the confluence of the Mohawk and Hudson rivers, near the present-day towns of Mechanicville and Stillwater, one of the most decisive battles of world history was fought in the early days of October 1777. The Battle of Saratoga holds its place in history as a watershed, a turning point in the prolonged and peripatetic series of military campaigns that made up the American Revolution. The battle, the sites of which are commemorated in ❖ **Saratoga National Historical Park,** offered the first conclusive proof that American forces could triumph over the British in a major engagement and led to the French entering the war on behalf of the United States.

The Lake Champlain and Hudson River valleys were a major north-south route in the eighteenth century and consequently provided a natural highway for the movement of troops. British Gen. John Burgoyne planned, early in 1777, to move his forces southward from Canada to Albany, from which point he would be able to act in concert with the British army headquartered in New York to cut the New England colonies off from the Middle Atlantic region.

But Burgoyne's plan ran into trouble from the start. He was denied the support of a detachment under Col. Barry St. Leger proceeding east from Lake Ontario, after St. Leger retreated back to Canada in the face of an expected attack by Gen. Benedict Arnold (Arnold was not yet the traitor of historical record). Burgoyne also suffered a surprise defeat when he sent part of his army into the field against New England militia at the Battle of Bennington, August 16. By the time he reached the west bank of the Hudson at Saratoga (present-day Schuylerville) on September 13, the prospect of "Gentleman Johnny" Burgoyne making

The Saratoga Monument
Saratoga National Historical Park

an easy progress to Albany was considerably dimmed by the presence of 9,000 American troops, with artillery, guarding the Hudson River route at Bemis Heights.

Burgoyne was stopped in a standoff battle on September 19. He regrouped his forces a mile north of the American lines for a three-week period of waiting for reinforcements from New York. But help didn't arrive, and rather than allow his supplies to become even more depleted and his men more demoralized, Burgoyne again engaged the Americans in battle on October 7. The fighting ended with a thousand British casualties (the Americans suffered fewer than half that number) and a Redcoat retreat north to the Saratoga heights. It was there that Burgoyne, his 6,000 troops surrounded by 20,000 Americans, surrendered on October 17.

A 9-mile tour road in the 2,800-acre Saratoga National Historical Park encompasses the sites that were crucial during those fateful weeks in September and October 1777. The 1777 Philip Schuyler House and the Neilson House can be toured in summer months.

Saratoga National Historical Park Visitor Center, 648 Route 32, Stillwater 12170, (518) 664–9821, is open daily in July and August from 9:00 A.M. to 5:00 P.M. Admission is $4 per car for the tour road; $2 for hiking. Children 16 and under are admitted free.

Tradition says the Indians of the Saratoga region visited High Rock Spring as early as 1300 to gain strength from the "Medicine Spring of the Great Spirit." Four hundred and seventy years later, in 1771, Sir William Johnson, suffering from a wound received in the Battle of Lake George, was carried on a litter by Mohawk Indians from Johnstown to High Rock Spring. After a short stay his health improved noticeably, and the reputation of the spring quickly grew.

The first person to recognize the commercial value of the mineral waters at Saratoga Springs may well have been John Arnold, who in 1774 purchased a crude log cabin built on a bluff overlooking High Rock Spring, improved it, and opened an inn. Thirteen years later, in 1787, revolutionary war hero Alexander Bryan purchased the inn. He is generally recognized as the first permanent white resident of Saratoga Springs, and his inn was the only Saratoga hotel until 1801, when Gideon Putnam built the Grand Union Hotel. Throughout the years the inn has operated sporadically as a lodge, tavern, restaurant, and private dwelling. Today, although it is in the process of being restored, you can enjoy stir-fried chicken Maui, fettuccini Lily, or a host of other delicious dishes at **The Olde Bryan Inn.**

The Olde Bryan Inn, 123 Maple Avenue, Saratoga Springs 12866, (518) 587–2990, is open Monday through Friday from 11:30 A.M. until 11:00 P.M.; Friday and Saturday until midnight. The tavern is open daily until 1:00 A.M.

After the word got out about the restorative powers of the water at Saratoga Spring, it didn't take long for the convinced and the merely curious to come. At ◆**Saratoga Spa State Park,** you'll learn how, by 1880, the town had become an elegant resort.

Twenty-two separate mineral wells currently bubble up from the ground in and around Saratoga Spa State Park. All of their waters are naturally carbonated, although they are significantly different in taste, alkalinity, salinity, and the effects they produce (some are decidedly laxative). A hundred years ago the springs were tapped and the waters served at salons built for the purpose; "taking the waters" became as much a part of summering at Saratoga as frequenting the racetrack.

In 1910 New York State acquired the rights to the mineral waters of Saratoga—a measure that was required to prevent the eventual depletion of the supply—and began to purchase the land that would become the state park. Although the springs still flow and some of the waters are bottled (some are available for drinking on-site), the principal means of enjoyment for latter-day enthusiasts is in the famous Saratoga baths. Open all year, the Roosevelt Baths offer private rooms, reasonable rates for mineral baths and soothing massages, and even hydrocollator and hot-pack treatments.

There's a lot more to Saratoga Spa State Park than the waters. The Gideon Putnam Hotel, on the park grounds, is within a short walk of the baths, as are a fine golf course, tennis courts, and cross-country ski trails. There are two swimming pools and, in the winter, three ice-skating rinks. The Saratoga Performing Arts Center is the summer home of both the Philadelphia Orchestra and the New York City Ballet, as well as the venue for a full schedule of pop concerts and dramatic performances in the Little Theater.

Saratoga Spa State Park, Saratoga Springs 12866, (518) 584–2000, is open throughout the year. For information on the baths and related treatments, call (518) 584–2011. For ticket information for the Saratoga Performing Arts Center, call (518) 587–3330.

Along with the convinced and the curious came the entrepreneurs. Between 1823 and 1889 mineral waters from approximately thirty springs in Saratoga County were bottled and distributed around the world, and an industry was born. The **National Bottle Museum,** housed in a 1901 former hardware store in Ballston Spa's historic district, documents the rise and decline of that industry. Through exhibits of antique bottles and glassmaking tools, videos, and artifacts, it tells the story of a time past, when young men were indentured to the owners of glass factories and apprenticed for fifteen years in order to become glassblowers in the glass houses that made bottles and jars by hand. It re-creates an industry and a way of life that have vanished from the American scene.

The National Bottle Museum, 76 Milton Avenue, Ballston Spa 12020, (518) 885–7589, is open daily from June 1 to September 30, 10:00 A.M. to 4:00 P.M.; October 1 to May 31, open Monday through Friday, 10:00 A.M. to 4:00 P.M., and closed weekends. Admission is $2 for adults, $1 for children ages 6 to 12, and free for children under 6.

After a nice mineral bath, massage, and dinner, you'll be all set for a night at the track. Horse racing is Saratoga's other raison d'etre, and the history and traditions of the sport are thoroughly chronicled at the ◆**National Museum of Racing and Thoroughbred Hall of Fame,** directly across from the Saratoga Race Course. Patrons enter the museum through an actual starting gate, complete with life-size representations of a horse, jockey, and starter. Some of the highlights: paintings of outstanding horses, the saddle and boots used by jockey Johnny Loftus on Man o'War, a Hall of Fame, and the actual skeleton of a thoroughbred. *Race America*, filmed at racetracks and stud farms across the country, is shown in the theater. Video booths lining the walls provide films of some of racing's greatest.

The National Museum of Racing and Thoroughbred Hall of Fame, Union Avenue, Saratoga Springs 12866, (518) 584–0400, is open year-round. From January 1 through the end of July, open Monday through Saturday, 10:00 A.M. to 4:30 P.M., and Sunday, noon to 4:30 P.M.; racing season, open daily, 9:00 A.M. to 5:00 P.M.; and September 1 through December 31, open Monday through Saturday, 10:00 A.M. to 4:30 P.M., and Sunday, noon to 4:30 P.M. Admission is $2 for adults and $1 for senior citizens, students, and children 5 to 18.

Before leaving Saratoga stop in at **The Casino,** which actually was one back in the days when it was perfectly legal to lose your shirt at the blackjack tables in New York State. The handsome Victorian structure was built in 1870–71 by John Morrissey, a colorful local character who was equally at home in the boxing ring and the state senate and who was one of the founders of the first racetrack at Saratoga Springs in 1863. Morrissey and the next owner, Richard Canfield, both ran a lucrative gambling establishment here, especially after Canfield's 1894 remodeling of the building. But Saratoga Springs was not to become Las Vegas, and when casino gambling was outlawed in New York, Canfield sold The Casino to the city. A year later, in 1912, the Historical Society of Saratoga Springs took up permanent residence in these lavish quarters.

The collections of the society concentrate largely upon the Victorian age during which Saratoga Springs flourished. The Hall of History traces the growth of the town from a frontier outpost to a grand resort. The Belter Room contains splendid specimens of the work of John Henry Belter, whose elaborately carved furniture stands as the epitome of Victorian interior design.

The Casino also houses the **Walworth Memorial Museum,** with nineteenth-century furnishings and personal effects belonging to the family of Reuben H. Walworth, the last chancellor of New York State.

The Casino, Congress Park, Saratoga Springs 12866, (518) 584–6920, is open during June, September, and October from 10:00 A.M. to 4:00 P.M. Monday through Saturday and from 1:00 to 4:00 P.M. Sunday. During July and August The Casino is open daily from 10:00 A.M. to 4:00 P.M. From November 1 through Memorial Day, The Casino is open Wednesday through Sunday from 1:00 to 4:00 P.M. Admission is $2 for adults, $1.50 for students and senior citizens, and 25 cents for children under 7.

Just outside Saratoga Springs are the **Petrified Gardens,** consisting of the exposed remains of a sea reef that thrived here beneath the Cambrian Sea 500 million years ago, give or take a year or two. Known since 1825 and properly identified in 1883, the "gardens" are the fossilized remains of cabbagelike plants related to modern algae. The reef they formed when alive teemed with trilobites, brachiopods, and rudimentary snails, the fossils of some of which are visible among the plant fossils at this site. When the primordial seas receded, the vegetation was exposed, fossilized beneath layers of sediment, and eventually exposed again by the shearing action of the glaciers. These cryptozoons, as they are called, are found elsewhere only at sites in northeastern Asia and western Australia.

At the Petrified Gardens visitors can walk among these ancient plants, which can easily be distinguished by the untrained eye. Just look for gray, layered nodules that look as if they might be broken, protruding sections of petrified cabbage. Among the vegetation is the "Iroquois Pine," one of the largest in the Adirondacks and estimated to be 300 years old. There are hands-on activities for children in the nature center.

Petrified Gardens, Petrified Gardens Road, off Route 29, Saratoga Springs 12866, (518) 584–7102, is open Mother's Day to November, daily, 10:00 A.M. to 5:00 P.M. Admission is $2 for adults, $1.80 for senior citizens, and $1 for children 8 to 16. Call for group rates.

In June 1885, suffering from throat cancer and longing for fresh air and a healthier climate, President Ulysses S. Grant left his home in New York City for Saratoga County. He and his family moved into a summer cottage on top of Mt. McGregor, 8 miles from Saratoga Springs. At the cottage he continued work on his memoirs and, two weeks after completing them, died on July 23, 1885.

The house at **Grant Cottage State Historic Site** is preserved as Grant left it, from the bed where he died to the floral pieces sent from around the country. It is operated by The Friends of the Ulysses S. Grant Cottage, in cooperation with the New York State Office of Parks, Recreation, and Historic Preservation.

Grant Cottage State Historic Site, Mt. McGregor, Wilton (mailing address: P.O. Box 990, Saratoga Springs 12866), (518) 587–8277, is open from Memorial Day to Labor Day, Wednesday through Sunday, 10:00 A.M. to 4:00 P.M.; September, open weekends, 10:00 A.M. to 4:00 P.M. Groups, by advance reservation, are accepted year-round. Admission is $2 for adults, $1.50 for senior citizens, and $1 for children.

Just north of Saratoga, where so much turn-of-the-century money was spent on the sporting life, is the town of Glens Falls,

35

where a small fortune was instead disbursed on a remarkable collection of art. Glens Falls was the home of Charlotte Pruyn, heiress to a local paper fortune, who married Louis Fiske Hyde of Boston in 1901. In 1907 the Hydes returned to Glens Falls, and in 1912 they began building the Florentine villa that today houses the ◆Hyde Collection. Influenced by the home-as-museum philosophy of the Boston Brahmin tastemaker Isabella Stewart Gardner, and with the help of connoisseurs such as Bernard Berenson, the Hydes filled their home with an eclectic and assiduously acquired collection of American and European art spanning five centuries.

The Hydes bought art with experts' eyes, concentrating not so much upon any individual period or school but upon the most expressive work of whichever painter or sculptor caught their attention. The end result was a collection that appears to have been amassed not by members of the upstate gentry but by a prince with a state treasury at his disposal.

Even before Louis Hyde's death in 1934, the Hydes had begun making plans to make their art collection accessible to the public someday. Employing curators to help round out her acquisitions (including the addition of twentieth-century work), Mrs. Hyde spent the next three decades working toward the day when her Adirondacks home would become an exquisite museum. Drawing upon a trust established by Mrs. Hyde in 1952, the Hyde Collection opened its doors to the public after her death, at the age of ninety-six, in 1963.

And so it is that in Glens Falls you can enjoy works by artists such as Rubens, Botticelli, Rembrandt, Seurat, Degas, Homer, Whistler, Picasso, Cézanne, and Matisse.

The Hyde Collection, 161 Warren Street, Glens Falls 12801, (518) 792–1761, is open Tuesday through Sunday, 10:00 A.M. to 5:00 P.M.; closed Mondays and national holidays. Admission is $4.50 for adults, $3.50 for students and senior citizens, and free for children 5 and under. Admission is free on Sundays from 10:00 A.M. to 2:00 P.M.

At the age of nineteen, Marcella (Kochanska) Sembrich made her operatic debut in Athens, singing in a number of the great opera houses in Europe before joining New York's Metropolitan Opera Company for its first season in 1883. She returned to Europe until 1898 and then rejoined the Metropolitan Opera until 1909, when her farewell was the occasion for the most sumptuous gala in the Met's history. She was founder of the vocal departments of the Juilliard School in New York and the Curtis Institute in Philadelphia and was a preeminent teacher of singing for twenty-five years. She often brought students to a studio near her summer home on Bolton Landing in Lake George. **The Marcella Sembrich Opera Museum,** in Mme. Sembrich's converted studio, displays operatic memorabilia she collected from her debut to her death in 1935.

The Marcella Sembrich Opera Museum, Bolton Landing-on-Lake George 12814, (518) 644–9839 (office: 3236 Congress Street, Fairfield, CT 06430; 203–259–2994), is open daily July 1 through Labor Day, 10:00 A.M. to 12:30 P.M. and 2:00 to 5:30 P.M. Admission is free.

EASTERN ADIRONDACKS

◆**Fort Ticonderoga,** which stands on a promontory jutting into the southern end of Lake Champlain, is remembered by Americans mostly because of its brave capture by Col. Ethan Allen and his Green Mountain Boys, after which Henry Knox hauled its cannons overland for Washington to use in the siege of Boston. But "Fort Ti" was actually built twenty years earlier, when the French colonial administration in Quebec needed a southern defense in its struggle against Great Britain for control of Canada. Called Fort Carillon, it was built of earth and timbers but later upgraded to the classic French fortress design, with four pointed bastions offering an interlocking field of fire against attackers.

The attackers showed up in early July 1758, in the form of 15,000 British and American colonial troops bent on taking the fort from the Marquis de Montcalm and his 3,500 defenders. Montcalm held the British off and managed to withdraw most of his troops and blow up part of the fort before its eventual capture the following summer by Gen. Jeffrey Amherst. Amherst had the fort rebuilt, and the British maintained it with a light garrison until it was peacefully surrendered to Col. Allen sixteen years later.

For two years Ticonderoga was an American fort, until British Gen. John Burgoyne forced its surrender during the southward march that ended in his defeat at Saratoga. A British garrison held it until October 1777, when it was finally abandoned to the Americans and to time after a useful life of only twenty-two years. It was never again permanently manned.

Fort Ticonderoga might be little more than an exhausted rubble quarry and a roadside marker had it not been for the remarkable efforts of the Pell family to restore and maintain the historic structure over the past century and a half. William Ferris Pell of New York City bought the fort grounds in 1820, and in 1908 his descendant Stephen Pell began its complete reconstruction (Stephen Pell's son, John Pell, presided over the Fort Ticonderoga Association until his death in 1988.) Today visitors can walk through the stone buildings, stride along the ramparts, and examine the barracks. The museum contains exhibits of Indian and early military artifacts, maps, and firearms and watercraft of the colonial and revolutionary periods, as well as a collection of materials relating to the career of Ethan Allen. One of North America's best collections of cannons is also on display.

As a sidelight to a Fort Ticonderoga visit, drive to the nearby summit of **Mt. Defiance,** which figured in the British action against Ticonderoga's American defenders in 1777.

Fort Ticonderoga, Route 74, Ticonderoga 12883, (518) 585–2821, is open daily from mid-May through mid-October. May, June, September, and October hours are 9:00 A.M. to 5:00 P.M.; July and August hours are 9:00 A.M. to 6:00 P.M. Admission is $7 for adults, $5 for children ages 10 to 13, and free for children under 10.

For some distance north of Ticonderoga, Lake Champlain remains narrow enough for a single military installation to have commanded both shores and governed the passage of ship traffic in the eighteenth century. This was the purpose of the fortifications that now lie in ruins at ◆ **Crown Point State Historic Site.**

In the late 1600s the staging area for French raids on English settlements in New England and the Hudson Valley, Crown Point became the location of the French Fort St. Frederic, begun in 1734 and finished in 1737. The fort was designed as a stone citadel within outer walls, defended by 50 cannons and swivel-mounted guns and a garrison of 80 to 120 soldiers.

In 1755 Fort St. Frederic was targeted by the British as one of four strategic French forts to be taken as part of the final surge toward hegemony in North America. Four years later Gen. Jeffrey

Amherst seized Crown Point and its fortress after it had been abandoned and partially destroyed by the French, who had used it as a fallback position after similarly abandoning Ticonderoga.

Amherst immediately ordered the construction of a much larger British fortress at Crown Point, which was substantially completed when the so-called French and Indian Wars ended in 1763. With hostilities ended, the fort began to deteriorate from neglect and was devastated by a 1773 fire. In 1775, a small British garrison there was captured by American militiamen under Seth Warner, after which Crown Point became the staging area for the abortive American attack on Canada. Until American forces withdrew in October 1776, after the Battle of Valcour Island, it was the headquarters of the American Navy under Benedict Arnold. After that a small British naval force occupied Crown Point on a seasonal basis until the end of the revolution.

The survival of the walls, foundations, and partial structures that we see at Crown Point today is due to the 1910 conveyance of the property to the state by private owners who wished to see the ruins preserved. In 1975 the area officially became a state historic site. The following year the new visitor center and museum were opened. Highlights of the museum exhibits include artifacts uncovered at the site during extensive archaeological digs.

Crown Point State Historic Site, at the Lake Champlain Bridge, 4 miles east of Routes 9N and 22, Crown Point 12928, (518) 597–3666, is open May through October, Wednesday through Saturday, 10:00 A.M. to 5:00 P.M.; Sunday, 1:00 to 5:00 P.M. Also open Memorial Day, Independence Day, and Labor Day. Open during the rest of the year by appointment only. Grounds are accessible all year. Admission is free. Group visits by advance reservation.

Most museums seek to interpret a particular era, if history is their subject, or the artifacts surrounding a particular event or series of events. Not so the ◆ **Adirondack Museum** at Blue Mountain Lake in the heart of the mountain region. This institution's ambition, at which it has succeeded admirably, is the chronicling of the entire Adirondacks experience throughout the years in which the area has been known to humanity. Located on a peninsula jutting into Blue Mountain Lake, the museum rambles through twenty-two separate exhibit buildings on a 30-acre compound and has been called the finest regional museum in the United States.

The museum takes as its focus the ways in which people have related to this incomparable setting and made their lives here over the past two centuries. As befits an institution that began in an old hotel, the museum tells the story of how the Adirondacks were discovered by vacationists in the nineteenth century, especially after the 1892 completion of the first railroad through the region.

Examples of nineteenth-century hotel and cabin rooms are shown, and a restored turn-of-the-century cottage houses a large collection of rustic "Adirondack Furniture," currently enjoying a revival among interior designers. Financier August Belmont's private railroad car *Oriental*—a reminder of the days when grand conveyances brought the very wealthy to even grander Adirondack mansions and clubs—is also on exhibit.

The workaday world of the Adirondacks is also recalled in mining, logging, and boat-building exhibits. The museum possesses an excellent collection of handmade canoes and guideboats, including some of the lightweight masterpieces of nineteenth-century canoe-builder J. H. Rushton. The lovely sloop *Water Witch* is preserved under its own glass dome.

Special attention is given to what has been written and painted using Adirondacks subjects. The museum's picture galleries display the work of artists from the Hudson River School and later periods.

The Adirondack Museum, Route 28N/30, Blue Mountain Lake 12812, (518) 352–7311 or 352–7312, is open daily from Memorial Day through mid-October, 9:30 A.M. to 5:30 P.M. Admission is charged.

Studying a subject in a museum is a great way to learn about it. But experience is often the best teacher—even the best museum in the world can't convey how it *feels* to walk among mountains that are 1.3 billion years old. **Siamese Ponds Wilderness Region** in western Warren County is a wilderness area in the true sense of the word: There are hundreds of miles of state-maintained trails and tote roads winding over hills and mountains, past streams, ponds, and lakes. Rockhounds will love exploring the endless passageways and valleys through a wide variety of rock formations. They were carved by glaciers of the Ice Age and by erosion caused by aeons of tumbling rocks carried along mountain streams, and hikers have found numerous exposed veins of minerals and semiprecious stones.

Siamese Ponds Wilderness Region has entrance points from Stony Creek, Thurman, Wevertown, Johnsburg, North Creek, and North River. Information is available in the *Guide to Adirondack Trails: Central Region,* published by the Adirondack Mountain Club, RD 3, Box 3055, Luzerne Road, Lake George 12845; (518) 668–4447. Or contact the Gore Mountain Region Chamber of Commerce, P.O. Box 84, North Creek 12853; (518) 251–2612.

◈ **Mt. Van Hoevenburg Recreational Area,** 6 miles south of Lake Placid, is the only place in the Western Hemisphere with separate luge and bobsled runs—and you can ride them both. The Olympic training facility is open year-round, although mid-March through mid-June is off-season and there may not be much to see. But visitors are invited to wander about and watch Olympic hopefuls at work. From mid-June through mid-December a tour of the facility and trolley ride are offered. Olympic training on the bobsled takes place almost every day in season from 10:00 A.M. to 4:00 P.M. Training hours on the luge are Tuesday through Friday, 10:00 A.M. to 3:30 P.M.

Rides on both the luge and the bobsled are contingent upon conditions. The sled in the 0.5-mile bobsled ride is steered by a professional and is offered Tuesday through Sunday, 2:00 to 4:00 P.M. The ride lasts thirty-five to forty seconds, costs $25 per person per trip, and you must sign a waiver (if you're under 18, a parent must sign for you). For the luge, riders are given instruction on how to go down the 1,200-foot run and then do so alone. It is open Saturday and Sunday, 2:00 to 4:00 P.M., and the cost is $15 per person per trip. You must sign a waiver, and those under age 18 need the permission of a parent or guardian.

In winter there are 35 miles of groomed trails open for cross-country skiing. The cost is $9 for adults and $7 for seniors and children between the ages of 7 and 14. After 1:30 P.M. the cost is $6 per person.

Mt. Van Hoevenburg Recreational Area, Lake Placid 12946, (518) 523–4436 or 523–3325, is open year-round. There is a $3 admission charge to the complex.

Having been immersed in Adirondacks history and lore at Blue Mountain Lake, it is surprising to drive north and find a spot near Lake Placid and Saranac Lake whose principal connections are with events that occurred hundreds of miles from these mountains. Here are the homestead and grave of the militant

John Brown Farm

abolitionist John Brown, who was executed for his part in the 1859 raid on the U.S. arsenal at Harper's Ferry, Virginia. The homestead and grave are maintained today as the ◆**John Brown Farm State Historic Site.**

Brown and several of his sons had organized their followers to stage the raid in the hope that the captured arms might be used to launch a war of liberation on behalf of black slaves in the South. But his involvement in the abolitionist cause began years before the failed Harper's Ferry attack. His sons had homesteaded in Kansas during the period in the 1850s when the territory earned the name "Bloody Kansas" because of the struggle to decide whether it would be admitted to the Union as a slave or a free state; Brown went to fight on the abolitionist side and took part in the desperate struggle at Osawatomie. But Brown wasn't a Kansan himself. Inasmuch as he had a permanent home during that turbulent period, it was his farm at North Elba, near Lake Placid. He had moved here in 1849 to participate in a plan to settle free blacks in an agricultural community called Timbucto. The benevolent scheme hadn't worked, but Brown still considered North Elba home and had requested that he be buried there. Two of his sons, killed at Harper's Ferry, are also interred at the farm, as are several of his followers, whose remains were moved here in 1899.

The farmhouse at the John Brown Farm State Historic Site, Route 73, Lake Placid 12946, (518) 523–3900, is open from late May through late October, Wednesday through Saturday, 10:00 A.M. to 5:00 P.M.; Sunday, 1:00 to 5:00 P.M. Also open Memorial Day, Independence Day, and Labor Day. The grounds are open all year. Admission is free.

The Adirondacks and, in fact, much of New York State were once the territory of the Iroquois Confederation. Perhaps the most politically sophisticated of all the tribal groupings of North American Indians, the Iroquois actually comprised five distinct tribes—the Mohawks, Senecas, Onondagas, Oneidas, and Cayugas—who were later joined by the Tuscaroras to form the "six nations" of the confederation. The history and contemporary circumstances of the Iroquois are documented in the ◆ **Six Nations Indian Museum** near Onchiota, 14 miles north of Saranac Lake.

The cohesiveness of the five original nations of the Iroquois Confederation was already apparent at the time of the first European explorations of North America, although even greater solidarity among the tribes was no doubt fostered by their early perception of the French as a common enemy. This unfortunate turn in the history of the Quebec settlements began when Samuel de Champlain, leading an expedition of French explorers and Algonquin allies along Lake Champlain early in the seventeenth century, shot and killed an Iroquois chief. While this act of bravado may have further endeared him to the Algonquins, traditional enemies of the Iroquois, it made the Iroquois an implacable enemy of the French and an eventual ally of the British in their struggle for control of North America.

A visit to the Six Nations Indian Museum, though, is a reminder that Iroquois culture and history have far deeper roots than are evident in the story of their involvement in the white man's conflicts. For centuries the Iroquois had been making their way through the forests of what is now New York State, building a society whose artifacts survive in the museum's collections. The Six Nations Indian Museum also houses examples of the contemporary craftwork of Iroquois tribespeople, as well as models of typical Iroquois villages of the pre-European period.

The Six Nations Indian Museum, Rhokedale Road, Onchiota 12968, (518) 891–0769, is open daily from July 1 through Labor Day, 10:00 am. to 6:00 P.M. Admission is $2 for adults and $1 for children.

Once a part of the corridor used by trading and war parties in the days of the French and Indians, the area around Plattsburgh, on Lake Champlain, had settled into a peaceful mercantile existence by the end of the eighteenth century. It was in Plattsburgh that the **Kent-Delord House** was built in 1797 as a residence for William Bailey. Following several changes of ownership, the house was purchased in 1810 by Henry Delord, a refugee from the French Revolution who had prospered as a merchant and served in a number of local political offices in Peru, New York, before moving to Plattsburgh. Delord remodeled the house in the fashionable Federal style of the era and moved in in 1811, thus beginning more than a century of his family's residence here.

Just three years after the Delords moved into their new home, the War of 1812 came to Plattsburgh in the form of a southward thrust by British forces along Lake Champlain. The family—Delord, his wife, Betsey, and their daughter, Frances—were even displaced during a week in September 1814 when the British appropriated their house to billet troops. But the enemy was repelled later that month by the Delords' friend Commodore Thomas Macdonough in the Battle of Plattsburgh—the only major naval engagement ever fought on Lake Champlain.

Henry Delord was well connected. In addition to Commodore Macdonough, whose portrait hangs in the house today, the immigrant-turned-squire entertained such early nineteenth-century notables as Gen. Winfield Scott, Col. Zebulon Pike (discoverer of Pike's Peak), and even President James Monroe. Several of the rooms in the house have been restored to their appearance during the days when these dignitaries paid their visits.

Aside from the wartime seizure of the house and the presidential visit, the story of the Kent-Delord House might be that of any home of a provincial bourgeois family during the nineteenth century. The difference, of course, is that this house has survived remarkably intact. It offers a fine opportunity to see how an upper-middle-class family lived from the days just after the revolution through the Victorian age and, not incidentally, houses a distinguished collection of American portrait art, including the work of John Singleton Copley, George Freeman, and Henry Inman.

The Kent-Delord House Museum, 17 Cumberland Avenue, Plattsburgh 12901, (518) 561–1035, is open for guided tours Tuesday through Saturday at noon, 1:30, and 3:00 P.M. and by appointment. Admission is $3 for adults, $2 for students and senior citizens, and $1 for children under 12. The museum is closed during January and February.

WESTERN ADIRONDACKS

When nations aren't running about occupying the homes of each other's citizens, they can accomplish quite a bit by acting in concert—as witness the ◆ **St. Lawrence Seaway,** an example of construction and administrative cooperation between the United States and Canada that has linked the Atlantic Ocean with the ports of the Great Lakes for more than three decades.

As the French fur traders of the seventeenth and eighteenth centuries knew, the St. Lawrence River forms a natural highway between the farthest reaches of the Great Lakes and the tidal waters of the Gulf of St. Lawrence. But modern commerce depends upon vessels with deeper drafts than the canoes of the voyageurs, and the rapids that characterize many sections of the St. Lawrence between Lake Ontario and Montreal impeded all but the lightest and most maneuverable craft. Shippers and planners on both sides of the border were long aware of the need for a continuous deep-water channel to link the ocean with the lakes, but it wasn't until the early 1950s, when it appeared that Canada would go ahead with its own section of the seaway without U.S. participation, that the U.S. Congress finally passed legislation to authorize construction of the American portions of the project. The St. Lawrence Seaway formally opened in 1959 and has since been operated by U.S. and Canadian commissions closely cooperating on maintenance, traffic regulation, and the setting of fees for passage.

The 2,342-mile distance that separates the open Atlantic from Duluth, on Lake Superior, also entails a vertical rise of 602 feet. Of the fifteen massive locks that enable ore and grain freighters and other cargo vessels to negotiate this passage, seven are located along the 190-mile stretch between Montreal and Lake

Ontario. Two belong to the United States—the Bertrand H. Snell and Dwight D. Eisenhower locks, which are connected by a 3-mile canal at Massena. Adjacent to the **Eisenhower Lock** is a visitor center that affords excellent views of ships passing through the lock and also provides interpretive exhibits showing how the gates at either end of the structure take in and release water to lift and lower vessels passing through this section of the seaway.

The Eisenhower Lock Visitor Center, off Route 37 in Massena 13662, (315) 764–3200, is open from May to October, roughly corresponding to the seaway shipping season. For information on the times at which ships are expected to be passing through the lock, call (315) 769–2422.

New York State, as was mentioned in the Introduction to this book, was somewhat of a staging area for America's westward expansion during the last century. It thus seems fitting that the greatest chronicler of the West in painting and sculpture was a New Yorker, who grew up in the town of Ogdensburg on the St. Lawrence River halfway between Massena and Lake Ontario. His name was Frederic Remington, and a splendid collection of his work and personal effects is today housed in the ◆**Frederic Remington Art Museum** in that community.

Born in 1861, Remington quit Yale at the age of nineteen and went west, where he spent five years garnering the experiences and images that would come across so powerfully in his paintings and sculpture. Success as an illustrator and later as a fine artist came after 1885; when Remington died suddenly following an operation in 1909, he was still riding the crest of his popularity. His wife moved from the Remington home in Connecticut in 1915 and settled in the artist's boyhood home of Ogdensburg, in a rented house that had been built in 1810. Mrs. Remington willed her husband's art collection, along with those of his own works in his possession at the time of his death, to the Ogdensburg Public Library, and five years after her own death in 1923, the museum exhibiting this collection was opened in the house where she had lived.

The Remington works housed in the museum include fifteen bronzes, sixty oil paintings, ninety watercolors, and several hundred pen-and-ink sketches. Selections of works from his own collection, among them paintings by Charles Dana Gibson and the American impressionist Childe Hassam, are also on display. There is also a re-creation of Remington's last studio as it stood in Ridgefield, Connecticut, at the time of his death in 1909.

The Frederic Remington Art Museum, 303 Washington Street, Ogdensburg 13669, (315) 393–2425, is open from May 1 through October 31, Monday through Saturday, 10:00 A.M. to 5:00 P.M., and Sunday, 1:00 to 5:00 P.M. Closed legal holidays. Admission is $3 for adults, $2 for children ages 13 to 16 and senior citizens, and free for children under 12.

Around the turn of the century, when Frederic Remington looked west for artistic inspiration, hotel magnate George C. Boldt turned instead to his native Germany. Boldt's creativity wasn't a matter of putting paint to canvas or molding bronze, however. He was out to build the 120-room ◆ **Boldt Castle,** Rhineland-style, on one of the Thousand Islands in the St. Lawrence River.

Boldt, who owned the Waldorf-Astoria in New York and the Bellevue-Stratford Hotel in Philadelphia, bought his island at the turn of the century from a man named Hart, but that isn't why it is named Heart Island. The name derives from the fact that the hotelier had the island physically reshaped into the configuration of a heart, as a token of devotion to his wife, Louise, for whom the entire project was to be a monumental expression of his love.

Construction of the six-story castle and its numerous outbuildings began in 1900. Boldt hired masons, woodcarvers, landscapers, and other craftspeople from all over the world to execute details ranging from terra-cotta wall inlays and roof tiles to a huge, opalescent glass dome. He planned and built a smaller castle as a temporary residence and eventual playhouse, and he built an underground tunnel for bringing supplies from the docks to the main house. There were bowling alleys, a sauna, an indoor swimming pool—in short, it was to be the sort of place that would take years to finish and decades to enjoy.

But there weren't enough years left. Mrs. Boldt died suddenly in 1904, and George Boldt, heartbroken, wired his construction supervisors to stop all work. The walls and roof of the castle were by this time essentially finished, but crated fixtures such as mantels and statuary were left where they stood, and the bustling island fell silent. Boldt never again set foot in his empty castle, on which he had spent $2.5 million.

Boldt died in 1916, and two years later the island and its structures were purchased by Edward J. Noble, the inventor of Life Savers

47

candy. Noble and his heirs ran the deteriorating castle as a tourist attraction until 1962, when it was sold to the Treadway Inns Company; today it belongs to the Thousand Islands Bridge Authority.

Boldt Castle, Heart Island, Alexandria Bay 13607, (315) 482–2520 or 800–8ISLAND is accessible via water taxi from the upper and lower docks on James Street in Alexandria Bay, as well as to tour-boat patrons departing from both the American and the Canadian shores. The Castle is open from mid-May through mid-October, daily from 10:00 A.M. to 6:00 P.M. For information call ahead, or write 1000 Islands International Council, P.O. Box 400, Alexandria Bay 13607. Admission is $3.25 for adults and $1.75 for children ages 6 to 12. Groups of twenty or more, senior citizens, and military personnel receive a discount.

If you find the most appealing aspect of George Boldt's heyday to be the sleek mahogany runabouts and graceful skiffs that plied the waters of the Thousand Islands and other Gilded Age resorts, make sure you find your way to ◆ **The Antique Boat Museum** in Clayton. The museum is a freshwater boat lover's dream, housing slender, mirror-finished launches, antique canoes, distinctive St. Lawrence River skiffs, handmade guideboats—more than 150 historic small craft in all.

The Antique Boat Museum takes no sides in the eternal conflict between sailing purists and "stinkpotters," being broad enough in its philosophy to house a fine collection of antique outboard and inboard engines, including the oldest outboard known to exist. The one distinction rigidly adhered to pertains to construction material: All of the boats exhibited here are made of wood.

The Antique Boat Museum, 750 Mary Street, Clayton 13624, (315) 686–4104, is open from May 15 to October 15 daily, from 9:00 A.M. to 4:00 P.M. Admission is $5 for adults, with reduced rates for senior citizens, students, and children.

The international cooperation exemplified by the St. Lawrence Seaway and the peaceful coexistence that allows pleasurecraft to sail unimpeded along the boundary waters of the St. Lawrence River and Lake Ontario are things we take for granted today, but this state of affairs has hardly existed since time immemorial. Barely more than a century ago, the U.S. Navy kept an active installation at ◆ **Sackets Harbor Battlefield,** on Lake Ontario's Henderson Bay, against the possibility of war with Canada. And during the War of 1812, this small lakeport actually did see combat between American and Anglo-Canadian forces.

At the time the war began, Sackets Harbor was not yet a flourishing American naval port and the site of a busy shipyard and supply depot. It was from here, in April 1813, that the Americans launched their attack upon Toronto; a month later the tables were turned when the depleted American garrison at the harbor was beleaguered by a British attack upon the shipyard. The defenders repulsed the attack but lost most of their supplies to fire in the course of the struggle.

Today's visitor to Sackets Harbor can still see many of the facilities of the old naval base, including officers' homes and sites associated with the 1813 battle.

Sackets Harbor Battlefield, 505 West Washington Street, Sackets Harbor 13685, (315) 646–3634 or 646-3636, is open from Memorial Day to Labor Day, Wednesday through Saturday from 10:00 A.M. to 5:00 P.M. and Sunday from 1:00 to 5:00 P.M. Also open Independence Day and Labor Day. Grounds are open all year from 8:00 A.M. to sunset. Admission is free.

An even larger and more long-lived Lake Ontario military installation was located farther south, at Oswego. ◆ **Fort Ontario,** also a state historic site, dates back to the eighteenth-century struggles for control of the Great Lakes waged by Britain and France and saw use as a refugee processing center managed by the U.S. Army as recently as the 1940s. During the intervening years this site at the mouth of the Oswego River has been defended beneath the flags of France, Britain, and the United States.

The first fort in this vicinity was built by the British in 1727. In 1755 the first Fort Ontario was built on the east shore of the Oswego, opposite the new Fort George. Both forts were destroyed by a French force under Montcalm only a year later, although the British were back by 1758 and built a larger and more permanent fort the following year.

Instrumental as a staging area for British forces in the French and Indian Wars, which ousted the French from Canada, Fort Ontario fell only briefly to the Americans during the revolution and was not finally relinquished by the British until 1796, thirteen years after the formal cessation of hostilities.

Fort Ontario figured in the warfare along the Lake Ontario front during the War of 1812, when it was captured and destroyed (1814) by Gen. Gordon Drummond and his British forces. It was rebuilt in what was to become its final form between 1839 and 1844, during which time the American government feared that the anti-British rebellion in Upper Canada known as the Patriot War might involve the United States. Defenses were updated during the Civil War, when it was felt that the British, in keeping with their Confederate sympathies, might invade the northern states from Canada.

Fort Ontario was used as a training camp and hospital during World War I and again as a training facility during World War II. Between 1944 and 1946 refugees from German concentration camps were housed at the fort, which was finally decommissioned in the latter year.

In 1985 a major $300,000 restoration project of the fort buildings and their surroundings was completed by the state of New York. Visitors can now see 1840s barracks and officers' quarters, bastions, parapets assaulted by the British in 1814, and Civil War artillery casements. Between July 1 and Labor Day, the costumed Fort Ontario Guard performs drills, fires cannons, and marches to the sounds of fifes and drums. Company F, Forty-second U.S. Infantry, Veteran Reserve Corps reenacts daily life at the fort as it was in the summer of 1868.

Fort Ontario State Historic Site, off Route 104 in Oswego 13126, (315) 343–4711, is open from mid-May through early fall (call for exact dates), Wednesday through Saturday and on Monday holidays, 10:00 A.M. to 5:00 P.M.; Sunday, 1:00 to 5:00 P.M. Admission is charged.

The completion of our counterclockwise tour through the Adirondacks takes us east to a point just north of Utica, to the ◆ **Steuben Memorial State Historic Site,** in the foothills of the mountains. Frederick von Steuben was a Prussian officer who, at the age of forty-seven, emigrated to the United States in 1777 to help drill the soldiers of the Continental Army. His first assignment was a challenging one. He was sent to the American winter encampment at Valley Forge, where morale was flagging and discipline, in the face of elemental hardship such as hunger and bitter cold, was virtually nonexistent.

As might be expected of a good Prussian officer, von Steuben rose to the occasion. Washington's troops at Valley Forge might not have had boots, but they learned how to march in file, as well

Steuben Memorial

as proceed through the other elements of classic military drill and perform effectively with the eighteenth-century frontline weapon of choice, the bayonet. The German émigré even found time to write a masterful treatise on military training, *Regulations for the Order and Discipline of the Troops of the United States*.

Having served as inspector general of the Continental Army until the end of the war, von Steuben was richly rewarded by the nation of which he had lately become a citizen. Among his other rewards was a New York State grant of 16,000 acres of land. Allowed to pick his own site, he chose the area partially occupied today by the Steuben Memorial State Historic Site and built a simple, two-room log house.

In 1936 the state erected a replica of von Steuben's house on a site located within the 50 acres it had recently purchased as his memorial (the drillmaster is buried beneath an imposing monument not far from here, despite his wish that he lie in an unmarked grave). The cabin is open to visitors. Encampments and historical interpretations reflecting the military life of the revolutionary war soldier are held at the memorial, and docents are available to discuss the baron's life.

The Steuben Memorial State Historic Site, Starr Hill Road, Remsen 13438, (315) 831–3737, is open from late May to Labor Day, Wednesday through Saturday, from 10:00 A.M. to 5:00 P.M.; Sunday, 1:00 to 5:00 P.M. Admission is free.

THE MOHAWK VALLEY

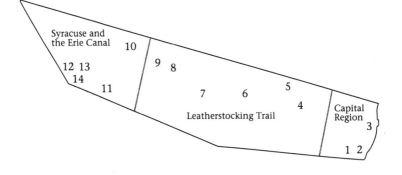

Syracuse and the Erie Canal

Leatherstocking Trail

Capital Region

1. Albany Institute of History and Art
2. Schuyler Mansion State Historic Site
3. Waterford
4. National Shrine of the North American Martyrs
5. Fulton County Museum
6. Fort Klock Historic Restoration
7. Remington Firearms Museum
8. Munson-Williams-Proctor Institute
9. Oriskany Battlefield State Historic Site
10. Erie Canal Village
11. Lorenzo State Historic Site
12. Erie Canal Museum
13. Everson Museum of Art
14. Mid-Lakes Navigation Company, Ltd.

THE MOHAWK VALLEY

Drums along the Mohawk . . . Leatherstocking . . . "I had a mule and her name was Sal / Fifteen miles on the Erie Canal"—the lore of the Mohawk Valley has long been a part of the national consciousness. The reasons are plain: The valley has been an important highway between the East and the Great Lakes for centuries, and countless Americans have passed through here via Indian trails, the Erie Canal, Commodore Vanderbilt's "Water Level Route" of the New York Central railroad, and today's New York State Thruway. Here was where Jesuit missionaries met their end at the hands of the Iroquois, where James Fenimore Cooper's Deerslayer stalked, and where those who were to homestead the Midwest struck out along a water-filled ditch, in barges pulled by draft animals. Surely, this is one of the most storied corridors of the Republic.

Yet between Albany and Syracuse, there are plenty of places where people settled down to make things . . . guns in Ilion, pots and pans in Rome, gloves, as you might suspect, in Gloversville. They nevertheless left no shortage of open land, as you can see when you crest one of the gently rolling hills in the dairy country near Cooperstown. If you are coming from the East, what you see here is a harbinger of the next 1,500 miles. It isn't prairie yet, but the land is opening up, and the horizon is growing more distant. This is where midwestern vistas begin.

This chapter begins in Albany, very much an eastern city and the capital of New York State. From here the direction followed is east to west, corresponding closely to the route of the Mohawk River itself and, conveniently, the New York State Thruway.

CAPITAL REGION

The conventional, foursquare approach to Albany is by way of the public facade it presents—the massively beautiful and ornate State Capitol building, partly designed by H. H. Richardson, or the four monolithic, marble-clad state office towers so closely associated with the grandiose visions of the late Nelson Rockefeller. But in order to see a subtler side of the city and surrounding area and to learn more of its antecedents and historic persona than is revealed by those gargantuan examples of power frozen in masonry, visit the ❖**Albany Institute of History and Art.** Descended from lyceums and art galleries that date back to 1791, the institute has followed an acquisitions policy geared to the furnishings, household articles, folk art, and fine art of Albany and the upper Hudson River Valley.

Hudson River art, of course, means the Hudson River School, which is well represented here with works by painters such as Kensett, Cropsey, and Cole. But the institute possesses fine examples of an even older regional genre, the sometimes-anonymous portraits of the Dutch burghers and their families who dictated the tone of Hudson Valley life during the seventeenth and eighteenth centuries. The Dutch in Holland had become the world masters of portraiture in the 1600s, as patrons and artists collaborated to compile a magnificent pictorial record of bourgeois life when the concept itself was still something new. It is fascinating to see how their New World counterparts worked a hundred years later. The experience is heightened by the institute's collection of early Hudson Valley furniture and silver, which formed the day-to-day surroundings of the people in the portraits.

The Albany Institute of History and Art, 125 Washington Avenue, Albany 12210, (518) 463–4478, is open Tuesday through Friday, 10:00 A.M. to 5:00 P.M.; Saturday and Sunday, noon to 5:00 P.M. The galleries are closed on Monday and certain holidays. Admission is by donation.

The Schuylers were among the earliest of the Dutch settlers of the upper Hudson Valley and were involved throughout the colonial period in trading, agriculture, land development, and local politics. The most renowned member of the family was Philip Schuyler (1733–1804), whose manorial home is today preserved as the ❖**Schuyler Mansion State Historic Site.**

Although Albany has grown up around the mansion and deprived it of its once-rural hillside setting, it stands as a monument not only to its talented and versatile builders but also to the best in eighteenth-century taste.

Philip Schuyler chose his then 80-acre homesite in 1760, by which time he had already served as a captain in the French and Indian Wars and married one of the neighboring Van Rensselaers. He designed the mansion himself in the Georgian style, with rose-colored brick walls, graceful fenestration, and double-hipped roof (the awkward octagonal brick entry vestibule is an

1818 addition), and furnished it largely with purchases he made during a 1761–62 trip to England.

But like George Washington's Mt. Vernon, the Schuyler Mansion was not to be a place of quiet retirement for its owner during his middle years. When the revolution broke out, Schuyler became a delegate to the Continental Congress and was soon commissioned a major general in the new nation's army. Since his command was the Northern Department, he was able to operate out of his own Albany home—with the result that the parlors and drawing rooms of the Schuyler Mansion were visited by the likes of Washington, Franklin, Benedict Arnold, and Alexander Hamilton. Hamilton, in fact, wed Schuyler's daughter Elizabeth at the mansion in 1780.

After Schuyler died in 1804, his house and much of the family land in Albany were sold and used as a private residence and later an orphanage. The Schuyler Mansion was acquired by the state in 1912, restored, and opened to the public.

The Schuyler Mansion is as fine a place as New York State offers to learn about life as it was lived among the most fortunate levels of society in the mid-1700s. The mansion is an architectural gem, and it houses an excellent collection of colonial- and Federal-period furnishings.

The Schuyler Mansion State Historic Site, 32 Catherine Street, Albany 12202, (518) 434–0834, is open April through October, Wednesday through Saturday from 10:00 A.M. to 5:00 P.M. and Sunday from 1:00 to 5:00 P.M.; November through March, by appointment only. Also open on Memorial Day, Independence Day, and Labor Day. Admission is free.

One of Philip Schuyler's interests during his later years was the development of a canal and lock system in New York State. It was in the three decades after his death that canal building really hit its stride in the United States, turning formerly sleepy villages into canal boomtowns, involved in the lucrative trade between New York City and points west. Once such town is ◆ **Waterford,** located near Cohoes just upriver from Albany.

Founded by the Dutch as Halfmoon Point in the early 1620s at the point where the Mohawk River flows into the Hudson, Waterford was incorporated under its present name in 1794 and is today the oldest incorporated village in the United States. In 1799 it became the head of sloop navigation on the Hudson, but its glory days of commerce came later, in the 1820s, when the new Champlain and Erie canals made the town not merely a backcountry terminus but an important waystation and transfer point on a statewide transportation system.

Unfortunately for Waterford and many of its sister communities, not all major canal towns became major railroad towns after the iron horse ended the brief supremacy of the artificial waterways. Waterford did prosper as a small manufacturing center during the nineteenth century, however, and the legacy of this era is the village's lovely residential architecture, much of it in the regionally significant "Waterford" style characterized by Federal details and Dutch-inspired single-step gables. Such architectural distinctions have earned the village center a place on the National Register of Historic Places. The historic district is the subject of tours given during "Canalfest" the second Saturday of May each year. It features boat rides, hayrides, a boat show, a craft fair, food, and entertainment.

From April through October in the village center at Erie Canal Lock 2, a series of outdoor exhibits details the history of the 1823 canal and the present-day barge canal.

Waterford attractions outside the village center include the **Champlain Canal,** this section of which was dug in 1823 and is still filled with water; the **Waterford Flight,** a series of five locks on the still-operating New York State Barge Canal, whose 169-foot total rise is the highest in the world; a state park at **Lock 6;** and **Peebles Island State Park. Waterford Historical Museum and Cultural Center,** 2 Museum Lane, off Saratoga Avenue, Waterford 12188, (518) 270–8667, is open weekends from 2:00 to 4:00 P.M. Admission is free.

LEATHERSTOCKING TRAIL

The Erie Canal and the feats of engineering that its building entailed are also the focus of **Schoharie Crossing State Historic Site,** farther up the Mohawk, at Fort Hunter. Seven canal-related structures dating from three periods of the waterway's construction or expansion are preserved here and provided with interpretive displays that explain their use. Of particular interest are the original canal bed, circa 1825; a guardlock from the original canal; and the Schoharie crossing itself, consisting of a

Schoharie Crossing

massive arched aqueduct that carried the canal and its adjacent towpath across Schoharie Creek. This structure, dating from the enlargement of the canal in the 1840s, looks almost as if it might be a Roman ruin tucked into the hills of southern Europe. The visitor center has an exhibit on the Erie Canal and information on the site and surrounding area. **Putman's Canal Store,** at Yankee Hill Lock 28 on Queen Anne's Road (about 2.2 miles east of the visitor center), was built during the 1850s and served as a store along the enlarged Erie Canal for many years. It now houses an exhibit on Erie Canal stores. Guided walking tours of the site are given at 11:00 A.M. and 2:00 P.M. on Wednesday, Thursday, and Friday during the season. Mule-drawn guided wagon tours are given from 11:00 A.M. to 2:00 P.M. every Saturday in July and August.

Along the old canal towpath are views of modern-day barge traffic on the Mohawk River, the depth of which in this area allows it to be used as a link in the New York State barge canal system.

Schoharie Crossing State Historic Site, 129 Schoharie Street, P.O. Box 140, Fort Hunter 12069, (518) 829–7516, is open mid-May through October 31 and Memorial Day, Independence Day, and Labor Day, Wednesday through Saturday, 10:00 A.M. to 5:00 P.M., and Sunday, 1:00 to 5:00 P.M. The grounds are open all year during daylight hours. Admission is free.

Long before there were canals or barges in this part of New York State, the waters of the Mohawk and its tributaries were plied by the canoes of the Iroquois. The Mohawk Valley was the heart of the empire of the five nations, one of which was the tribe that gave the river its name. In what is today the town of Auriesville stood the palisaded village of Mohawk longhouses called Ossernenon in the seventeenth century; here, in 1642, a raiding party of Indians returned with three French and twenty Huron captives in custody. Among the French were a Jesuit priest, Isaac Jogues, and his lay assistant, Rene Goupil.

Enemies captured by the Iroquois—Hurons and French were enemies by definition in those days—were lucky if they died quickly. Jogues and Goupil survived their tortures and were kept as slaves, although Goupil was tomahawked to death barely a month later when his attempt to teach a child the sign of the cross was interpreted as the casting of an evil spell. Jogues was rescued by the Dutch during a Mohawk trading foray to Fort Orange, and he returned to Europe and eventually Quebec. But he volunteered to go back to Ossernenon in May 1646, as part of a group attempting to ratify a peace treaty with the Mohawks, and was captured near the village by a faction of the tribe favoring a continuation of hostilities. Both he and a lay companion, Jean Lalande, were murdered by tomahawk-wielding braves in October of that year. Canonized by the Roman Catholic church in 1930 along with five Jesuit missionaries martyred in Canada, Jogues, Goupil, and Lalande are honored at the ◆**National Shrine of the North American Martyrs** in Auriesville.

The shrine, which occupies the hilltop site of the original Mohawk village of Ossernenon amid 600 verdant acres, is maintained by the New York Province of the Society of Jesus, the same Jesuit order to which Isaac Jogues belonged. Founded in 1885, the shrine accommodates 40,000 to 50,000 visitors each year during a season lasting from the first Sunday in May to the last Sunday in October. Mass is celebrated in the vast "Coliseum," the central altar of which is built to suggest the palisades of a Mohawk village; there are also a Martyrs' Museum, rustic chapels, and a retreat house.

For information on the schedule of observances at the National Shrine of the North American Martyrs, Auriesville 12016, call (518) 853–3033.

The French Catholic missionaries working among the Indians in the seventeenth century were not without their successes. The most famous name among Mohawk converts of that era is Kateri Tekakwitha, the "Lily of the Mohawks," born at Ossernenon and baptized at what is now the village of Fonda, where the **Fonda National Shrine of Blessed Kateri Tekakwitha** is now located. Maintained by the Conventual Franciscan Order, the shrine commemorates the life of the saintly Indian girl who lived half of her life here, before removing to the community of converted Indians established by the French at Caughnawaga, near Montreal, where she died in 1680 at the age of twenty-four. (In 1980, on the tercentenary of her death, Pope John Paul II announced the beatification of Kateri Tekakwitha, which is the last step before canonization in the Catholic church.)

Aside from its religious connections, the Fonda site of the Tekakwitha shrine is interesting because of its identification by archaeologists as the location of a Mohawk village, also called Caughnawaga. Artifacts dug from the village site are exhibited in the shrine's Native American Exhibit, located on the ground floor of a revolutionary-era Dutch barn that now serves as a chapel. Indian items from elsewhere in New York State and throughout the United States are also part of the exhibit.

The Fonda National Shrine of Blessed Kateri Tekakwitha, off Route 5, Fonda 12068, (518) 853–3646, is open daily, May through October, from 9:00 A.M. to 4:00 P.M. Admission is free.

Just north of Fonda and nearby Johnstown is Gloversville, home of the ◆ **Fulton County Museum.** Gloversville was originally called Kingsborough, but the townspeople adopted the present name in 1828 in homage to the linchpin of the local economy in those days—tanning and glovemaking. It is the glove industry that provides the Fulton County Museum with its most interesting exhibits, housed in the Glove and Leather Room. Here is the state's only glove-manufacturing display—a complete small glove factory of the last century, donated to the museum and reassembled in its original working format.

There is also a Weaving Room that demonstrates the technique from raw flax to the finished product; an Old Country Kitchen; a nineteenth-century Lady's Room, complete with costumes and cosmetics; a Country Store; an old-time Candy Store; an Early Farm display; and an old-time Country Schoolroom. Don't miss the Indian Artifact exhibit on the first floor.

The Fulton County Museum, 237 Kingsboro Avenue, Gloversville 12078, (518) 725–2203, is open May and June, Tuesday through Saturday, 10:00 A.M. to 4:00 P.M.; July and August, Tuesday through Sunday, noon to 4:00 P.M.; and September through mid-November, Tuesday through Saturday, 10:00 A.M. to 4:00 P.M. Admission is free.

Fate plays a capricious hand in deciding which industries a town will be noted for. Gloversville got gloves; Canajoharie, our next stop along the Mohawk, got chewing gum—specifically the Beech-Nut Packing Company, of which town native Bartlett Arkell was president in the 1920s. Because of Mr. Arkell and his success in business, Canajoharie also came into possession of the finest independent art gallery of any municipality its size in the United States—the **Canajoharie Library and Art Gallery.**

Arkell's beneficence to his hometown began with his donation of a new library in 1924. Two years later he donated the funds to build an art gallery wing on the library, and over the next few years he gave the community the magnificent collection of paintings that forms the bulk of the gallery's present holdings. In 1964 yet another wing was added, paid for by the Arkell Hall Foundation.

This institution has become not merely an art gallery with a library attached but an art gallery with a small town attached. The roster of American painters exhibited here is astounding, totally out of scale with what you would expect at a thruway exit between Albany and Utica. The Hudson River School is represented by Albert Bierstadt (*El Capitan*), John Kensett, and Thomas Doughty. There is a Gilbert Stuart portrait of George Washington. The Winslow Homer collection is the third largest in the United States. The eighteenth century is represented by John Singleton Copley; the nineteenth, by luminaries such as

Thomas Eakins, George Innes (*Rainbow*), and James McNeill Whistler (*On the Thames*). Among twentieth-century painters are Charles Burchfield, Reginald Marsh, and the painters of the Ash Can School: N. C. Wyeth and his son Andrew (*February 2nd*), Edward Hopper, Thomas Hart Benton, and even Grandma Moses. There is also a Frederic Remington bronze, *Bronco Buster*. Add a collection of eighty Korean and Japanese ceramics, the gift of the late Col. John Fox, and you have all the more reason—as if more were needed—to regard Canajoharie as a destination in itself rather than a stop along the way.

The Canajoharie Library and Art Gallery, 2 Erie Boulevard, Canajoharie 13317, (518) 673–2314, is open Monday through Wednesday, 10:00 A.M. to 4:45 P.M.; Thursday, 1:30 P.M. to 8:30 P.M.; Friday, 1:30 to 4:45 P.M.; Saturday, 10:00 A.M. to 1:30 P.M.; and Sunday, from Memorial Day to Labor Day, 1:00 to 3:45 P.M. Admission is free.

Art played little part in the life of the Mohawk Valley in the year 1750, when Johannes Klock built the farmhouse-fortress preserved today as the ◆**Fort Klock Historic Restoration.** Located above the river at St. Johnsville, Fort Klock is a reminder that the building of stout-walled outposts capable of being held defensively was by no means confined to the "wild West" of the late 1800s. In 1750 the Mohawk Valley *was* the wild West, and a man like Klock found it necessary to build a home that could serve just as easily as a fortress. The enemy was not only the Indians but also the French; and twenty-five years later the valley would become a theater of warfare involving American rebels, Tories, British regulars, and mercenary Indians.

Like his neighbors at scattered sites along the river, Johannes Klock engaged in fur trading and farming. Canoes and bateaux could tie up in the cove just below the house, yet the building itself stood on high enough ground and at a sufficient distance from the river to make it easily defensible should the waters of the Mohawk bring foes rather than friendly traders. The stone walls of Fort Klock are almost two feet thick and are dotted with "loopholes" that enabled inhabitants to fire muskets from protected positions within.

Johannes Klock's descendant John Klock lived here during the revolution, in which he fought on the American side. The war was hard on the area: 700 homes were burned, and a third of the population of the valley, some 10,000 people, left for the safety of Canada. Those who remained, and who survived the hostilities, often had the strong walls of structures such as Fort Klock to thank for their security.

Now restored and protected as a registered National Historic Landmark, Fort Klock and its outbuildings tell a good part of the story of the Mohawk Valley in the eighteenth century—a time when the hardships of homesteading were made even more difficult by the constant threat of the musket, the tomahawk, and the torch.

Fort Klock Historic Restoration, Route 5, St. Johnsville 13452, (518) 568–7779, is open from June through October, Tuesday through Sunday, 9:00 A.M. to 5:00 P.M. An admission fee is charged.

One of the best known of all Mohawk Valley towns (it's actually a good deal south of the river, on Otsego Lake) is Cooperstown, named for the family of novelist James Fenimore Cooper and synonymous with ultimate achievement in America's national pastime. The Baseball Hall of Fame and Museum is what brings most visitors to Cooperstown—but when they get there, they are often surprised to find that the community also harbors an equally engaging museum dedicated to the experience of rural life in days gone by. This is **The Farmers' Museum,** part of the New York State Historical Association's Cooperstown holdings that also include **Fenimore House,** which presents collections of American folk and academic art.

The particular focus of The Farmers' Museum is the period between the American Revolution and the Civil War, when most Americans still lived in rural areas. Many tasks associated with farming and homemaking had not yet been subject to mechanization in those days, and country people had to rely not only upon their own ingenuity and capacity for hard work but also upon a small-scale infrastructure of blacksmiths, weavers, and other craftspersons. The museum's "Village Crossroads" gathers these and other town fixtures together in a community of more than a dozen early nineteenth-century buildings, all built within a hundred miles of Cooperstown and moved here as life-size, working exhibits. The village includes a blacksmith's shop, church, tavern, country store, one-room schoolhouse, lawyer's and doctor's offices, print shop, druggist's shop, barn, and homestead. Museum interpreters work as did the craftspeople of the 1800s, making horseshoes or brooms, setting type by hand, or cooking at an open hearth.

Yet these were agricultural communities, and whatever else had to be done, farmwork itself was most important. The Lippitt Farmstead, a nineteenth-century farm at the museum, presents the farming practices of the day. The Main Barn, which houses the museum's principal indoor exhibits, offers displays of farm, craft, and household implements of the era.

Annual events held at the museum include seminars on American culture, old-time Fourth of July celebrations, a Harvest Festival, and a Candlelight Evening at Christmastime.

The Farmers' Museum and Fenimore House (headquarters of the New York State Historical Association), Cooperstown 13326, (607) 547-2593 for the museum, 547-2533 for Fenimore House, are open daily from May 1 through October 31, 9:00 A.M. to 6:00 P.M. Call regarding off-season schedules. Admission to the museum is $8 for adults and $3 for children 7 to 12. Fenimore House admission is $6 for adults and $2.50 for children 7 to 12. Inquire about discount tickets for admission to both attractions or to all three (museum, Fenimore House, and Baseball Hall of Fame).

It was an environment very much like the one depicted at The Farmers' Museum's Village Crossroads that produced one of the great American toolmakers, inasmuch as dependable firearms were indispensable tools of frontier life and westward expansion. In 1816 Eliphalet Remington was twenty-four years old and in need of a new rifle. He made a barrel at his father's village forge and then walked into the Mohawk Valley town of Utica to have it rifled (rifling is the series of twisting grooves inside a gun barrel that give the bullet spin—and therefore accuracy—and distinguish it from the smoothbore muskets of earlier days). He may not have known it then, but gunmaking was to be his life's work and the Remington Arms Company his creation. You can learn the history of America's oldest gunmaker at the ◆ **Remington Firearms Museum** in Ilion, which houses an impressive collection of rifles, shotguns, and handguns dating back to Eliphalet Remington's earliest flintlocks. Here are examples of the first successful breech-loading rifles, for which Remington held the initial 1864 patents; rare presention-grade guns; and company firsts including bolt-action and pump rifles, autoloading rifles and shotguns, and the Model 32 over-and-under shotgun of 1932.

Other displays include explanations of how firearms are built today, advertising posters and other firearms ephemera, and even

Antique Double Derringer
Remington Firearms Museum

antique Remington typewriters—yes, it was the same company.

The Remington Firearms Museum, Catherine Street, off Route 5S, Ilion 13357, (315) 895–3200, is open Monday through Saturday, 9:00 A.M. to 4:00 P.M. From May through October the museum is also open on Sunday, 1:00 to 4:30 P.M. Admission is free.

From Ilion, it's just a short hop down the thruway to Utica and a pair of worthwhile museums. The ◆ **Munson-Williams-Proctor Institute** is the sort of thing small cities do well, given farsighted founders and the right endowment. The institute is a multifaceted operation that places a good deal of emphasis on community accessibility and service, with free group tours, a speakers' bureau, and children's art programs, as well as free admission and a modestly priced performing arts series (some performances take place at the nearby Stanley Performing Arts

Center). But you don't have to be a Utica resident to enjoy the major holdings, which include a collection of paintings strong in nineteenth-century genre work and the Hudson River School, as well as moderns such as Calder, Picasso, Kandinsky, and Pollock; comprehensive art and music libraries; a sculpture garden; and even a children's room where patrons can leave their kids for supervised play while they enjoy the museum. Also on the grounds of the institute is **Fountain Elms,** a beautifully restored 1850 home in the Italianate Victorian style, which was once the home of the philanthropic Williams family. Four period rooms on the ground floor exemplify Victorian tastes. At Christmastime the house is resplendent with Victorian ornamentation.

The Munson-Williams-Proctor Institute, 310 Genesee Street, Utica 13502, (315) 797–0000, is open Tuesday through Saturday, 10:00 A.M. to 5:00 P.M. Admission is free.

Having retrieved your little ones from the children's room at the institute, take them next to a museum of their own. Outside of New York City, Utica's **Children's Museum** is now the largest such institution just for kids in the state, having grown like Topsy since its founding by the city's Junior League. Since 1980 it has occupied its own five-story, 30,000-square-foot building, which it keeps chock-full of participatory and hands-on exhibits concentrating on natural history, the history of New York State, and technology. Installations designed for children ages 2 to 12 and their families include a Dino Den; Childspace, for preschoolers; Iroquois longhouse and artifacts; a natural history center; and bubbles, architecture, and dress-up areas. The museum also offers special exhibitions on a monthly basis and special programs for children and their families on Saturdays beginning at 2:00 P.M., from October through July. Portions of the permanent Railroad Exhibit, which includes a Sante Fe dining car and diesel locomotive, are on display next to the museum.

The Children's Museum, 311 Main Street, Utica 13501, (315) 724–6128, is open between July 4 and Labor Day, Tuesday through Sunday: Wednesday, 10:00 A.M. to 4:30 P.M.; Thursday through Friday, noon to 4:30 P.M.; Saturday and Sunday, 10:00 A.M. to 4:30 P.M. The museum is closed on most major holidays. Admission is $2 per person; children 2 and under are admitted free.

Like other eighteenth-century conflicts, the American War of Independence was not the sort of all-out bloodbath to which we have become inured in the century that gave us Verdun and Stalingrad. But given the right ingredients—a British ambush, tomahawk-wielding Iroquois mercenaries, a patriot force that fought like cornered wolverines—a summer day in the Mohawk Valley could turn nasty indeed. Such is the story told at the ◆ **Oriskany Battlefield State Historic Site.**

The British strategy for the summer of 1777 called for dividing the Middle Atlantic colonies from the New England colonies via a three-pronged attack in New York. Gen. John Burgoyne, as we saw earlier in this book, was to descend on the Hudson Valley from Canada, while another of His Majesty's armies was to head north from New York. The central thrust of this three-way attack was to be made by Col. (temporarily Brig. Gen.) Barry St. Leger, who would attack Albany from Lake Ontario by way of the Mohawk Valley.

The northward attack from New York City was never made, and we saw what happened to Burgoyne at Saratoga. What of St. Leger? His army bogged down at the siege of western New York's Fort Stanwix, which the patriot defenders held much more tenaciously than the British had expected. To make matters worse for the attackers, a relief party of 800 men and boys under the Continental Army's Gen. Nicholas Herkimer had begun to march toward Fort Stanwix in hope of lifting the siege. St. Leger decided to seize the initiative and meet the fort's would-be rescuers before they could reach his main position. To this end he dispatched two Tory leaders, Sir John Johnson and Col. John Butler, to lead a contingent of Loyalists and Iroquois warriors (under Chief Joseph Brant) to intercept Herkimer's force in ambush.

The Tories and Indians fell upon Herkimer and his men as they emerged from a ravine near Oriskany on August 6, 1777. The first volley brought down General Herkimer, who, with a mortal musketball wound in his leg, continued to shout orders to his troops. Both sides closed in too quickly for successive musket volleys to be exchanged by orderly lines of soldiers in classic eighteenth-century fashion, and the fighting quickly descended to hand-to-hand grappling with bayonets and tomahawks. The patriots fought fiercely—so fiercely that the Indians gave up the field, followed soon after by the Tories and British regulars, in whose behalf they had joined the fray. The British survivors retreated to Fort Stanwix, where their absence during the

Oriskany battle had done St. Leger's cause no good. The siege of the fort was abandoned, and the British returned to Canada. Their Mohawk Valley thrust had been thwarted, thanks largely to the bravery of General Herkimer—dead of his wound within a few days after the battle—and his militia of farmers and their sons.

The bloodiest of American revolutionary battles is commemorated at the Oriskany site by an audiovisual show, by guided walking tours of the battlefield, and by a memorial obelisk built in 1884.

Oriskany Battlefield State Historic Site, Route 69, 2 miles west of Oriskany 13424, is open from early May through Labor Day, due to the efforts of the Oriskany Battlefield Volunteer Community. Any questions should be directed to (315) 736-8823. The battlefield is open to the public daily from 9:00 A.M. until dusk. Staff is on-site Saturdays and Sundays. Tours can be arranged. An anniversary celebration is held every August 6.

On a lighter note . . . just to the southwest of Oriskany and Utica, in the small town of Deansboro, is the extraordinary **Musical Museum,** operated by the Sanders family since 1948. The very idea of such a place might be enough to keep a layperson in the fast lane on the thruway, but don't make that mistake. This is *not* a collection of old oboes in glass cases but a seventeen-room agglomeration of the kinds of instruments anyone can play: player pianos, ancient jukeboxes, harmoniums and melodeons, and just about every sort of early phonograph and music box. Anyone *can* play the exhibits—literally. Restored to operating condition, most of the musical contraptions at the museum are there for the cranking, pumping, or whatever else is required of the curious visitor to make sound come out.

Among the items exhibited at the museum are an incredible mechanical violin player built in 1912, the coin-operated player pianos that were the first "jukeboxes," an 1,800-pound Wurlitzer band organ that reproduces the sound of an entire twenty-piece band, and even a compressed-air calliope. (The original steam calliopes were enormous, cumbersome affairs with their own boilers; only seventy-five or so ever operated in the United States.)

The Musical Museum, Route 12B, Deansboro 13328, (315) 841-8774, is open daily April 1 through December 31, 10:00 A.M. to 4:00 P.M. Admission is $5 for adults, $4 for children 6 to 12, and free for children under 6.

SYRACUSE AND THE ERIE CANAL

If a parlor organ can carry you back in time, think of what a ride on a horse-drawn canal boat will do. That was the original idea behind the ◆ **Erie Canal Village,** which opened in Rome in 1973 near the site where the first spadeful of dirt for the Erie Canal was dug on Independence Day in 1817.

It's difficult for us to make modern-day comparisons with the Erie Canal in terms of national pride, public excitement, and the sense of heroic accomplishment that the project inspired in the new Republic. The space program? Our pride in U.S. space accomplishments is necessarily more vicarious, since few of us are going up there ourselves. But imagine building the first commercial pathway into the heart of the continent—a level water-road that would replace the treacherous footpaths and wagon routes that had stifled trade and settlement in earlier years. The short-lived canal era may have been only a prologue to the age of the railroad—but in the 1820s New Yorkers felt the Erie Canal was one of the wonders of the world.

The *Chief Engineer,* which keeps to a regular schedule of thirty-five-minute trips on the restored section of the original canal at the village, was built of Mohawk Valley oak to the same specifications as the passenger-carrying packet boats of the canal's early years. The core attraction of the village, it has since been joined by a narrow-gauge, one-half-scale steam locomotive, the *Edward Nolan,* and the Harden Carriage Museum, which comprises a varied collection of horse-drawn vehicles used on roads and snow. Other buildings in the village—nearly all of which are more than a hundred years old and were moved here from other communities in the area—include a tavern, church, smithy, canal store, settler's house, barn, and the New York State Museum of Cheese. The Erie Canal Museum, housed in a building of a newer construction, contains exhibits explaining the technological and social importance of the Erie Canal. Fort Bull, dating from the French and Indian Wars, is also on the premises.

The village, now managed by the Rome Historical Society, presents historical craft demonstrations, interpretive programs, and seasonal festivals, with the primary focus on canal and harvest activities.

69

Erie Canal Village, Routes 49 and 46, Rome 13440, (315) 337–3999, is open daily, 9:30 A.M. to 5:00 P.M., from mid-May through September. Admission is charged. Boat rides are an additional $1 per person.

If a visit to the Erie Canal Village has brought you to Rome, stop in at the **Corning-Revere Factory Store.** The store offers terrific bargains on slightly irregular and factory-closeout items from the company's standard line of copper-clad stainless steel, as well as aluminum-slab stainless steel and copper-slab stainless steel. It also carries Corning Ware and other selected kitchen equipment.

The Corning-Revere Factory Store, 137 Liberty Plaza, Rome 13440, (315) 337–7828, is open Monday through Saturday, 9:00 A.M. to 5:00 P.M.

Back before the Erie Canal was built, years before anyone thought of putting a copper bottom on a steel pot, this part of New York State was the western frontier, ripe for settlement, agriculture, and the development of manufacturing. During those first decades of American independence, land development companies operated much as they had in colonial times, securing rights to vast sections of virgin territory and undertaking to bring in settlers and get them started. One such outfit was the Holland Land Company, which in 1790 sent its young agent John Lincklaen to America to scout investment possibilities. Two years later he reached the area around Cazenovia Lake, between present-day Rome and Syracuse, and his enthusiasm for the area's prospects led his firm to invest in 120,000 acres here. A village, farms, and small businesses soon thrived, with Lincklaen remaining in a patriarchal and entrepreneurial role that demanded the establishment of a comfortable family seat. The result was Lincklaen's 1807 building of his magnificent Federal mansion, Lorenzo, today preserved at the ◆**Lorenzo State Historic Site.**

The little fiefdom of Lorenzo offers an instructive glimpse into why New York is called the Empire State. Lincklaen and the descendants of his adopted family, who lived here until 1968 (the same year that the house, with its contents, was deeded to the state), were involved with many of the enterprises that led to the state's phenomenal growth during the nineteenth century—road building, canals, railroads, and industrial development.

Lorenzo

The mansion, surrounded by 20 acres of lawns and formal gardens, sits on the shores of a 4-mile-long lake. It is rich in Federal-era furnishings and the accumulated possessions of a century and a half of Lincklaens. In 1992 several of the rooms at Lorenzo were restored. The southwest bedroom was wallpapered with a reproduction of the original Jeffrey and Company of London paper, first hung in the room at the turn of this century. The downstairs drawing room was repapered with a reproduction of the original 1901 wallpaper, and new matching drapes, upholstery, and carpets were chosen to match the original as closely as possible. These projects are part of an ongoing process to fully restore the site to its turn-of-the-century beauty.

Lorenzo State Historic Site, Route 13, Cazenovia 13035, (315) 655–3200, is open May 15 through October 31, Wednesday through Saturday and on Monday holidays, 10:00 A.M. to 5:00 P.M.; Sunday, 1:00 to 5:00 P.M. The grounds are open all year, 8:00 A.M. to dusk. Admission is free.

A swamp northwest of Cazenovia was destined for an even grander future as the nineteenth century began. This was the site of Syracuse, which would be lifted to prominence by the salt industry and the Erie Canal, and which today contains the last of the "weighlock" buildings that once dotted the waterway. Built in 1850 in Greek Revival style, this weigh station for canal boats today houses the ◆ **Erie Canal Museum.**

How did they weigh canal boats? The procedure used here can be more clearly understood if you begin by envisioning the Erie Canal flowing along the present route of Erie Boulevard. Boats were towed into a "weighlock chamber" on the open, canal-side section of the building, after which lock gates were closed at the front and the rear. When the water was drained out of the chamber, the boat came to rest on a wooden cradle that constituted the bed of an enormous scale. The boat was weighed, tolls were assessed accordingly, and water was readmitted to the chamber to float the boat along its way when the gates were reopened.

Exhibits in the Weighlock Building, which houses the museum, include a 65-foot replica of a canal boat. The *Frank Buchanan Thomson,* named after a late museum director, offers a look at a typical Erie Canal vessel's crew quarters, immigrant accommodations, and cargo storage. Immigration along the canal is a special focus of the museum's exhibits, particularly with regard to its effects upon Syracuse. The museum experience also includes a hands-on display of canal equipment and explanations of the engineering involved in connecting Albany and Buffalo by means of a 363-mile artificial waterway, with eighty-three locks and eighteen aqueducts. The job wasn't easy, but the result was the longest and most successful canal in the world.

The Erie Canal Museum, 318 Erie Boulevard East, Syracuse 13202, (315) 471–0593, is open daily from 10:00 A.M. to 5:00 P.M.; closed holidays. Admission is free.

Having passed through the stages from swamp to canal boomtown to major commercial and industrial center by the end of the nineteenth century, Syracuse was ready for an art museum. The idea for the institution that was to become today's ◆ **Everson Museum of Art** came from George Fisk Comfort, a lion of the

American art establishment who had been instrumental in establishing New York City's Metropolitan Museum and served as founder and dean of the College of Fine Arts at Syracuse University. Comfort organized the museum as the Syracuse Museum of Fine Arts, and in 1900 the first exhibition took place. A progressive policy toward acquisitions was in evidence even at that early date, with the initial show featuring, among older and more recognized masters, the work of impressionists such as Monet, Sisley, and Pissarro.

Renamed the Everson Museum in 1959 following a large bequest from the estate of Syracuse philanthropist Helen Everson, the museum moved in 1968 into its present quarters, a massive, modernist concrete structure that was architect I. M. Pei's irst museum building. Its three exhibition levels contain nine galleries and a 50-foot-square, two-story sculpture court.

The emphasis at the Everson is heavily American, particularly with regard to ceramics. The museum's Syracuse China Center for the Study of Ceramics houses the nation's premier collection in this field, with holdings dating from A.D. 1000 to the present. Here are pre-Columbian Native American vessels, colonial and nineteenth-century pieces, and contemporary functional and art pottery, as well as some 1,200 examples of ceramic craftsmanship from cultures outside the Western Hemisphere.

The Everson's holdings also include anonymous colonial portraits (and one very famous and not so anonymous one of George Washington), the works of nineteenth-century genre and luminist painters, and paintings by twentieth-century names such as Robert Henri, John Sloan, Grandma Moses, Maxfield Parrish, Reginald Marsh, and Grant Wood. The museum possesses a good graphic art collection and a small but comprehensive photography section.

The Everson Museum of Art, 401 Harrison Street, Syracuse 13202, (315) 474–6064, is open Tuesday through Friday, noon to 5:00 P.M.; Saturday, 10:00 A.M. to 5:00 P.M.; and Sunday, noon to 5:00 P.M. Admission is free, although a suggested donation of $2 is welcome.

If your curiosity about canals has not yet been sated, you might want to sign on for a grand tour—a two- or three-day journey down the Cayuga-Seneca, the Oswego, the Champlain, and the Erie canals. ◆**Mid-Lakes Navigation Company, Ltd.** offers

Lockmaster Hireboat
Mid-Lakes Navigation Company

escorted, navigated, and catered cruises, with departures from Buffalo, Syracuse, and Albany. During the day passengers travel and dine aboard *Emita II,* a reconverted passenger ferry. At night the ferry ties up on shore, and passengers check into a local hotel. It's a perfect blending of the nineteenth and twentieth centuries.

The company also runs week-long bare-boat charters from the town of Cayuga aboard European-style Lockmaster hireboats.

Mid-Lakes Navigation Company, Ltd., is headquarted at 11 Jordan Street, P.O. Box 61, Skaneateles 13152; (315) 685–8500 or (800) 545–4318.

THE FINGER LAKES

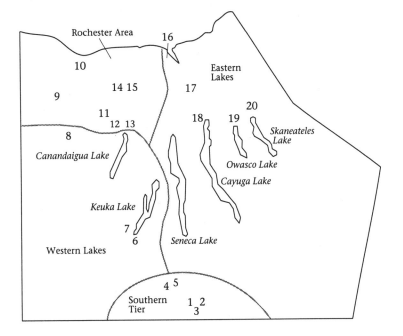

Rochester Area

16

10

Eastern
Lakes

14 15   17

9

11
12 13

18   19   20

Skaneateles
Lake

8

Canandaigua Lake

Owasco Lake

Cayuga Lake

Keuka Lake

7

6   Seneca Lake

Western Lakes

4 5

Southern
Tier   1 2
3

1. Mark Twain Study
2. Hill Top Inn
3. National Soaring Museum
4. Ice Cream Works
5. The Rockwell Museum
6. Glenn H. Curtiss Museum of
   Local History
7. Wine and Grape Museum of
   Greyton H. Taylor
8. National Warplane Museum
9. Genesee Country Village
   and Museum
10. Strong Museum

11. Electronic Communication
    Museum
12. Granger Homestead and
    Carriage Museum
13. Sonnenberg Gardens
14. Hill Cumorah
15. Historic Palmyra
16. Sodus Bay
17. Grape Hill Gardens
18. National Women's Hall
    of Fame
19. Cayuga Museum
20. The Krebs

THE FINGER LAKES

Here, between New York's "northern seaboard" along Lake Ontario and the Pennsylvania border, lies the region that many visitors consider to be the most beautiful part of the state. South of the Lake Ontario plain, the land appears to have been furrowed on a vast scale, with hilly farmland descending toward each of the Finger Lakes only to rise again before the next. The aptly named elongated lakes extend roughly north and south across an 80-mile swath of the state, offering vistas so reminiscent of parts of Switzerland that it's no wonder the city at the northern end of Seneca Lake was named Geneva.

Another distinctly European aspect of the Finger Lakes area is its status as New York State's premier wine-growing region. No longer limited only to the cultivation of native grape varieties, New York's vintners have come a long way, as visits to individual vineyards and the wine museum described below will demonstrate.

Scenes of well-tended vines in rows along steep hillsides may put you in mind of Europe, but the Finger Lakes region is rich in Americana. Here are museums of coverlets, Victorian dolls, and horse-drawn carriages. You'll even find Mark Twain's study and a museum devoted to Memorial Day.

We'll approach this area from the south, beginning near the Pennsylvania border and continuing up toward Rochester, then heading east along the New York State Thruway and the northern Finger Lakes.

THE SOUTHERN TIER

In the city of Elmira, there is a site with significant associations in the life of Mark Twain but one that many Americans—including Twain aficionados familiar with his haunts in Hannibal, Missouri, and Hartford, Connecticut—know little about. This is the ◆**Mark Twain Study,** a charming little summer house on the campus of Elmira College.

Mark Twain married an Elmira woman named Olivia Langdon in 1870, and for many years the author and his family took leave of their palatial Hartford home to spend summers outside Elmira with Olivia's sister, Mrs. Theodore Crane. Mrs. Crane and her husband lived on a farm, where in 1874 they built Twain a free-standing octagonal study, with windows on all sides and a massive stone fireplace. Here Twain wrote *Tom Sawyer* and completed sections of *Huckleberry Finn, Life on the Mississippi, A Connecticut Yankee in King Arthur's Court,* and other works. It was, he said, "the loveliest study you ever saw."

Twain spent his last summer in Elmira in 1903 and returned the following year for his wife's funeral. The author himself was buried in Woodlawn Cemetery, on Walnut Street in Elmira, in 1910.

Difficult to maintain and protect from vandalism, the study was donated to Elmira College by the Langdon family in 1952, whereupon it was removed to its present site on the campus. A Mark Twain exhibit in nearby Hamilton Hall includes a typewriter identical with the one Twain once used and memorabilia relevant to his summer home.

The Mark Twain Study, on the Elmira College Campus off Main Street, Elmira 14901, is open during the summer months on Monday through Saturday, 9:00 A.M. to 5:00 P.M., and on Sunday, noon to 5:00 P.M. To arrange off-season visits write The Center for Mark Twain Studies, Quarry Farm, Box 900, Elmira College, Elmira 14901, or call (607) 732–0993.

Every summer at the **Mark Twain State Park,** America's most popular humorist is remembered in a lively **Musical Drama** the *New York Times* described as "an extravaganza of singing, acting and dancing." A cast of more than sixty—both professional Broadway performers and local talent—perform dramatizations of Twain's life and works on lavish sets, which include a life-size replica of his Quarry Farm home and study, a real horse and carriage, and Jim and Huck's raft floating down the Mississippi. Performances are held inside a 1,500-seat, airconditioned geodesic dome.

Eight performances of the Mark Twain Musical Drama at Mark Twain State Park, Route 14, P.O. Box 265, Elmira 14902, (607) 796–4111 or (800) 395–MARK, are held every week during July and August. Matinees are at 2:00 P.M. on Wednesday, Thursday, Saturday, and Sunday. Evening performances are at 7:30 P.M. on Tuesday, Thursday, Friday, and Saturday. Call for ticket information and/or reservations.

If you're in town and thirsty or hungry for some great Buffalo chicken wings or a super sandwich, stop in at **Bernie Murray's,** a favorite neighborhood watering hole and restaurant. Bernie's is at 500 S. Main Street, Elmira, (607) 734–1299. If the kids are hungry for more than a Big Mac, **Granny's Restaurant** in the Diven Plaza, 1622 Lake Street, Elmira, (607) 733–8874, puts out a super family-style buffet and salad bar. (Closed Monday.)

Head up Jerusalem Hill in Elmira to the ◆**Hill Top Inn's** outdoor terrace and deck for a great view of the Chemung Valley and some delicious continental fare. The Sullivan family has been greeting and feeding patrons since 1933. The Hill Top Inn is open for lunch Monday through Friday, 11 A.M. to 2:00 P.M. during the summer. Dinner is served year-round Monday through Saturday, 5:00 P.M. to 10:00 P.M. Closed most holidays. Reservations are recommended. Call (607) 732–6728.

The three-story Italianate mansion **Lindenwald Haus** has been a popular overnight stop for travelers for more than 115 years. Owners Sharon and Michael Dowd are in the process of renovating the B & B's forty-four rooms, and those they've completed are cozy, clean, and comfortable. Fruit trees dominate the home's 5 acres, and guests are welcome to walk, bike, or cross-country ski.

Lindenwald Haus, 1526 Grand Central Avenue, Elmira 14901, (607) 733–8753, has varying hours; call for information.

When Mark Twain's study was at its original site on the Quarry Farm belonging to his in-laws, it commanded a lovely view of the undulating hills along the Chemung River Valley. Little did Twain suspect that within a few decades after his death, these same hills would attract recreationists content not merely to walk the trails and pastures but instead to soar quietly far above them. By the 1930s Harris Hill, outside Elmira, had become the "Soaring Capital of America." The science and sport of motorless flight is today kept vigorously alive at the ◆**National Soaring Museum,** which offers visitors earthbound exhibits *and* the opportunity to go aloft in sailplanes piloted by experienced professionals.

Regardless of whether you agree with the museum's philosophy that soaring is "flying as nature intended," a visit to the facility offers a good introduction to this often-overlooked aspect of modern aviation. The museum houses the world's largest exhibit of contemporary and historic sailplanes, along with displays explaining the development of soaring and its relation to the parallel fields of meteorology and aerodynamics. You can even climb into a cockpit simulator, similar to those used to teach soaring, and learn what the experience of controlling a motorless plane is like.

Well, almost. To really understand soaring, you have to get off the ground. This can easily be arranged at the museum or at the Harris Hill Soaring Corp. Visitors' Center, which has a staff of competent pilots licensed by the FAA. Just check in at the Harris Hill Gliderport—the rides are available all summer long and on weekends throughout the year, weather permitting. Even if you don't go up yourself, it's fun to watch the graceful, silent flights and landings of the sleek sailplanes.

The National Soaring Museum, Harris Hill, RD 3, Elmira 14903, (607) 734–3128 (office) or 734–0641 (glider field), is open daily 10:00 A.M. to 5:00 P.M. Call regarding schedules and cost of sailplane flights.

Upstream along the Chemung River is Corning, indelibly associated in most travelers' awareness with the Corning Glass Company and its Corning Glass Center and Museum and Steuben Glass Factory. If you'd prefer a more intimate environment in which to watch magnificent glass pieces being created by traditional glassblowing techniques, visit **Vitrix Hot Glass Studio** in Corning's historic Market Street district. Since 1959 Vitrix has been turning out some of the country's finest handblown glass pieces.

Vitrix Hot Glass Studio, 77 West Market Street, Corning 14830, (607) 936–8707, is open Monday through Friday, 10:00 A.M. to 6:00 P.M.; Saturday, 10:00 A.M. to 5:00 P.M.; and Sunday, noon to 5:00 P.M. Summers the studio stays open Monday through Saturday until 8:00 P.M.

Buffalo lays claim to chicken wings and beef on weck, and in the Chautauqua region goat's-milk fudge is the regional delicacy. And now some folks in Corning hope to put the Finger Lakes on the map with wine ice cream. Mick Balock, co-owner of the ◆ **Ice Cream Works,** invented the recipe and turned to Hunt Country Vineyards in nearby Branchport for product assistance: Foxy Lady wine ice cream was the result. As far as Mick knows, no similar recipe exists anywhere. The ice cream, hand-dipped or served through a soft-serve unit, has a subtle wine taste and is served in—you guessed it—a wine glass. The less adventurous can order up other ice cream house specialties such as Custer's Last Stand or a Sweet Ruthie at the authentically restored 1880s ice cream parlor.

The Ice Cream Works, West Market Street and Centerway Square, Corning 14830, (607) 962–8481, is open daily year-round, in summer from 9:00 A.M. to 10:00 P.M. and in winter from 11:00 A.M. to 5:00 P.M., serving food and desserts.

Also in Corning is the ◆ **Rockwell Museum**, an institution that owes its existence almost entirely to a single individual whose collection it comprises. Robert F. Rockwell is an area native and former proprietor of a small department store chain whose interest in western art dates to his youth spent on a Colorado ranch. He began collecting seriously in the late 1950s, over the years acquiring works not only by universally recognized masters of "cowboy" art such as Charles M. Russell and Frederic Remington but also by landscapists of the caliber of Albert Bierstadt and Thomas Hill and by animal artists A. F. Tait and Carl Rungius.

Rockwell's protean interests went beyond western art and sculpture to include an area dear to him as a Corning resident— the beautiful art glass created by Frederic Carder, cofounder of the Steuben Glass Works, which was later incorporated into Corning Glass Works, now Corning, Inc. Rockwell even collected antique toys.

By the beginning of the 1980s, Rockwell's collections, particularly of western art and Carder Steuben glass, were too extensive to be casually shown in his department stores and as part of exhibitions loaned to other institutions. He needed a museum, and one arrived in the form of Corning's old city hall, a Romanesque Revival structure built in 1893. The Corning Company acquired the building from the city for $1, renovations were undertaken, and in 1982 The Rockwell Museum opened. At present it houses the largest collection of western art on the East Coast, more than 2,000 pieces of Carder Steuben glass, Navajo weavings, antique firearms, Indian artifacts, and the toy collection as well.

The Rockwell Museum, Cedar Street at Denison Parkway, Corning 14830, (607) 937–5386, is open September through June, Monday through Saturday, 9:00 A.M. to 5:00 P.M.; Sunday, noon to 5:00 P.M. During July and August the hours are Monday through Friday, 9:00 A.M. to 7:00 P.M.; Saturday, 9:00 A.M. to 5:00 P.M.; and Sunday, noon to 5:00 P.M. The museum is closed Thanksgiving, Christmas Eve, Christmas Day, and New Year's Day. There is an admission fee.

WESTERN LAKES

The southern Finger Lakes region is a tranquil, easy-paced corner of the world that nevertheless nurtured one of twentieth-century America's great speed demons. At Hammondsport, on the southern tip of Keuka Lake, the ◆ **Glenn H. Curtiss Museum of Local History** chronicles the lifework of this native son, who was also a serious pioneer in motorcycling and aviation.

Glenn Hammond Curtiss started out, as did the Wright brothers, in the bicycle business. He quickly turned to motorcycles, building a V-8–powered bike on which he went over 136 miles per hour in 1907. He also built engines that powered lighter-than-air craft, and in that same year he became involved with Dr. Alexander Graham Bell and other enthusiasts in the "Aerial Experiment Association." Curtiss's engineering helped lift the association's airplane *Red Wing* off the ice of Keuka Lake on the first public flight (as opposed to the Wrights' secret 1903 experiment) of a heavier-than-air craft in the United States.

Glenn Curtiss's accomplishments over the next twenty years dominated the adolescence of aeronautics. In 1910 he landed a plane on water for the first time, and in 1911 he became the first American to receive a pilot's license. In 1919 a Curtiss "flying boat" made the first transatlantic crossing by air. Meanwhile he had built his Curtiss Aeroplane and Motor Company into an industrial giant, employing 10,000 men at the peak of production during World War I. Sensing the traveling trends of the motor age, he even manufactured the first successful house trailers. The museum, founded in 1960, houses seven historic aircraft and two reproductions, one of the latter of which is a flyable replica of the inventor's 1908 *June Bug II*.

The Glenn H. Curtiss Museum of Local History, Route 54, 0.5 mile south of Hammondsport 14840, (607) 569–2160, is open from May 1 through October 31, Monday through Saturday, 9:00 A.M. to 5:00 P.M., and Sunday, 11:00 A.M. to 5:00 P.M.; from November 1 through April 30, it is open Monday through Saturday, 10:00 am. to 4:00 P.M., and Sunday, noon to 5:00 P.M. Admission is $4 for adults, $3.50 for senior citizens, $2.50 for students, and free for children ages 6 and under.

The Finger Lakes region is New York's wine country, and the area around Keuka Lake is in many ways its heart. It was along the shores of Keuka Lake that the late Dr. Konstantin Frank established his Vinifera Vineyards and proved to the world that the European grapes could survive New York State winters when grafted to hardy American rootstocks. Keuka Lake is also the home of Bully Hill Vineyards, owned by a man who calls himself Walter S. _____. Why? It's a long story, involving the purchase of the Taylor Wine Company by the Coca-Cola Company a few years back (at that time, Mr. _____ was no longer associated with Taylor) and Coke's successful legal action barring the Taylor name from appearing on any labels or promotional literature connected with the products of Mr. _____'s Bully Hill. Can you guess his name now?

In any event, Walter S. _____ is the proprietor not only of Bully Hill but of the ◆ **Wine and Grape Museum of Greyton H. Taylor,** G. H. having been none other than his father. (Oops, now we gave it away.) The museum recounts the story of a century and a half of winemaking in New York State, particularly in the Finger Lakes area.

The Wine and Grape Museum of Greyton H. Taylor, G. H. Taylor Memorial Drive, Hammondsport 14840, (607) 868–4814, is open from May 1 through October 31, Monday through Saturday, 10:00 A.M. to 4:30 P.M.; Sunday, noon to 4:30 P.M. A moderately priced restaurant next door specializes in homemade pasta and dishes prepared with wine. The Bully Hill winery can also be visited for tours and tastings; call (607) 868–3210.

And now for a completely different kind of craft (art?)—pottery, hand-thrown and hand-decorated by "The Wizard of Clay," master potter Jim Kozlowski, and his assistants at **The Wizard of Clay Pottery** in Bristol. Jim's production facilities and retail stores are housed in seven geodesic domes he designed himself.

The potter's wheel and eight kilns are in the workshop. All pieces are fired at a temperature of 2,265 degrees F., which makes them extremely hard and durable, then treated with a specially formulated glaze that gives them a richly colored finish. The Wizard's most original pottery is decorated with delicate imprints from real leaves gathered from the Bristol hills.

The Wizard of Clay Pottery, Route 20A in Bristol, 3 miles east of Honeoye Lake (mailing address: 7851 Route 20A, Holcomb 14469), (716) 229–2980, is open daily from 9:00 A.M. until 5:00 P.M.

Heading northwest away from the Finger Lakes toward the Lake Ontario lowlands, we find the ◆**National Warplane Museum** in Geneseo, dedicated to the restoration and maintenance of flying-condition World War II aircraft. The museum now has twenty-five aircraft in its collection dating from World War II and the Korean Conflict, including an ME-109 Messerschmitt, a Boeing B-17 Flying Fortress, and a Spitfire. Several of the planes, including the B-17, a PBY 6-A Catalina, and a Fairchild C-119 Boxcar, are open to visitors for inspection.

If you're lucky enough to be in the area the third weekend of August, be sure to attend the "1941 Wings of Eagles" air show, featuring more than a hundred World War II–vintage aircraft.

The National Warplane Museum, Geneseo Airport, Geneseo 14454, (716) 243–0690, is open year-round, Monday through Friday, 9:00 A.M. to 5:00 P.M.; Saturday and Sunday, 10:00 A.M. to 5:00 P.M. Before going, call ahead—at times the aircraft may be off the field attending other air shows. Admission is $5 for adults and $1 for children under 12.

ROCHESTER AREA

"Spend a day in the nineteenth century," reads the ◆**Genesee Country Village and Museum**'s invitation—but what's different about this reconstructed village in Mumford, on the southern outskirts of Rochester, is that the properties mean the *whole* nineteenth century, not just a small part of it. The fifty-plus buildings originally standing on or relocated to this site—all of them restored—represent virtually every stage of the development of upstate New York, from frontier days to late Victorian times.

The rail-fenced pioneer settlement reveals what rural living was like up near Lake Ontario around 1800. Just twenty-five years later the region had prospered to the extent that sumptuous Greek Revival homes such as Livingston Manor, also on the village grounds, could reflect the rapidly cultivated tastes of the upstate gentry. Turn the pages of another half-century, and you find the Victorian quirks and fussy comforts of the 1870 Octagon House, with its tidy cupola and broad verandas. Other village buildings include a carriage barn containing a collection of forty horse-drawn vehicles; a Gallery of Sporting Art, showcasing paintings

Richard Greeve's *Kiowa*
Genesee Country Village Museum

and sculpture inspired by wildlife and the hunt; and the George Eastman birthplace, moved here in homage to the man who made nearby Rochester a "film capital" of an entirely different sort than Hollywood, California.

The Genesee Country Village and Museum, off Route 36 in Mumford, (mailing address: P.O. Box 310, Mumford 14511), (716) 538–6822, is open from mid-May through mid-October: July and August, open daily, 10:00 A.M. to 5:00 P.M.; spring and fall, open daily, 10:00 A.M. to 4:00 P.M., except Mondays. Admission is $10 for adults, $8.50 for senior citizens, $6 for children ages 13 to 17, $5 for children ages 6 to 12, and free for children under 5.

If you picture a little girl in crinoline playing in the parlor of the Genesee Country Village's Octagon House, you can well imagine the sort of dolls she might have for companions. Up near Rochester, in North Chili, Linda Greenfield has assembled a wonderful collection of these delicate and elaborately dressed playthings in her **Victorian Doll Museum.** The hundreds of dolls at the museum not only reflect the tastes of the Victorian era but also show many types of doll construction that have faded from the picture in these days of molded plastic doll faces and bodies.

The Victorian Doll Museum premises are also the home of the **Chili Doll Hospital,** also run by Linda, who is an expert at doll restoration and repair. Dolls are appraised by appointment, and a collector's gift shop offers fine modern and period reproduction specimens.

The Victorian Doll Museum and Chili Doll Hospital, 4332 Buffalo Road, North Chili 14514, (716) 247–0130, are open Tuesday through Saturday, 10:00 A.M. to 4:30 P.M.; Sunday, 1:00 to 4:30 P.M. Admission to the museum is $2 for adults and $1 for children ages 12 and under.

There are dolls and a whole lot more at Rochester's ◆ **Strong Museum.** This remarkable institution, the legacy of one woman's interests and devotion to collecting, takes as its theme the artifacts not only of childhood but of all of American life during the decades of our national expansion and industrialization. Since its founding the museum has expanded its scope up through the present day, using its impressive collections to explore contemporary topics in the light of history.

Margaret Woodbury Strong's (1897–1969) family owned one of the largest buggy-whip concerns in the United States. This fact in itself might not have led to twentieth-century prosperity had the proceeds not been invested wisely. But Margaret's father did so, buying stock in a new venture being started by a young Rochester bank clerk named George Eastman, who had a notion that the fun of photography might be spread among the masses. At the time of her death, Margaret Woodbury Strong was the largest individual stockholder in the Eastman Kodak Corporation, and the bequest with which she endowed her museum amounted to $60 million.

The Strong collections offer a virtual one-stop education in the development of American taste over a century and a quarter of rapid economic growth and social adjustment. Here is one of the largest and best collections of Victorian furniture in the United States, along with a vast sampling of decorative objects—glass, silver, ceramics, and Oriental objects of virtu. There are lithographs, engravings (including much of Winslow Homer's magazine work), rare books, early bicycles, and dollhouses, along with eighty miniature rooms. The sampling of antique dolls is drawn from the 30,000 that Mrs. Strong owned at the time of her death. Other aspects of the collection include mechanical toys, paper ephemera, and costumes.

Dynamic exhibits tell the remarkable stories of the people and events that have shaped everyday life in America since 1820. Permanent exhibits include "Great Transformations, 1820–1920" (how the industrial revolution reshaped the lives of Americans) and "Changing Patterns: Household Furnishings, 1820–1939."

One of the museum's most popular exhibits is an interactive learning/play area designed especially for children. Called "One History Place," it features original and reproduction artifacts from the turn of the century, arranged in kitchen, parlor, and attic settings that allow the children to imagine life in the time of their parents and grandparents. The children can also pretend to travel on a child-size locomotive.

The Strong Museum, One Manhattan Square, Rochester 14607, (716) 263–2700, is open Monday through Saturday from 10:00 A.M. to 5:00 P.M., and Sunday from 1:00 to 5:00 P.M.; closed Thanksgiving, Christmas, and New Year's Day. Admission is $4 for adults; $3 for senior citizens and students with school I.D., and $2 for children 3 to 16.

South and east of Rochester is a monument to another important development in the history of American popular culture:

the shopping mall. Not the steel-and-glass malls of the 1950s, but a sturdy wooden structure erected in 1879. It was built by Levi Valentine as an all-purpose market and community center for the settlement he was developing, and thus it lays claim to being the first multistore "shopping center" in the United States. Today it houses the **Valentown Museum,** a collection of nineteenth-century small-town memorabilia that includes a reconstruction of the first railroad station in the Rochester area and a "Scientific Exhibition," which traveled around the country in a covered wagon from 1825 to 1880.

Valentown Hall, as Valentine called his "mall," had front doors opening into a general store, meat market, cobbler shop, barber shop, bakery, and harness shop. Upstairs were a grange lodge, rooms where classes in the arts and trades were held, and a community ballroom. The ambitious scheme lasted only thirty years, since the promised railroad connection never materialized (the restored station interior belonged to an earlier rail operation). The building was saved from demolition and restored in 1940 by J. Sheldon Fisher, a member of the Fisher family that gave its name to the town of Fishers, in which the hall is located. For information on when the museum can be visited, contact Mr. Fisher at the Valentown Museum, Valentown Square, Fishers 14453, (716) 924–2645.

Along with shopping malls, what could be more intrinsic to American civilization than the electronic media? The early days of our fascination with the vacuum tube (a device, young readers, that brought us our news, sports, and "Top 40" before the invention of the transistor) are chronicled in the Antique Wireless Association's ◆**Electronic Communication Museum** south of the thruway in East Bloomfield. The museum's collections, housed in the handsome 140-year-old quarters of the East Bloomfield Historical Society, have been amassed by AWA members throughout the world. They include nineteenth-century telephones (in working order!), some of Marconi's original wireless apparatus, early shipboard wireless equipment, and the crystal radio sets that brought the first broadcast programs into American living rooms. A special attraction is a fully stocked replica of a circa 1925 radio store; another is wireless station W2AN, an actual broadcast operation staffed by AWA members.

The AWA Electronic Communication Museum, just off Routes 5 and 20 in East Bloomfield 14443, (716) 657–7489, is open May 1 to October 31, Sunday, 2:00 to 5:00 P.M.; also open Saturday, 2:00 to 4:00 P.M., and Wednesday, 7:00 to 9:00 P.M., during June, July, and August.

Preserved Americana seems to be the order of the day in this part of upstate New York, and the theme is carried along nicely at the ✦**Granger Homestead and Carriage Museum** in Canandaigua. *Homestead* is actually a bit too homespun a term for this grand Federal mansion, which must have been the talk of Canandaigua and all the farms around when it was built in 1816 by Gideon Granger, a lawyer who had served as postmaster general under Jefferson and Madison. Granger came here to spend the life of a country squire in his retirement, and his descendants lived here until 1930, when they willed many of the furnishings to Rochester's Memorial Art Gallery. The furnishings have been returned to the house on loan since it reopened in 1948. Nine restored rooms contain the furniture of the nineteenth century, including Federal, Empire, and Victorian styles. Decorative objects, original artworks, and China Trade porcelain are also displayed.

A distinctive attraction of the Granger Homestead is the Carriage Museum, which exhibits more than fifty horse-drawn vehicles made or used in western New York. The sociological implications of the various conveyances on display are explained in an informative exhibit titled "Sleighs and Surreys and Signs and Symbols."

The Granger Homestead and Carriage Museum, 295 North Main Street, Canandaigua 14424, (716) 394–1472, is open May through October. Guided tours are offered on the hour Tuesday through Saturday, 1:00 to 5:00 P.M., and also on Sunday, 1:00 to 5:00 P.M., in June, July, and August. Admission is $3 for adults and $1 for children.

✦**Sonnenberg Gardens** are part of an estate built around a mansion representative of a much bolder and more expressive architectural aesthetic than Granger's Federal style—this is a Gilded Age extravaganza, part Tudor Revival, part Queen Anne, built in 1887 by Frederick Ferris Thompson, who founded the First National Bank of the City of New York. The forty-room mansion is well worth a tour—but even more impressive than the heavily carved Victorian furniture and fine

**Japanese Hill Garden with Tea House
Sonnenberg Gardens**

Oriental rugs contained beneath the house's multicolor slate roof are the gardens themselves.

Frederick Thompson died in 1899, and in 1902 his widow, Mary Clark Thompson, began the extensive formal and informal plantings on the estate as a memorial to her husband. She worked at creating the gardens for the next fourteen years and held occasional "public days" so that her Canandaigua neighbors (she had spent her youth in the town) could enjoy them as well. Since 1973 the gardens have been undergoing restoration, and they appear today much as they did during the first decades of the century.

What sets Sonnenberg Gardens apart is the sheer eclecticism. While many estates of the turn-of-the-century period were planted in a single style, usually formal French or the more naturalistic English, the gardens here represent just about every major mode of horticultural expression. There are a Japanese Garden, a rock garden, an Italian Garden, a sunken parterre display in a Versailles-inspired fleur-de-lis motif, an Old-Fashioned Garden, a garden planted entirely in blue and white flowers, and a Rose Garden containing more than 2,600 magnificent bushes blossoming in red, white, and pink. There are also a Roman bath, a thirteen-house greenhouse complex with a domed palm house conservatory, and fountains and statuary everywhere. After a while the mansion itself almost seems like an afterthought.

Sonnenberg Gardens, off Route 21N, Canandaigua, 14424 (716) 394–4922, is open daily mid-May through mid-October, 9:30 A.M. to 5:30 P.M. Admission is $6 for adults, $5 for senior citizens, and $2 for children ages 6 to 16.

In the rolling farm country east of Rochester, there is a drumlin—a round, glacially deposited hill—called Cumorah. According to the beliefs of the Church of Jesus Christ of Latter Day Saints, it was on ◆ **Hill Cumorah** in September 1823 that an eighteen-year-old farmboy was told of the existence of a golden book of revelations, buried on the hill fourteen centuries earlier. The boy's name was Joseph Smith, and he said that the messenger who told him about the book was the angel Moroni.

So began the Mormon faith. Or, according to the church's doctrines, so resumed the ministry of Jesus Christ in the New World, because the revelations contained in the Book of Mormon tell of a vanished civilization in upstate New York, among whose members Christ preached after his time on earth in Palestine. The golden leaves of the book were purportedly buried by Moroni—then a mortal—after an apocalyptic battle had taken place around Hill Cumorah in the year A.D. 421.

The modern part of the Mormon story continues with Joseph Smith's annual meetings with the angel on Hill Cumorah, the culmination of which, according to Smith, was Moroni's directing him to unearth the scriptures in 1827.

Though seated now in Salt Lake City, the church maintains a strong presence in Palmyra in the form of a large visitor center at Hill Cumorah and an imposing statue of the angel Moroni atop the hill. The visitor center features exhibits, paintings, dioramas, and films explaining Mormon history and beliefs.

Other historical sites maintained by the LDS church in and around Palmyra include the Joseph Smith home in Manchester; the "Sacred Grove," where the Book of Mormon was first revealed; and the Peter Whitmer farm near Waterloo, where the church was organized. For information on the schedules and locations of each of these sites, as well as on Hill Cumorah itself and the annual pageant, contact the Hill Cumorah Visitor Center, Palmyra 14522, (315) 597–5851.

Palmyra is not without its secular points of interest, one of the most unusual of which is the **Alling Coverlet Museum,** part of ◈ **Historic Palmyra** in the village's downtown business district. One never knows where the nation's largest collection of this or that is going to turn up, but when it comes to coverlets, the answer is Palmyra.

The bed coverings displayed here were collected over thirty years by Mrs. Merle Alling of Rochester. Heirlooms all, they represent both the simple spreads hand-loomed by farmwives and the somewhat more sophisticated designs woven on multiple-harness looms by professionals during the nineteenth century. The collection also includes a number of handmade nineteenth-century quilts and antique spinning equipment.

The Alling Coverlet Museum (Historic Palmyra, Inc.), 122 William Street, Palmyra 14522, (315) 597–6737, is open June through mid-September, daily 1:00 to 4:00 P.M.; also by appointment. Admission is free, although donations are welcome.

Another facet of Historic Palmyra is the **William Phelps General Store Museum.** Erected in 1826–28, this commercial building was purchased by William Phelps in 1868 and remained in his family until 1977. Having remained virtually unchanged over the past 125 years, the store, along with its stock, furnishings, and business records, amounts to a virtual time capsule of nineteenth- and early twentieth-century Palmyra. An unusual note: The gaslight fixtures in the store and upstairs residential quarters were used by a Phelps family member until 1976, electricity never having been installed in the building.

The William Phelps General Store Museum, 140 Market Street, Palmyra 14522, (315) 597–6981, is open June through September, Saturday, 1:00 to 4:00 P.M. Admission is free.

Historic Palmyra, Inc.'s final holding is the **Palmyra Historical Museum,** which was erected about 1900 as a hotel. It is now a museum housing a unique display of elegant furniture, children's toys and dolls, household items, tools, gowns, and other artifacts of bygone ages.

The Palmyra Historical Museum, 132 Market Street, Palmyra 14522, (315) 597–6981, is open June through September, Saturday, 1:00 to 4:00 P.M., and by appointment. Admission is free.

For a fabulous day of fishing, head for ◆**Sodus Bay** on the shore of Lake Ontario. In season more than twenty-five charter boat companies offer their services in this small fishing paradise. Stop for a bite at **Papa Joe's Restaurant** on Sodus Point. The only restaurant open here year-round, it has a children's menu and entertainment on the deck on summer weekends. During fishing season, Papa Joe's starts serving breakfast at 5:30 A.M. Lunch and dinner are served from 11:30 A.M. until 10:00 P.M. (315) 483–6372. The **Carriage House Inn,** featured in Rand McNally's *The Best B & Bs & Country Inns/Northeast,* overlooks the lake and is a great place to spend a night. Sixty dollars for a double room includes a full breakfast, private bath, TV, and a room overlooking the lake (if one is available). The inn is at the corner of Ontario and Wickham, Sodus Point 14555, (315) 483–2100 or (800) 292–2990. The lighthouse at **Sodus Bay Lighthouse Museum** on Sodus Point was built in 1871 and was in use until 1901. It's open daily May 1 through October 31 from 10:00 A.M. until 5:00 P.M.

One of the world's largest private lilac collections is open for viewing during May and June at ◆**Grape Hill Gardens** in Clyde. Collections of magnolias, peonies, flowering crabs and other herbaceous garden plants and flowering trees, all at varying stages of development, are also on display. The gardens, 1232 Devereaux Road, Clyde 14433 (315) 923–7290, are handicapped accessible and open daily from 8:00 A.M. to 8:00 P.M. in season. There is no charge for admission.

From coverlets to clocks . . . the northern Finger Lakes region seems to be New York State's attic, filled with interesting collections of things we might otherwise take for granted. In Newark the **Hoffman Clock Museum** comprises more than a hundred clocks and watches collected by local jeweler and watchmaker Augustus L. Hoffman. Housed in the Newark Public Library, the collection includes timepieces from Great Britain, Europe, and

Japan, although the majority of the clocks and watches are of nineteenth-century American manufacture, with more than a dozen having been made in New York State. Each summer the museum's curator mounts a special exhibit devoted to a particular aspect of the horologist's art.

The Hoffman Clock Museum, Newark Public Library, 121 High Street, Newark 14513, (315) 331–4370, is open weekdays, 9:30 A.M. to 9:00 P.M., and Saturday, 9:30 A.M. to 5:30 P.M. Admission is free.

EASTERN LAKES

"To honor in perpetuity these women, citizens of the United States of America, whose contributions to the arts, athletics, business, education, government, the humanities, philanthropy and science have been the greatest value for the development of their country." Thus were the parameters for entry outlined when the women of Seneca Falls created the ◆National Women's Hall of Fame in 1969, believing that the contributions of American women deserved a permanent home.

And, indeed, the list of members reads like a "Who's Who": Marian Anderson, Pearl S. Buck, Rachel Carson, Amelia Earhart, Billie Jean King, Sally Ride, Dorothea Dix, and a host of others who have left their mark on American history and the American psyche.

Exhibits, housed in the bank building in the heart of the Historic District II, include a panel celebrating Elizabeth Cady Stanton, who led the way to rights for women, and artifacts and mementos about the members, events, and activities significant to women's history.

The National Women's Hall of Fame, 76 Fall Street, Seneca Falls 13148, (315) 568–8060, is open from May through October, daily from 9:30 A.M. to 5:00 P.M.; November through April, Wednesday through Saturday, 10:00 A.M. to 4:00 P.M., and Sunday, noon to 4:00 P.M. Closed Thanksgiving, Christmas, and New Year's Day. Admission is $3 for adults, $2 for senior citizens and students, and $1 for children over 10.

For a small town, Waterloo, New York, is large on preserving history and has two museums well worth a visit. It was in the village of Waterloo, in the summer of 1865, that a patriotic businessman named Henry C. Welles put forward the idea of honoring the soldiers who fell in the Civil War by placing flowers

93

on their graves on a specified day of observance. On May 5 of the following year, thanks to the efforts of Welles and Civil War veteran Gen. John B. Murray, the village was draped in mourning, a contingent of veterans and townspeople marched to the local cemeteries and, with appropriate ceremonies, decorated their comrades' graves. Thus Memorial Day was born.

In 1966 President Johnson signed a proclamation officially naming Waterloo the birthplace of Memorial Day. On May 29 of that same Memorial Day centennial year, Waterloo's new **Memorial Day Museum** was opened in a reclaimed mansion in the heart of town. The twenty-room, once-derelict brick structure is itself a local treasure, especially distinguished by the ornate ironwork on its veranda. Although built in the early Italianate Revival era of 1836–50, the house is being restored to its appearance circa 1860–70—the decade of the Civil War and the first Memorial Day observances.

The museum's collections cover the Civil War and the lives and era of the originators of the holiday, as well as memorabilia from both world wars and the Korean Conflict.

The Memorial Day Museum, 35 East Main Street, Waterloo 13165, (315) 539–9611, is open Memorial Day weekend, July, and August, Mondays and Thursdays, 1:00 to 4:00 P.M., and Saturdays, 10:00 A.M. to 2:00 P.M. Admission is by donation. Tours are given by appointment.

Just a block from the Memorial Day Museum is the **Terwilliger Museum,** where the "antique and elegant" combine with the "long-lasting and functional" to tell the story of Waterloo and surrounding areas. The collection includes everything from Native American artifacts to Roaring Twenties fashions. Authentic full-size vehicles and a replica of a general store offer a slice of life as it used to be; and five rooms, decorated down to the last detail, each depict a specific era.

The Terwilliger Museum, 31 East William Street, Waterloo 13165, (315) 539–0533, is open all year, Monday from 2:00 to 5:00 P.M. and Wednesday from 7:00 to 9:00 P.M. Donations are welcome. Tours are given by appointment.

Some institutions have a pinpoint focus; others follow a more eclectic pattern of acquisiton and education. Occasionally, a small institution finds its focus as it matures, as is the case with the ◆ **Cayuga Museum** in Auburn, which is really two museums in one.

Founded in 1936, the Cayuga Museum contains the rich history of both Auburn, "the village that touched the world," and Cayuga County. Exhibits include business timekeeping devices manufactured by Auburn's Bundy brothers, whose Binghamton, New York, operation evolved into IBM. Other notables from Cayuga County who are highlighted at the museum include President Millard Fillmore; E. S. Martin, founder of the original, pre-Luce *Life* magazine; prison reformer Thomas M. Osborne; and Ely Parker, the Seneca Indian who penned the surrender at Appomattox.

In 1911 Theodore W. Case proved that recording sound on film was possible, and in late 1922 he made it a reality with the assistance of E. I. Sponable. Newly restored in 1993 after being forgotten for sixty years, the **Case Research Lab Museum** opened its doors to the public on the second floor of the Cayuga Museum's carriage house in June of that year. Exhibits include the laboratory building, the sound stage, and many examples of the early history, inventions, and laboratory equipment developed to commercialize sound on film.

The Cayuga Museum and the Case Research Lab Museum, 203 West Genesee Street, Auburn 13621, (315) 253–8051, are open Tuesday through Sunday from noon to 5:00 P.M., and Monday holidays. Admission is free, but a donation is welcome.

Just south of Auburn at Emerson Park on Owasco Lake is the **Owasco Teyetasta,** a museum of the Northeast Woodland native peoples who first dwelled in what is now Cayuga County. Operated by the Cayuga Museum, the facility counts among its exhibits artifacts of the native peoples, as well as the skeleton of a 12,000-year-old woolly mammoth.

The Owasco Teyetasta, Route 38A, adjacent to Emerson Park, Owasco Lake 13130, (315) 253–8051, is open Memorial Day to Labor Day, Wednesday through Sunday, 1:00 to 5:00 P.M. Admission is free, but a donation is welcome.

In the town of Skaneateles, on the Finger Lake of the same name, is a restaurant that serves as a living museum of a certain style of American eating, back before obsessive slenderness became a national preoccupation. This is ◆ **The Krebs,** a place where it is always Sunday afternoon and your grandmother is always fixing dinner.

The Krebs began back in 1899, when Mr. and Mrs. Fred Krebs first opened their doors to a local clientele. Since then the menu has remained fixed upon the dining preferences of 1899 small-town America. As for the setting, think "parlor" instead of "living room" and you'll be on the right track. The nouvelle minimalist approach is no more in evidence here in the furnishings than it is on the plates.

Dinner at the Krebs (aside from Sunday brunch, dinner is the only meal served) is always table d'hote, with a minimum of choices. You can choose from among simple starter courses such as shrimp cocktail, fruit cup, and (not *or*) clear or cream soups, but then the serious, standard menu kicks in: lobster Newburg, followed by half a broiled chicken and roast beef. Accompaniments include homemade breads, rolls, and relishes, candied sweet potato, fresh vegetables, creamed mushrooms . . . all good, honest Sunday-dinner fare. Then they bring out the homemade pies, and brownies, and cake.

The Krebs, 53 West Genesee Street (Route 20), Skaneateles 13152, (315) 685–5714 or 685–7001, is open from early May through late October. Dinner is served from 6:00 to 9:00 P.M. Monday through Thursday, from 6:00 to 10:00 P.M. Friday and Saturday, and from 4:00 to 9:00 P.M. Sunday; Sunday brunch, from 10:30 A.M. to 2:00 P.M. Reservations are strongly recommended.

Now what you need is a walk—preferably to Nebraska, if you want to work off every last calorie, although a day at the **Beaver Lake Nature Center** in Baldwinsville will do. The center is an Onandaga County park incorporating several different ecosystems, all connected by 9 miles of well-maintained hiking trails. A 200-acre lake, offering beautiful vistas but no recreational facilities, is a migration-time magnet for up to 30,000 Canada geese. Guided canoe tours of the lake are available during the summer; rental canoes are available for these tours, and you must preregister. The entire center is a great place for birders; more than 180 species have been sighted here over the years. The informative Beaver Lake Visitor Center is the starting point for a regular schedule of hour long guided tours of the trails, given by professional naturalists each weekend.

Beaver Lake Nature Center, 8477 East Mud Lake Road, Baldwinsville 13027, (315) 638–2519, is open all year, daily, dawn to dusk. Admission is $1 per car and $10 per bus. Call ahead to register for guided group nature tours.

NIAGARA-ALLEGANY REGION

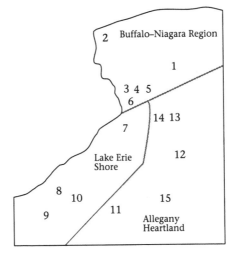

1. Iroquois National Wildlife Refuge
2. Old Fort Niagara
3. Allentown
4 Theodore Roosevelt Inaugural National Historic Site
5. Frank Lloyd Wright houses
6. Buffalo Museum of Science
7. Original American Kazoo Company
8. Stockton Sales
9. Chautauqua Institution
10. Lock, Stock & Barrel Country Store
11. Allegany State Park
12. Arcade and Attica Railroad
13. Roycroft Campus
14. Elbert Hubbard-Roycroft Museum
15. Stull Observatory

NIAGARA-ALLEGANY REGION

Ever since the Erie Canal was opened a century and a half ago, New York City and Buffalo have assumed a front door–back door status in New York State. New York City became the Empire State's gateway to the world, a capital of international shipping and finance. The docksides and railyards of Buffalo, meanwhile, were the portals through which the industrial output and raw materials of the Midwest flowed into the state. Buffalo became an important "border" city between the East Coast and the hinterlands, a center of manufacturing and flourmilling whose fortunes have risen and fallen with the state of the nation's smokestack economy.

But don't write Buffalo off as an old lunchbucket town that gets too much snow in the winter. Buffalo has some impressive architecture, from Louis Sullivan's splendid Prudential Building and the art deco City Hall downtown to the Frank Lloyd Wright houses described below. South Park, with its conservatory, and Riverside Park on the Niagara offer welcome open spaces, and there are even culinary treasures like Buffalo chicken wings and beef on weck (roast beef on a delicate caraway seed roll).

The countryside at the western tip of New York provides further evidence as to why Niagara Falls isn't the only reason to drive to the end of the thruway. The Pennsylvania border country boasts giant Allegany State Park, a hiking and camping paradise, and the byways along the Lake Erie shore wander through a picture-pretty territory dotted with vineyards, cherry orchards, and roadside stands selling delicious goat's-milk fudge. Yes, goat's-milk fudge. It's the little serendipities that make traveling fun.

BUFFALO-NIAGARA REGION

Just to mix things up a bit, we'll venture out into the sticks to begin our tour of the Niagara-Allegany region. Only 40 miles northeast of Buffalo is a pristine tract of some 19,000 acres, the core of which (11,000 acres) makes up the federal ◆**Iroquois National Wildlife Refuge.** On either side of the refuge are the **Oak Orchard** (east) and **Tonawanda** (west) **Wildlife Management Areas,** operated by the state of New York's Department of Environmental Conservation. Both the Oak Orchard and the Tonawanda areas are primarily wetlands, with plenty of access trails on high ground, that offer superb opportunities not only for hunters (during designated seasons) but for hikers and birders as well.

Both the 5,600-acre Tonawanda tract and the 2,500-acre Oak Orchard area owe their status as superb waterfowl habitats to human intervention in what was already a natural wetland. The Oak Orchard Swamp, after which the smaller area is named, is the result of a limestone outcrop that substantially blocks the flow of Oak Orchard Creek near the town of Shelby Center, thus creating a vast upstream wetland. Tonawanda (not to be confused with the city near Buffalo) lies just to the southwest, on the Tonawanda Creek floodplain. Before the state took control of these lands, the flooding that made the area so attractive to migrating waterfowl was largely a spring phenomenon. But the building of dikes and other water-level control structures has resulted in the creation of a total of 3,000 acres of permanent marshland, allowing birds to nest here even after late spring and to use the areas as a resting stop on their fall migration as well.

The best time for birders to visit Tonawanda and Oak Orchard is from early March to mid-May. That's when more than 100,000 Canada geese, along with lesser numbers of black, pintail, and mallard ducks, American wigeon, teal, and shoveler and ringnecked ducks, pause on their northward migration, with some staying to nest. The transitional habitat along the borders of the marsh attracts shore and wading birds and migrating spring warblers.

The Iroquois National Wildlife Refuge headquarters, 1101 Casey Road, Alabama 14003, (716) 948–5445, is open Monday through Friday from 7:30 A.M. to 4:00 P.M. There are self-guided exhibits and an observation tower at the Oak Orchard Education Center on Knowlesville Road, just north of the town of Oakfield. The center is open daily from sunrise to sunset and is the starting point for four nature trails. For additional information contact the regional wildlife manager of the New York State Department of Environmental Conservation, 6274 East Avon-Lima Road, Avon 14414; (716) 226–2466.

It seems as if it isn't possible to tick off too many miles in this state without encountering one of the string of forts that once defended the thirteen colonies' northwestern frontier and played so prominent a role not only in the struggles between the British and the French for North American supremacy but in our own

Drummer at Old Fort Niagara

War of Independence as well. The westernmost of these (in New York, at least) is ◆ **Old Fort Niagara,** located in Fort Niagara State Park downstream from Niagara Falls at the point where the Niagara River flows into Lake Ontario.

Fort Niagara occupies what was, in the days of conventional warfare, one of the most strategic locations in all of the interior of North America. The first European to realize that whoever held this spot would control traffic between Lakes Erie and Ontario was René-Robert Cavalier, Sieur de La Salle, the great French explorer. Here, in 1678, he built Fort Conti, the first of the site's defenses. Abandoned the following year, Fort Conti was followed by Fort Denonville (1687–88) and finally by the great "French Castle" erected here in 1726. The castle served as the core of Fort Niagara's defenses through nearly a century of intermittent warfare and was in use as officers' housing as recently as World War I. Now restored to its eighteenth-century appearance, it is the focal point of Old Fort Niagara.

The French Castle and its outer defenses fell to the British in 1759, following a nineteen-day siege. A British garrison held the fort throughout the American Revolution, having strengthened its defenses with the addition of the North and South Redoubts, which survive today. It was 1797 before a treaty finally forced Great Britain to cede Fort Niagara to the United States, but the installation was seized again by British troops in 1813. Returned to American control in 1815, it has been peaceful ever since, although it continued as a commissioned fort throughout the period of tensions with Canada in the mid-1800s. Finally relegated to service as a training facility, the fort was closed by the U.S. government in 1963—just fifteen years short of the tercentennial of La Salle's Fort Conti.

Restored between the years 1927 and 1934, the older buildings of Fort Niagara are maintained by the nonprofit, private Old Fort Niagara Association in cooperation with the state of New York. Beyond the silent military structures are broad vistas of Lake Ontario and, in clear weather, the rising mists of Niagara Falls 14 miles to the south.

Old Fort Niagara, Fort Niagara State Park, Youngstown 14174, (716) 745–7611, is open daily, July 1 through Labor Day, 9:00 A.M. to 7:30 P.M.; during the rest of the year, although daily opening is at 9:00 A.M., seasonal closing times vary. Closed Thanksgiving, Christmas, and New Year's Day. During the summer there are frequent costumed reenactments of military drills, with musket and cannon firings. Admission is $5.75 for adults, $4.75 for senior citizens, and $3.50 for children ages 6 to 12.

Heading upriver (or more likely, down Route I–190) we pass Niagara Falls and come to the terminus town of the Erie Canal, in its day, and the New York State Thruway, in ours—Buffalo. For a quick introduction to this sprawling inland port, head downtown to reconnoiter the city and Lake Erie from the twenty-eighth-floor observatory of **City Hall** (open weekdays from 9:00 A.M. to 3:00 P.M.) and then visit the nearby historic neighborhood of ❖ **Allentown.** In 1827, when Lewis Allen bought 29 acres of farmland here, this was just beyond the northern boundaries of the young village of Buffalo. In those days what is now Allen Street was a path used by the farmer's cows, but the successive

101

development of rural estates, suburban subdivision, and finally full-scale urbanization made Allentown the residential heart of the growing city. In a scenario repeated throughout the northeastern United States, the middle of our century found Allentown run-down and forgotten—but by the 1980s community activists and rehabilitation specialists, organized as the Allentown Association, had become determined not to let the neighborhood slip into oblivion. The result of their efforts has been the substantial revival of the blocks surrounding Allen Street, east of Main, and the iden-tification of a number of formerly neglected points of interest.

The works of a number of important architects and the homes of several famous people are tucked into the compact Allentown neighborhood. Representative of the district's myriad building styles are the Kleinhans Music Hall on Symphony Circle, designed in 1938 by Eliel and Eero Saarinen; the 1869 Dorsheimer Mansion, 434 Delaware Avenue, an early work of the peerless Henry Hobson Richardson; Stanford White's 1899 Butler Mansion (672 Delaware) and 1895 Pratt Mansion (690 Delaware); and a lovely example of the Flemish Renaissance style at 267 North Street. As for the haunts of the famous, there are the childhood home of F. Scott Fitzgerald, 29 Irving Street; the home of artist Charles Burchfield (once a designer for a Buffalo wallpaper company) at 459 Franklin Street; and, at 472 Delaware Avenue, the carriage house belonging to the now-vanished house occupied circa 1870 by the editor and part-owner of the *Buffalo Morning Express,* a man who hated Buf-falo: Samuel Langhorne Clemens, whom we met back in Elmira under the name of Mark Twain.

One house in the Allentown neighborhood stands above all others in historic importance. For fifty years the home of promi-nent Buffalo lawyer Ansley Wilcox, the Greek Revival house at 641 Delaware Avenue became part of American legend on Sep-tember 14, 1901, when a vigorous young man who had just rushed from a vacation in the Adirondacks stepped into the library to take the oath of office as president of the United States. William McKinley was dead, the victim of an assassin; the era of Theodore Roosevelt was about to begin.

The story of that fateful day and the tragic event that preceded it is told at the ◆ **Theodore Roosevelt Inaugural National Historic Site,** as the Wilcox House has been known since its restoration and opening to the public in 1971. Perhaps the most interesting aspect of the tale concerns the mad dash Roosevelt made from the Adirondacks to Buffalo. He had gone to the city and stayed for a few days at the Wilcox House after McKinley was shot by an anarchist at the Pan-American Exposition but had left to join his family at their mountain retreat after being assured by the president's doctors that his condition had stabilized. Notified several days later of McKinley's worsening state, the vice president made an overnight journey by horse and wagon to the nearest train station, where he learned that the president was dead. Roosevelt and his party then raced to Buffalo in a special train. Within two hours after his arrival, he was standing in Wilcox's library, wearing borrowed formal clothes as he took the oath of office as the nation's twenty-sixth president.

The Theodore Roosevelt Inaugural National Historic Site, 641 Delaware Avenue, Buffalo 14202, (716) 884–0095, is open Monday through Friday, 9:00 A.M. to 5:00 P.M.; weekends, noon to 5:00 P.M. It is closed on Saturdays, January through March. Closed January 1, Good Friday, Memorial Day, July 4, Labor Day, Thanksgiving Day, Christmas Eve, and Christmas Day. Admission is $2 for adults and $1 for children under 12.

The residential neighborhoods north of the downtown and Allentown areas of Buffalo boast five examples of the work of America's greatest architect, Frank Lloyd Wright. Wright's residential architecture is generally distributed within the central and upper Midwest, where he brought his "prairie style" to maturity. The fact that there exists a pocket of the master's work in Buffalo is due to his having designed a house in Oak Park, Illinois, for the brother of John D. Larkin, founder of the Larkin Soap Company of Buffalo. Larkin liked his brother's house and brought Wright to Buffalo to design the company headquarters. The Larkin Building, a light, airy masterpiece of commercial architecture, stood on Seneca Street from 1904 until it was unconscionably demolished in 1950. But fate was kinder to the five Buffalo houses built for Larkin Soap Company executives following Wright's arrival in town, all of which survive to this day. Here is a list of the **Frank Lloyd Wright houses** in Buffalo and their locations:

• **William Heath House,** 76 Soldiers Place, corner of Bird Avenue, completed in 1906 and landscaped by Frederick Law Olmsted. (Private; not open to visitors.)

- **Darwin D. Martin House,** 125 Jewett Parkway, corner of Summit Avenue. Also completed in 1906, this expansive home was unfortunately left vacant for seventeen years prior to the mid-1950s, during which time half of the original Wright windows were lost. It was restored in 1970 by the State University of New York at Buffalo, which uses it for offices. For information regarding tours contact the School of Architecture and Planning, Hayes Hall, 125 Jewett Parkway, Buffalo 14214; (716) 831–3485.
- **George Barton House,** 118 Summit Avenue, a smaller brick structure with distinctive top-story casement windows and a broad roof overhang built in 1903–4. (Private; not open to visitors.)
- **Gardener's Cottage,** Martin Estate, 285 Woodward Avenue. Constructed in 1906, the cottage is one of the few surviving service buildings of the Martin Estate. (Private; not open to visitors.)
- **Walter Davidson House,** 57 Tillinghast Place. With the exception of Darwin Martin's 1926 summer house, built south of the city on a bluff above Lake Erie, the 1909 Davidson House is the last of Wright's Buffalo residences. (Private; not open to visitors.)

From what we know about Frank Lloyd Wright, we can surmise that if he ever caught a client putting a player piano in one of his houses, he would have rapped him across the knuckles with his walking stick. But the perennially old-fashioned machines began to flourish during the first decade of the twentieth century, when Wright was designing his radically modern houses, and they are with us still. Nowadays the most complete line of rolls for player pianos is manufactured and sold by a Buffalo institution called **Q-R-S Music Rolls.**

Q-R-S is one of the last (and also the oldest) manufacturers of player-piano rolls in the United States, having been founded in 1900 by Melville Clark, the man who perfected the player. During the heyday of the instrument in the 1920s, Q-R-S had plants in New York, Chicago, and San Francisco, but by 1966 only a small facility in the Bronx remained. A new owner bought the company and moved it to Buffalo, where subsequent ownership has kept it.

A piano-roll company like Q-R-S doesn't stay in business simply by cranking out reprints of "Sweet Adeline" and "You Are My Sunshine." Today you can buy rolls for Billy Ray Cyrus's "Achy

Breaky Heart," Whitney Houston's "I Will Always Love You," and other tunes penned long after your player was built.

But not all player pianos are antiques. The company is making a device that will enable any piano to play music programmed on special Q-R-S CDs You can order a copy of the company's current catalog through the mail, but if you're in the area it's a lot more fun to stop in at the factory and make your purchase after taking a tour.

Q-R-S Music Rolls, 1026 Niagara Street, Buffalo 14213, (716) 885–4600, is open Monday through Friday, 9:00 A.M. to 4:00 P.M., with a morning tour at 10:00 A.M. and an afternoon tour at 2:00 P.M. Admission fees, refunded with a purchase, are $2 for adults and $1 for children.

Just minutes from downtown the ◆ **Buffalo Museum of Science** houses an extensive collection of natural science exhibits. The museum was built in the 1920s and features a blend of classic dioramas and modern museum exhibitry. A stunning glass-enclosed atrium connects the museum to the Charles R. Drew Science Magnet School, one of the first science magnet schools in the nation to be physically and programmatically linked to a museum.

The museum's main exhibit hall is filled with exciting temporary exhibits. A visit to the permanent "Dinosaurs & Co." exhibit provides an exciting look at some of the favorite prehistoric giants. "Insect World" features insects six times life-size in two vastly different ecosystems—the cloud forest in the coastal Andean highlands of north central Venezuela and the Niagara frontier region of New York State. The only Tibetan Sand Mandala preserved and on exhibit in North America is in the museum's hall of Asian Art and Culture. Two halls of space provide detailed information about our world and the worlds around us; and observatories provide views of stars, planets, and our sun. The museum also features exhibits on endangered species, zoology, flora and fauna, gems and minerals, and technology.

The Buffalo Museum of Science is located at 1020 Humboldt Parkway (Best Street exit of the Kensington Expressway), Buffalo 14211; (716) 896–5200. Open Tuesday through Sunday from 10:00 A.M. to 5:00 P.M. Closed January 1, July 4, Thanksgiving Day, and Christmas Day. Admission is $4.75 for adults and $3.25 for children, students, and senior citizens.

The Buffalo Museum of Science also operates **Tifft Nature Preserve** just 3 miles from downtown. Billed as an "Urban Nature Sanctuary," the preserve is a 264 -acre habitat for animal and plant life, dedicated to environmental education and conservation. With miles of hiking trails, three boardwalks, and a self-guided nature trail, it's a wonderful place to spend the day hiking or fishing. For birdwatchers there's a 75-acre freshwater cattail marsh with viewing blinds. In winter the preserve rents snowshoes. Free guided nature walks are given every Sunday at 2:00 P.M. The Makowski Visitor Center has some wonderful exhibits on ecology, animals, and plant life.

The Tifft Nature Preserve and Makowski Visitor Center, 1200 Fuhrmann Boulevard, Buffalo 14203, (716) 825–6397 or 896–5200, is open Tuesday through Sunday from 9:00 A.M. to 5:00 P.M. Closed January 1, Thanksgiving Day, December 24, and December 25. There is no admission charge.

LAKE ERIE SHORE

The southwestern tip of New York State is packed with as eclectic a mix of off-the-beaten-path sights as can be found anywhere. Remember kazoos—those funny little musical instruments you could play just by humming into them? They're still being made in Eden, at the ◆ **Original American Kazoo Company.** Established in 1916, it's now the only metal kazoo factory in the world—and it's still making them the same way they were made in 1916. The company used to produce everything from toy flutes and fishing tackle boxes to metal dog beds and peanut vending machines, but in 1965 the demand for kazoos became so great that the firm stopped manufacturing everything else.

The "working museum" at the Original American Kazoo Company shows how "America's only original musical instrument" is made, chronicles kazoo history, and regales visitors with such fascinating trivia as " 'Far, Far Away' is the most requested tune played on the kazoo."

The Original American Kazoo Company, 8703 South Main Street, Eden 14057, (716) 992–3360, is open Monday through Saturday, 10:00 A.M. to 5:00 P.M.; Sunday, noon to 5:00 P.M. Closed Thanksgiving, Christmas Day, New Year's Day, Memorial Day, Easter, Fourth of July, and Labor Day. Admission is free.

Although it's now just a short hop off I–90, its easy to imagine how isolated the **Dunkirk Historical Lighthouse** must have been when the lantern in the square, 61-foot tower first began guiding ships into Dunkirk Harbor in 1876. Today an automated light in the tower does the job, and the two story, stick-style keeper's dwelling has been converted into a **Veterans' Park Museum.**

Five of the museum's rooms are devoted to displays of each branch of the military; three are preserved to show how the lighthouse keeper used to live; one is a memorial to the Vietnam War; and the last is an exhibit of maritime history.

Displays on the grounds include a 40-foot lighthouse buoy tender, a 21-foot rescue boat, and a Civil War cannon. Visitors can take a tour of the lighthouse tower (there's a fee).

Dunkirk Historical Lighthouse and Veteran's Park Museum, off Point Drive North, Dunkirk 14048, (716) 366–5050, are open April through June, 10:00 A.M. to 2:00 P.M. daily, except Sunday and Wednesday; July and August, 10:00 A.M. to 4:00 P.M. daily; and September through November, 10:00 A.M. to 3:00 P.M. daily, except Sunday and Wednesday.

Ready for a little beef on weck? Order "The Kaiser." Something fancier, like angel hair pasta with roasted vegetable salsa? Stop at stately **White Inn** in Fredonia. Duncan Hines did, back in the 1930s, and was so taken with the food that he included it in his "Family of Fine Restaurants." Although the restaurant/inn has since undergone several transformations, it still proudly displays the Duncan Hines sign out front. And the building itself encompasses the original Victorian mansion built in 1868.

The White Inn, 52 East Main Street, Fredonia 14063, (716) 672–2103, is open daily year-round for lunch and dinner. Lunch is served Monday through Saturday, 11:30 A.M. to 2:00 P.M.; dinner is served Monday through Thursday, 5:00 to 8:00 P.M., Friday and Saturday until 9:00 P.M., and Sunday, 12:30 until 7:30 P.M.

Antiquing and basketmaking have long been favorite activities in Chatauqua County, and ◆**Stockton Sales** offers visitors a wealth of both. The building Dan and Carol Graziano bought in 1980 was originally known as the Stockton Basket Factory, and Carol still makes them today. Now calling her business Bear Lake Baskets, she uses maple and cherry to craft a wide variety of shapes and designs, often adding stenciled designs. Many of her basket weaves and designs are original, and all are utilitarian as well as lovely.

And the merchandise at Stockton Sales? There are five buildings packed with antiques as well as one-of-a-kind items, memorabilia, and just plain old "stuff." At any given time a rough inventory might include oil paintings, carousel horses, animal mounts, barber poles, a Chinese cradle, a mounted water buffalo head, 1,000 chairs, 50 sets of china, . . . and on, and on, and on. The Grazianos also have a terrific selection of old books and encourage visitors to browse at leisure.

Stockton Sales, 6 Mill Street, Stockton 14784, (716) 595–3516, is open June through August, Tuesday through Friday, 10:00 A.M. to 5:00 P.M., and Saturday and Sunday, 1:00 to 5:00 P.M.; September through May, Tuesday through Friday, 10:00 A.M. to 4:00 P.M., and Saturday, 10:00 A.M. to 5:00 P.M.; and closed Sundays from October 1 through March 1. Closed Monday.

At the northern tip of Lake Chautauqua in Mayville, the people at **Webb's Candy Factory** have been making goat's-milk fudge for more than thirty years. The goats are gone from out back now and the milk comes from cans, but the confection is just as rich and creamy as ever, and the chocolate fudge with pecans is a regional taste treat not to be missed. Webb's makes all its candies by hand, using the old-fashioned, copper-kettle method, and has added a host of other treats to its repertoire, including "frogs," hard suckers, chocolate bars, divinity, and chocolate clusters. If you own a goat and want to start production, take a short tour of the candy factory between 10:00 A.M. and 4:00 P.M. Monday through Friday.

Webb's Candy Factory, Route 394, Mayville 14757, (716) 753–2161 is open daily, year-round. In summer the hours are 9:00 A.M. to 10:00 P.M.; in winter, 9:00 A.M. to 6:30 P.M.

Lake Chautauqua is also the home of a 114-year-old enterprise that exemplifies the American penchant for self-improvement. The ◆ **Chautauqua Institution** gave its name to an endless array of itinerant tent-show lyceums around the turn of the century. A lot of us have forgotten, though, that the original institution is still thriving right where it was founded in 1874. Chautauqua's progenitors were Bishop John Heyl Vincent and the industrialist (and father-in-law of Thomas Edison) Lewis Miller, and their original modest goal was the establishment of a school for Sunday-school teachers. Chautauqua grew to become a village unto itself, offering not only religious instruction but a program of lectures and adult-education courses.

The largely secularized Chautauqua of today bears little resemblance to the Methodist camp meeting of a hundred years ago, although services in the major faiths are held daily. The character of the place in the 1990s owes at least as much to the founding here of the Chautauqua Literary and Scientific Circle, a turn-of-the-century self-education program based upon the great books of the Western tradition. The Chautauqua emphasis on culture and mental and spiritual improvement has led to an extensive annual summer calendar of lectures, classical and popular concerts, dramatic performances, and long- and short-term courses in subjects ranging from foreign languages to tap dancing to creative writing. It has its own 30,000-volume library.

For performing-arts enthusiasts there are four professional companies that perform throughout the season: the Chautauqua Symphony Orchestra, the Chautauqua Conservatory Theater Company, the Chautauqua Ballet Company, and the Chautauqua Opera Company.

To put it simply, Chautauqua is a vast summer camp of self-improvement, a place where you can rock (in chairs) on broad verandas, walk tree-lined streets that have no cars, and listen in on a chamber music rehearsal on your way to lunch. Recreational opportunities include a thirty-six-hole golf course, tennis, softball, fishing, sailing, waterskiing, wind surfing, boating, canoeing, cycling, lawn bowling, shuffleboard, volleyball, and swimming at four beaches.

The season at Chautauqua lasts for nine weeks each summer, but admission is available on a daily, weekend, or weekly basis.

For complete information on facilities and programs, contact Chautauqua Institution, 1 Ames Street, Chautauqua 14722; (716) 357–6200 or (800) 836–ARTS.

Head south along the lake for a few miles to catch a ride on one of the last surviving modes of pioneer transport—the **Bemus Point–Stow Ferry.** The cable-drawn ferry has traversed the "narrows" of the lake at these points for more than 177 years. Unfortunately (or, for animal rights activists, fortunately), the oxen that once pulled the ferry with the aid of a treadmill and manila rope retired quite a while ago. But the pace and charm of the primitive open barge still remain.

The Bemus Point–Stow Ferry, Stow 14757 (mailing address: 15 Water Street, Mayville 14757), (716) 753–2403, is open from 11:00 A.M. to 9:00 P.M. Saturdays and Sundays in June and daily in July and August. Admission is $3 per car and $1 per person for walk-ons.

You found that stuffed water buffalo head you wanted back at Stockton Sales, but where to go to buy a turkey call or a genuine crock pickle? ◆**Lock, Stock & Barrel Country Store,** serving the people of Ellington since 1833. Lock, Stock & Barrel is the country store of our youth—jam-packed with penny candy, spices, candles, roasted peanuts, hunting and fishing equipment, and antiques and collectibles.

The rooms are as packed with history as they are with merchandise. The shelves in the main part of the store are original, as are the wooden floors and the kerosene lanterns hanging from the ceiling (now converted to electricity). There's a reconstructed country kitchen from more than one hundred years ago. Be sure to check the guest book before you leave: To date, visitors from forty states and fourteen countries have found their way to this off-the-beaten-path attraction.

Lock, Stock & Barrel Country Store, Town Square, Ellington 14732, (716) 287–3886, is open daily, except Tuesdays, from 11:00 am. until 6:00 P.M.

You'll notice a lot of goods made by the Amish at Lock, Stock & Barrel. That's because Ellington borders on **Amish Country,** which encompasses several towns to the north and east. The Amish people first came to Cattaraugus County from Ohio in 1949. Although they prefer to live their own lifestyle, they're a friendly people who generally welcome questions about their way of life. (They do request, however, that you not take their picture.) There are a number of small shops on Route 62 in the town of **Conewango Valley** that offer products made by, or about, the Amish. **Franklin Graphics** sells Amish photos, books, and postcards. Stop at **Mueller's Valley View Cheese Factory** to sample swiss cheese and forty other varieties, made in Amish country. **Amish Country Fair** carries furniture and crafts.

ALLEGANY HEARTLAND

Salamanca is the only city in the world located on a Native American reservation; it is also home to the largest park in the state's park system. The **Seneca–Iroquois National Museum** on the Allegany Indian Reservation traces the cultural and historical heritage of the Seneca, known as "Keeper of the Western Door of the Iroquois Confederacy." The museum exhibits collections of artifacts beginning with prehistoric times and re-creates the culture and history of the Seneca people.

The Seneca-Iroquois National Museum, Broad Street Extension, Salamanca 14779, (716) 945–1738, is open April 1 through September 30, Monday through Saturday, 9:00 A.M. to 5:00 P.M., and Sunday, 10:00 A.M. to 5:00 P.M.; October 1 through March 31, Monday through Friday, 9:00 A.M. to 5:00 P.M. Closed for the month of January and on Easter, American Indian Day, Thanksgiving, and Christmas. An entry fee is charged.

With 65,000 acres, two 100-acre lakes, and 80 miles of hiking trails, ◆**Allegany State Park,** "the wilderness playground of western New York," is the largest of the state parks. It came into being on May 2, 1921, with the acquisition of 7,150 acres of land, largely through the efforts of Senator Albert T. Fancher of Salamanca. Land acquisition continues today so that eventually the park will comprise the 65,988 acres authorized by the state legislature.

Today the park is a mecca for both summer and winter outdoor enthusiasts. There are lakes for boating and swimming, ballfields, tennis courts, picnic areas, playgrounds, bike paths, and miles of cross-country and snowmobile trails. Rowboats and paddleboats can be rented at the Red House boathouse, where there are also a restaurant, tent and trailer area, and bicycle rental. The park has seasons for small game, turkey, archery deer, and big game. A special permit (free) is required to fish the park's waters.

Allegany State Park, off Route 17, Salamanca 14779, (716) 354–9101 or 354–9121, is open daily, year-round. There is no entrance fee.

Before you leave Salamanca, stop at the **Salamanca Rail Museum,** a fully restored passenger depot constructed in 1912 by the Buffalo, Rochester, and Pittsburgh Railroad. The museum uses exhibits, artifacts, and video presentations to re-create an era when rail was the primary means of transportation from city to city.

Throughout the summer and fall, the museum offers special three- to five-hour rail excursions along the historic route of the New York and Lake Erie Railroad. Call for the schedule and fares.

Salamanca Rail Museum, 170 Main Street, Salamanca 14779, (716) 945–3133, is open Monday through Saturday from 10:00 A.M. to 5:00 P.M. and Sunday from noon to 5:00 P.M. Closed the months of January and February. Closed Mondays in March, October, November, and December. Admission is free.

Most of us have heard about how, in an effort to force Indians out west onto reservations in the late 1800s, the buffalo they relied on for food, clothing, and protection were slaughtered en masse. In 1850 twenty million buffalo roamed the western plains. By 1900 only a couple of hundred could be found.

But research now shows that buffalo meat is lower in cholesterol than fish or chicken and has 25 percent more protein than beef. America's "original meat" is becoming *the* choice of health-conscious Americans, and buffalo are once again roaming the fruited plains (plums go particularly well with bison) in increasing numbers.

So when Glenn and Lorri Bayger decided to start a ranch and considered raising beef cattle, they were advised by experts to invest in buffalo instead. Today a herd of 300 roam over 610 open acres at the **B & B Buffalo Ranch** in Ellicottville. Visitors are invited to learn about buffalo and visit the store, which sells buffalo-related souvenirs, Indian jewelry, and, of course, buffalo meat.

The store at the B & B Buffalo Ranch, Horn Hill Road, Ellicottville 14731, (716) 699–8813, is open from May 1 through December 31, Tuesday through Saturday, 10:00 A.M. to 5:00 P.M., and Sunday, 11:00 A.M. to 5:00 P.M.; from January 1 through April 30, Thursday through Saturday, 10:00 A.M. to 5:00 P.M., and Sunday, 1:00 to 5:00 P.M.

Head north on Route 219 a short distance to Ashford Hollow to see one of the most unconventional sculpture "gardens" ever. For more than twenty years, local sculptor Larry Griffis has been integrating his art with nature—placing his monumental abstract/representational sculptures throughout a 400-acre woodland setting/nature preserve. More than 200 of his pieces, most made of steel and between 20 and 30 feet high, are on exhibit at **Griffis Sculpture Park.** Ten nudes ring a pond, sharing the banks with live swans and ducks. A towering mosquito awaits unwary hikers along one of the 10 miles of hiking trails. Giant toadstools grow in a field, waiting to be climbed on.

Arcade and Attica Railroad

Griffis Sculpture Park, Route 219, Ahrens Road, Ashford Hollow (mailing address: 6902 Valley Road, East Otto 14729), (716) 257–9344, is open daily, May through October, from 9:00 A.M. to 9:00 P.M. Closed November through April. Admission is free. Tours are given by appointment.

If you were heading off to a summer at Chautauqua three generations ago, you would have gotten there by rail—specifically by a steam-hauled train of the Erie, Pennsylvania, or New York Central railroads. Of course, Amtrak can get you there today (nearest station: Erie, Pennsylvania), but if you want steam, you'll have to head to a nostalgia operation like the ◆**Arcade and Attica Railroad,** headquartered just southeast of Buffalo in Arcade.

Maybe *nostalgia* isn't the right word, since the Arcade and Attica is a real working railroad with a healthy freight clientele. But the company's passenger operation is an unabashed throwback, relying for motive power on a pair of circa 1920 coalburners pulling old, open-window steel coaches that once belonged to the Delaware, Lackawanna, and Western.

113

Actually, the Arcade and Attica's tourist-oriented passenger run is the company's second venture into the business of hauling people as well as freight. In 1951 the firm abandoned its regular passenger operations, having discovered that ticket revenues for the first quarter of that year amounted to all of $1.80! (In those days the line did indeed connect Arcade and Attica, but service north of North Java was abandoned in 1957 after a washout just south of Attica.) But in 1962 the Arcade and Attica management decided that if it reinvested in previously abandoned steampower, people might come just to ride the train for fun. They did, and they still do. Arcade and Attica passengers enjoy a ninety-minute ride through some of upstate's loveliest farm country, ending right where they started by way of a trip back through time.

The Arcade and Attica Railroad, 278 Main Street, Arcade 14009, (716) 496–9877, operates weekends from Memorial Day through the end of October, with Wednesday and Friday trips during July and August. Call ahead for schedules. Tickets are available at the 278 Main Street office.

Along with steam engines and the Chautauqua, one of the true institutions of turn-of-the-century America was a self-made philosopher named Elbert Hubbard. In addition to writing a little "preachment" (as he called it) titled "A Message to Garcia" that dealt with the themes of loyalty and hard work, and publishing his views in a periodical called the *Philistine,* Hubbard was famous for having imported the design aesthetic and celebration of handcrafts fostered in England by the artist and poet William Morris. Elbert Hubbard became the chief American proponent of the arts and crafts movement, which touted the virtues of honest craftsmanship in the face of an increasing tendency in the late nineteenth century toward machine production of furniture, printed matter, and decorative and utilitarian household objects.

Visually, the style absorbed influences as diverse as art nouveau and American Indian crafts and is familiar to most of us in the form of solid, oaken, slat-sided Morris chairs and the simple "Mission" furniture of Gustav Stickley. Elbert Hubbard not only wrote about such stuff but also set up a community of craftspeople to turn it out—furniture, copper, leather, even printed books. He called his operation The Roycrofters, and it was headquarted on a "Campus" in East Aurora.

There are several ways the modern traveler can savor the spirit of Elbert Hubbard in modern East Aurora. One is by visiting the ✦ **Roycroft Campus,** on South Grove Street. The campus grounds, now a National Historic Site, feature a gift shop, working pottery, art gallery, and several antiques dealers, all housed in Hubbard-era buildings. For information, contact the East Aurora Chamber of Commerce, 666 Main Street, East Aurora 14052, (716) 652–8444.

Another window on the Roycroft era is the ✦ **Elbert Hubbard-Roycroft Museum,** recently located in a 1910 bungalow built by Roycroft craftsmen and now on the National Register of Historic Places. Part of the furnishings, including the superb Arts and Crafts Dining Room, are original and were the property of centenarian Grace ScheideMantel when she turned the house over to the museum in 1985. (Mrs. ScheideMantel's husband, George, once headed the Roycroft leather department.) Other Roycroft products on display at the house include a magnificent stained-glass lamp by Roycroft designer Dard Hunter and a saddle custom-made for Hubbard just prior to his death on the torpedoed *Lusitania* in 1915.

There is a wonderful period garden, complete with a sundial and a "gazing ball," maintained by "The Masters Gardeners" of the Erie County Cooperative Extension Service.

The Elbert Hubbard Museum (ScheideMantel House), 363 Oakwood Avenue, East Aurora 14052, (716) 652–4735, is open from June 1 to mid-October on Wednesday, Saturday, and Sunday, 2:00 to 4:00 P.M.; by appointment the rest of the year. A $1 donation is requested. Private or group tours also can be arranged, year-round, by appointment.

Before taking leave of East Aurora, we should stop in at the home of one of our least appreciated presidents, Millard Fillmore. Fillmore, who was born in the Finger Lakes town of Genoa in 1800, came to East Aurora to work as a lawyer in 1825. He built this house (since moved to its present Shearer Avenue location) on Main Street, in the village, in the same year and lived here with his wife until 1830. As restored and furnished by previous owners and the Aurora Historical Society, the **Millard Fillmore House National Landmark** contains country furnishings of Fillmore's era, as well as more refined pieces in the Greek Revival, or "Empire," style of the president's early years. A high desk to be

115

used while standing was part of the furnishings in Fillmore's law office; the rear parlor, added in 1930, showcases furniture owned by the Fillmores in later years, when they lived in a Buffalo mansion. The large bookcase was used in the White House during the Fillmore presidency.

The Millard Fillmore House National Landmark (Aurora Historical Society), 24 Shearer Avenue, East Aurora 14052, (716) 652–8875, is open from June 1 to mid-October, Wednesday, Saturday, and Sunday, 2:00 to 4:00 P.M.; by appointment the rest of the year. Admission is charged.

There's only one direction we haven't yet looked to in this chapter, and our final destination will remedy that. At the southeast corner of the Alfred University campus is the ◆ **Stull Observatory,** considered to be one of the finest teaching observatories in the Northeast. It exists largely through the efforts of John Stull, who built or rebuilt all of the telescopes and many of the buildings. There are five major telescopes at the observatory: a 9-inch refractor dating from 1863, a 16-inch Cassegrain reflector, and 14-, 20- and 32-inch Newtonian reflectors.

The Stull Observatory at Alfred University, Alfred 14802, (607) 871–2208, offers public viewings (weather permitting) at the following times: September, October, November, February, March, and April, Friday from 9:00 to 11:00 P.M.; May, June, and July, Thursday from 10:00 P.M. until midnight. Admission is free.

116

THE CATSKILLS

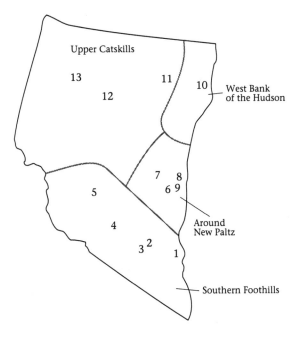

Upper Catskills

13

12

11

10   West Bank
      of the Hudson

5

7   8
6   9

4

3 2

1   Around
         New Paltz

Southern Foothills

1. Constitution Island
2. Brotherhood (winery)
3. Hall of Fame of the Trotter
   and Trotting Horse Museum
4. Wurtsboro Airport
5. Catskill Fly Fishing Center
   and Museum
6. Huguenot Street
7. Delaware and Hudson Canal
   Museum

8. Slabsides
9. Mohonk Mountain House
10. Bronck Museum
11. Durham Center Museum
12. Burroughs Memorial State
    Historic Site
13. Hanford Mills
    Museum

THE CATSKILLS

To many lifelong New York City residents for whom the Adirondacks might as well be the other side of the moon, the Catskills *are* upstate New York. At this point in our travels, we certainly know better—but nevertheless, if you had only a couple of days to get out of the city, the Catskills would be your best bet for a quick introduction to exurban New York.

The Catskills, of course, are "mountains" in the eastern rather than the western sense. Generally lower in elevation than the Adirondacks, these are old, worn peaks, part of the Appalachian Range. The higher elevations are to the north, where the larger ski areas are located. But some of the most dramatic Catskills scenery lies along the west shore of the Hudson, within 30 or 40 miles of the New York City line. Here are the majestic Palisades, brooding cliffs of volcanic basalt exposed by millions of years of water and weather; here also are Bear Mountain, Tallman, and Harriman state parks, with their thick forests and panoramic views. Farther west are the abrupt cliffs of the Shawangunk Mountains, where some of the world's greatest rock climbers perfect their technique.

A place of mystery to the early Dutch settlers, and later a virtual synonym for a certain style of resort entertainment, the Catskill region has a history as varied as its terrain. We'll start our exploration at the south, near the Hudson, and move north and then west toward the farther hills.

SOUTHERN FOOTHILLS

Just about everyone knows where West Point is, but how many Hudson Valley travelers or military buffs can locate ◆ **Constitution Island**? Geographic literalists might look for it in the first chapter of this book, since it's practically on the east shore of the Hudson, separated from the mainland only by marshes. But since visitors have to take a boat to get to the island, and since the boat leaves from West Point, we have it here among our Catskill sites.

Although Constitution Island never served any military purpose after the revolutionary war, it had an important part to play in General Washington's strategy for keeping British naval traffic out of the upper Hudson River. During the earlier part of the war, the fortifications on the island were relatively ineffectual; begun in 1775, **Fort Constitution** was still unfinished when it was captured by the British two years later. Largely destroyed by its American defenders before they retreated, the fort was never rebuilt.

By the following year, however, the island was back in American hands and was more valuable than ever in view of its position opposite the new American defenses constructed at West Point. Here was a place where British ships could be stopped dead in the water, and the way to do it was to stretch an immense iron chain across the river from West Point to Constitution Island. The chain was forged of stout New Jersey iron (a portion of it can be seen at the state reservation at Ringwood, New Jersey), floated across the river on rafts of logs, and securely anchored at either shore. Three redoubts and a battery were constructed on Constitution Island to protect the eastern end of the chain.

The chain did its job, and Constitution Island saw no further hostilities throughout the remaining five years of the war—no thanks to Benedict Arnold, who tried to hand over West Point and related defenses to the British in 1780. When the war ended in 1783, the barracks that had been built on the island were decommissioned, and civilian calm returned to this isolated spot on the Hudson.

Constitution gained fame in the nineteenth century as the home of the Warner sisters, Susan (1819–85) and Anna (1824–1915). Under pseudonyms the two sisters wrote a total of 106 books, collaborating on 18 of them. Susan Warner is most famous for her novel *Wide, Wide World,* which was on the Civil War era's best-seller list (second in popularity only to *Uncle Tom's Cabin*). Anna Warner wrote the words to the famous hymn "Jesus Loves Me." Part of the present-day tour of the island is a visit to the **Warner House,** fifteen rooms of which are furnished in the Victorian style of the Warner sisters' heyday. Costumed guides escort visitors on a tour of the house, while the rest of the tour consists of a walk to and around the ruined fort.

Constitution Island is open to guided tours from mid-June through the end of September. Boats leave West Point South Dock at 1:00 and 2:00 P.M. Wednesday and Thursday afternoons. Fare and admission to the house and fort are $7 for adults, $6 for senior citizens and students, and $2 for children under 5. For information contact the Constitution Island

Association, Box 41, West Point 10996; (914) 446–8676. Reservations are recommended.

In the 1830s John Jaques emigrated from Europe to the small town of Washingtonville. Trained as a shoe- and bootmaker, he planned to support himself with his trade. To augment his income he purchased 10 acres of land on Main Street and planted grapes in the rich, loamy Hudson Valley soil to sell at market. When he became a church elder, he used some of his grapes to make sacramental wine.

Today ◆**Brotherhood** is America's oldest winery, and the church where Mr. Jaques's wine was first served is the winery's gift shop. Brotherhood has been making wine continuously since 1839, having survived Prohibition by once again reverting back to the sale of sacramental wine. Its vast underground cellars, comparable to those of famous European wineries, are the largest in the country, and, in addition to sacramental wine, Brotherhood now makes specialty, table, dessert, and premium vintage wines—including Grand Monarque champagne.

A tour of the winery includes a visit to the underground cellars and a sampling of a half-dozen wines.

Brotherhood, 35 North Street, Washingtonville 10992, (914) 496–9101, offers guided wine-tasting tours daily, from May through October, and on weekend afternoons, from November through April. Admission is $4 for adults, $2 for children ages 15 to 20, and free for children under 15. Call for a calendar of weekend events.

Orange County is known for its fine standardbred horses, and it is quite fittingly the home of the ◆**Hall of Fame of the Trotter and Trotting Horse Museum.** Standardbreds are the horses of the harness track, and Orange County is the home not only of some of the greatest standardbreds (including the legendary Hambletonian, sire of virtually all of today's trotters) but also of the 153-year-old Historic Race Track, the only sporting site in the United States to have gained the status of a registered National Historic Landmark.

Adjacent to the Historic Race Track is what appears to be a lovely Tudor mansion, a half-timbered structure actually built as the Good Time Stable. In 1951 the stable became the home of the Trotting Horse Museum, in which the history of American harness racing is told through a series of exhibits housed in the former box stalls. In addition to antique sulkies and tack, the

Hall of Fame of the Trotter

displays include numerous fine examples of equestrian art, among them the famous Currier and Ives print of Hambletonian himself (1849–76).

The Hall of Fame of the Trotter honors the greats of harness racing—trainers, breeders, owners, and drivers. They're immortalized not by flat bronze plaques but by colorful, lifelike statuettes showing them in the garb of their professions.

The Hall of Fame of the Trotters and Trotting Horse Museum, 240 Main Street, Goshen 10924, (914) 294–6330, is open Monday through Saturday, 10:00 A.M. to 5:00 P.M.; Sundays, noon to 5:00 P.M.; and holidays, noon to 5:00 P.M. Closed Christmas, Thanksgiving, and New Year's Day. Admission is $1.50 for adults and 50 cents for children.

If you've worked up a thirst from your stroll out to the bandstand, head over to the Tin Pan Alley Room at the **Bodles Opera House** in nearby Chester. It's a Gay Nineties saloon, complete with gaslights, oak panels, and brass trimmings—a wonderful place to wash down track dust. The one hundred-year-old opera house is itself well worth a visit, and you may be tempted to stay for some southern fried chicken or Cajun blackened catfish—all served up by singing waiters and waitresses—and listen to old chestnuts such as "Shine on Harvest Moon" played by the Bodles Gang house band. The opera house also has a rotating schedule of performances, which include vaudeville, Broadway, country-and-western, and "Old Time Religion" shows.

Bodles Opera House, 39 Main Street, Chester 10918, (914) 469–4595, is open to the public Friday and Saturday evenings, 6:30 P.M. to 1:00 A.M. (Reservations are highly recommended.) The opera house is open to tour bus and senior citizens' groups by appointment the rest of the week.

The next time you eat an onion, consider this: It might well have been grown in black dirt formed 12,000 years ago in a glacial lake in an area now known as **Pine Island.** As the glaciers melted and the climate warmed, vegetation grew, died, and sank to the bottom of the lake. The lake area earned the nickname "the drowned lands" and remained a swamp until the early 1900s, when immigrants came, bought the land cheap, drained the lake by hand, built drainage ditches, and then planted onions in the rich black dirt. Today, with thousands of acres planted, the "black dirt" region is one of the country's leading producers of onions.

The cream of onion soup at **Ye Jolly Onion Inn** is made from Pine Island onions. So are the deep-fried onion blossoms, the onion rings, and the onion gravy on the Pine Island steak. And the vegetables on the salad bar are all from farms in the area (in season). After a visit to the "black dirt" region and Ye Jolly Onion Inn, you'll never again think lightly of the humble onion.

Ye Jolly Onion Inn, corner of Route 517, Pulaski Highway and Orange County Route 1, Pine Island 10969, (914) 258–4277, is open Wednesday and Thursday, 5:00 to 9:00 P.M.; Friday and Saturday, 5:00 to 10:00 P.M.; and Sunday, noon to 7:30 P.M.

If your interest in horses has been piqued by the Hall of Fame of the Trotter, head over to **New Hope Farms** in Port Jervis. With 80 acres it's one of the largest equestrian facilities in the nation and features indoor and outdoor arenas and permanent stabling for one hundred horses. Visitors are invited to stop by at any time to watch thoroughbreds and warmbloods being trained for show jumping competitions.

The first weekend in May, New Hope Farms hosts the Royal Dressage Festival (there's a gate charge), and the week after Labor Day, the Autumn Classic (free except for a charge for the Grand Prix Saturday night). And throughout the year there are events such as a tri-state rodeo, a family festival, and a championship dressage. The indoor arena, which seats 3,000, is the largest in the country.

New Hope Farms, 500 Neversink Drive, Port Jervis 12771, (914) 856–8384 or 856–4007, is open daily, year-round, from 8:00 A.M. to 5:00 P.M. From the end of January through March 15, most of the horses are moved south and there's very little activity. Admission is free.

Getting from one place to another quickly and with panache is an American preoccupation. In the nineteenth century a fast trotting horse might have done the trick; in the twentieth we have the option of zipping along on or off the ground. If you like the idea of slipping silently through the air and didn't get your chance at the National Soaring Museum in Elmira (see The Finger Lakes chapter), you'll find another opportunity in the southern Catskills at ◆ **Wurtsboro Airport.**

Established in 1927, Wurtsboro bills itself as the oldest soaring site in the nation. The airport's Flight Service is the largest soaring school in the United States, offering lessons for people with no flight experience as well as for those licensed to fly power planes. For the casual visitor, however, the big attraction is the demonstration rides. After being towed aloft by a single-engine Cessna, you'll glide high above the Catskills with an FAA-rated commercial pilot at the stick. The demonstration ride lasts fifteen to twenty minutes and costs $32. For $5 more you can turn your joyride into an introductory lesson.

Wurtsboro Airport and Flight Service, Route 209, Wurtsboro 12790, (914) 888–2791, is open daily, all year, 9:00 A.M. to dusk, weather permitting.

Many devotees of fly fishing believe that in North America, the sport began in the Catskills. And seeing the streams that run along the Beaverkill and Willowemoc valleys, it's hard to imagine a more suitable birthplace—or a more suitable location for a center devoted to preserving the heritage and protecting the future of fly fishing in the United States. That's the mission of the ✦ **Catskill Fly Fishing Center and Museum,** on the shores of the Willowemoc River between Roscoe and Livingston Manor.

From its inception in 1981, the founders of the center wanted their creation to be more than a museum of angling artifacts. They also had a strong commitment to environmental education. The center has grown from a small regional group to a nationwide organization of more than 3,000 members.

Hundreds of meticulously crafted flies, rods, reels, and other priceless artifacts from past and present masters of the art of fly fishing are on exhibit in the museum. Fly tying demonstrations are held throughout the season on Saturdays. And the center continues to teach the importance of a clean environment.

Catskill Fly Fishing Center and Museum, between Roscoe and Livingston Manor (mailing address: RD 1, Box 130C, Livingston, Manor 12758), (914) 439–4810, is open from April through September, 10:00 A.M. to 4:00 P.M. daily. Winter hours are Monday through Friday, 9:00 am. to 1:00 P.M., except holidays.

AROUND NEW PALTZ

The Tuthilltown gristmill at **Tuthilltown Gristmill & Country Store** has been grinding flour and meal without interruption since 1788: grinding while Napoleon fought in Austria . . . grinding through France's Reign of Terror . . . grinding through the War of 1812 . . . grinding while ether was invented . . . grinding when Abraham Lincoln was shot . . . grinding while the *Titanic* sank . . . grinding when Pearl Harbor was bombed . . . grinding when John F. Kennedy was shot . . . grinding when Richard Nixon resigned . . . and so on. And as one listens to the stones as they continue to grind flour and grain today, it's pleasant to contemplate that they'll still be grinding away 205 years from now.

The country store at the rear of the building sells a wide variety of flours and grains, as well as pancake and waffle mixes, natural dried fruits, nuts, spices, and other items for baking, along with antiques and gifts.

Tuthilltown Gristmill and Country Store, 1020 Albany Post Road, Gardiner 12525, (914) 255–5695, is open Wednesday through Friday, 9:30 A.M. to 5:30 P.M.; Saturday, 9:30 A.M. to

Abraham Hasbrouck House, Huguenot Street

6:00 P.M.; and Sunday, 11:00 A.M. to 4:00 P.M. An admission fee is charged to enter the mill.

Back in the old Hudson Valley town of New Paltz, we encounter one of those odd superlatives—something you might never have devoted a moment's curiosity to but is nonetheless fascinating once discovered. This is ◆ **Huguenot Street,** the oldest street in America that still has its original houses. Think about it: Find a street where each building lot has had only one house upon it, and chances are you're in a 1950s subdivision. But the stone houses on Huguenot Street were built between 1692 and 1712, and they'll look good for at least another 300 years.

Persecuted by the Catholic majority in their native France and displaced by the incessant religious warfare of the seventeenth century, many Huguenots—peaceful members of a Protestant sect—came to southern New York in pursuit of freedom and tolerance. In 1677 twelve of their number purchased the lands around present-day New Paltz from the Esopus Indians and built log huts as their first habitations. The name of their village is taken from *die Pfalz,* a section of Germany's Rhine-Palatinate region where they had formerly taken refuge.

As the twelve pioneers and their families prospered, they decided to build more permanent dwellings. And permanent they were. Here are five perfectly preserved houses, with additions that were built on by the settlers' descendants over the years. Only one, the 1692 Deyo House, was substantially remodeled, but even its 1890 wood-frame Queen Anne–style upper stories rest upon the solid stone foundations laid by its builder. The 1705 DuBois Fort is a handsome stone structure with a broad veranda and a covered balcony. All of the houses are maintained by the Huguenot Historical Society, which gives tours Wednesday through Sunday from Memorial Day weekend through September. Tours are available at varying rates and durations. For information contact the Huguenot Society, P.O. Box 339, New Paltz 12561; (914) 255–1660 or 255–1889.

Just north of New Paltz, at High Falls, is a museum dedicated to a great work of engineering brought about because of an energy crisis. No, this one had nothing to do with OPEC or Iranian crude—it was the crisis in coal supply brought about by America's 1812–14 war with Great Britain. When the two countries were at peace, the United States imported soft coal from England. But when hostilities broke out, the supply was cut off, and entrepreneurs on this side of the Atlantic scrambled to find a substitute. Two of them were the Wurts brothers, Maurice and William, who figured that a canal was the way to bring Pennsylvania anthracite (hard coal) from the mines to New York City and vicinity, thus avoiding future shortages brought about by depending on foreign suppliers.

The two men formed the Delaware and Hudson Canal Company in 1825, with the stated purpose of linking Honesdale, Pennsylvania, with the Hudson River port of Eddyville, New York. The surveying and engineering of the 100-mile-plus route was handled by Benjamin Wright, chief engineer of the Erie Canal. The Delaware and Hudson Canal, completed in 1828, was the first million-dollar enterprise in America. Between 1847 and 1852 it was enlarged and deepened to accommodate heavier traffic. A lot of coal came down in barges along the old route, but the company that built it made a bold move in 1829 that would soon doom canals and the way of life they represented. In that year the company began to work its gravity-operated rail line between Honesdale and Carbondale, Pennsylvania, with a new English contraption called a steam locomotive. Except for a few weedy stretches, the canal is gone—but the Delaware and Hudson Railroad survives to this day.

The ❖ **Delaware and Hudson Canal Museum** is a private institution established to tell the story of the old canal, and it does so not merely through glassed-in exhibits but by preserving the extant structures, channel, and locks in the High Falls vicinity. Visitors learn about the canal through sophisticated dioramas, photos, and technological exhibits, including models of a working lock and gravity railroad. There are five locks at High Falls. The Delaware and Hudson Canal Historical Society has done whatever restoration and preservation work is possible on them and has linked canal sites in the area with a system of hiking trails. Self-guided tours take in nearby canal segments as well as the remains of John Roebling's suspension aqueduct.

The Delaware and Hudson Canal Museum, Mohonk Road, High Falls 12440, (914) 687–9311, is open Memorial Day weekend through Labor Day, Thursday through Monday, 11:00 A.M. to 5:00 P.M. Also open weekends in May, September, and October, Saturday, 11:00 A.M. to 5:00 P.M., and Sunday, 1:00 to 5:00 P.M. A small donation is requested.

The prodigious industrial expansion made possible by canals and railroads in the America of the nineteenth century was often accomplished at the expense of the natural environment, a phenomenon that persists in our own day. Fortunately, the 1800s also produced great pioneers of the conservationist spirit, whose writings and example point the way for those who continue their struggle today. Among them, of course, are the Californian John Muir and his equally dedicated, near-contemporary John Burroughs, a native New Yorker who wrote twenty-five books on natural history and the philosophy of conservation. In 1895 Burroughs built a rustic log hideaway in the woods outside the village of West Park, barely 2 miles from the west bank of the Hudson. He called it ❖ **Slabsides,** and it is a National Historic Landmark today.

Burroughs, whose permanent home was only a mile and a half away, came to his little retreat to write and to quietly observe his

Sky Top Observation Tower
Mohonk Mountain House

natural surroundings. John Muir came here to talk with Burroughs, as did Theodore Roosevelt and Thomas Edison. They sat around the fire on log furniture of Burroughs's own manufacture, much of it still in the cabin.

Slabsides, which was deeded to the John Burroughs Association after the author's death in 1921, now stands within the 191-acre **John Burroughs Sanctuary,** a pleasant woodland tract that forms a most fitting living monument to his memory. The sanctuary is open all year; on the third Saturday in May and the first Saturday in October, the John Burroughs Association holds an open house from 11:00 A.M. to 4:00 P.M. In addition to an opportunity to see the cabin, the special days include informal talks and nature walks. Admission is free. For further information write the association at 15 West Seventy-seventh Street, New York City 10024, or call (914) 384–6320 or (212) 769–5169.

Nestled in the heart of a 4,000-acre natural area in the Shawwangunk Mountains, overlooking Lake Mohonk, is a sprawling Victorian castle-resort called the ◆Mohonk Mountain House. And above the Mohonk Mountain House stands Sky Top Tower, an observation tower built in 1923 of Shawangunk conglomerate that was quarried at its base. From the top of Sky Top Tower, on a clear day, you can see forever—or at least as far as the Rondout and Wallkill valleys, New Jersey, Connecticut, Vermont, Pennsylvania, and Massachusetts. The tower is also known as the Albert K. Smiley Memorial Tower in tribute to the founder of the Mohonk Mountain House, and even if you're not an overnight guest you can pay a day-visitor fee that will give you access to the tower; the many miles of hiking trails, paths, and carriage roads; and the lovely landscaped grounds.

Day visitors are also invited to visit the Barn Museum, in one of the largest barns in the Northeast. Built in 1888, it houses more than fifty nineteenth-century horse-drawn vehicles and many working tools made more than one hundred years ago. The Barn Museum, (914) 255–1000, ext. 2447, is open Wednesday, Saturday, and Sunday. In winter, day visitors can cross-country ski on more than 35 miles of marked, maintained cross-country ski trails. A shuttle ($2 per person round-trip) runs to and from Picnic Lodge—the day-visitor center—and the parking lot.

The Mohonk Mountain House, Lake Mohonk, New Paltz 12561; (914) 255–1000. Day-visitor pass cost is $5 for adults midweek and $8 weekends and holidays; $3 for children under 12 midweek and $4 weekends and holidays; and, for families with children under 12, $13 midweek and $20 weekends and holidays.

WEST BANK OF THE HUDSON

The state's highest waterfall, 3 miles west of Tannersville, is no broad Niagara but more a miniature version of Angel Falls in Venezuela. Kaaterskill Falls leaps from a rock ledge as a narrow curtain of white water, plunging past a natural grotto to a second scooped-out shelf at which it gathers force to finish its plunge toward the floor of Kaaterskill Clove.

Now little celebrated outside of hikers' guidebooks, the falls was once the Catskills' most celebrated natural wonder. Thomas Cole, founder of the Hudson River School of art, immortalized the falls in his painting *View of Kaaterskill Falls* in the early 1800s.

The path to the base of the falls is not particularly difficult, although in the spring, when its snow cover has melted and refrozen into glare ice, it requires a gingerly step. But it is a short trail, and it follows the ravine gouged by Kaaterskill Creek for less than a mile before reaching the base. For the less adventurous or those who prefer viewing waterfalls from the top, there is a path to the head of the falls from the North/South Lake State Campground on Route 18, roughly 2 miles east of Haines Falls. For information contact New York State Parks, Recreation, and Historic Preservation, Empire State Plaza, Agency Building 1, Albany 12238, (518) 474–0456.

Now we're going to the Broncks. No, it's not the wrong chapter—or the wrong spelling. Bronck was the family name of one of the original clans of Swedish settlers in New Amsterdam and the Hudson Valley. The farmstead of Pieter Bronck, who settled on the west bank of the Hudson near what is now Coxsackie, today makes up the ◆ **Bronck Museum.**

It is one thing to have a surviving seventeenth-century house, but it is the great good fortune of the Greene County Historical Society, owner of the Bronck Museum, to be in possession of an entire farm dating from those early years of settlement. The reason the Bronck property has come down virtually intact is that eight generations of the family lived there, working the farm, until Leonard Bronck Lampman willed the acreage and buildings to the historical society. Thus, we get to appreciate not only the oldest of the farm buildings but also all of the barns, utility buildings, and furnishings acquired over two centuries of prosperity and familial expansion. What it all amounts to is an object lesson in the changes in style, taste, and sophistication that took place between the seventeenth and nineteenth centuries.

The original stone house on the property was built by Pieter Bronck himself in 1663. It is believed that his widow was responsible for adding the stone west wing in 1685. The adjacent brick house, which reflects a more refined style, was built by a newer, more affluent generation of Broncks in 1738. In 1792 modifications to the original stone dwelling had to be made following a devastating storm, thus leaving us with examples of the early Federal mode. The little detached kitchen, opposite the main house in the rear courtyard, is also Federal in spirit. Of the barns on the property, the most unusual is a thirteen-sided structure typical of a fad for multisided barns and homes in the mid-1800s.

The Bronck Museum, Pieter Bronck Road, off Route 9W (mailing address: Greene County Historical Society, RD, Coxsackie 12051), (518) 731–8862 or 731–6490, is open from the last Sunday in June to the Sunday before Labor Day, Tuesday through Saturday, 10:00 A.M. to 5:00 P.M., and Sunday, 2:00 to 6:00 P.M. Admission, including scheduled guided tours, is $4 for adults, $3.50 for senior citizens, $2 for children 12 to 15, and $1 for children 5 to 11. Group tours, by prior arrangement, are available from mid-May through mid-October.

Imagine a field stretching as far as your eye can see and filled with flowers of every color and description, and you'll have some idea of the beauty and scope of **Blossom Farm.** Sixty varieties of country and wild flowers cover more than 30 acres of rolling fields overlooking the Catskill Mountains. There are a dried flower barn, country store, hayrides, farm tours, and, for kids, a petting zoo.

The opening date in the spring for Blossom Farm is dependent on the weather but comes sometime in mid-June. And the closing date too depends on the first frost, but the farm stays open through September—and into October, weather permitting.

Blossom Farm, Johnny Cake Lane, Greenville 12083, (518) 966–5722, is open daily from 10:00 A.M. to 5:00 P.M. during wildflower season. An admission fee of $2 is charged for adults when flowers are at their peak.

UPPER CATSKILLS

If you're heading west from the Hudson Valley into the upper Catskills, a stop at the ◆**Durham Center Museum** in East Durham provides an instructive look at the things a small community finds important—in many ways this museum is archetypical of the "village attics" that dot the land, and travelers could do worse than to take an occasional poke into one of these institutions. At the museum, which is housed in a circa 1825 one-room schoolhouse and several newer adjacent buildings, the collections run to Indian artifacts, portions of local petrified trees, old farm tools, and mementos of the 1800 Susquehanna Turn-pike and the 1832–40 Canajoharie-Catskill Railroad, both of which passed this way. There is also a collection of Rogers Groups, those plaster statuette tableaux that decorated Victorian parlors and played on bourgeois heartstrings before Norman Rockwell was born. Finally, don't miss the collection of bottled sand specimens from around the world, sent by friends of the museum. If you're planning a trip to some far-off spot not repre-sented on these shelves, don't hesitate to send some sand.

The Durham Center Museum, Route 145, East Durham 12423, (518) 239–4313 or 239–8461, is open June through August, Wednesday, Thursday, Saturday, and Sunday, from 1:00 to 4:00 P.M. Admission is $2 for adults and 50 cents for children under 12. Groups are welcome by appointment April through October. Genealogical researchers are welcome year-round by appointment.

While spending a summer day in East Durham, drop in at another local institution with a far more specialized collection: **Richter's Butterfly Museum,** a small monument to one man's lifelong interest in lepidoptera. Max Richter was born in Germany, where even as a young boy he was fascinated with butterflies. When he moved to East Durham in 1932, he named his new country property Butterfly Farm. Here he raised butter-flies, mounted them, and even made the mounted specimens into plaques. He opened his museum in 1953 and took great pride in showing his vast collection of butterflies to visitors over the next three decades. Mr. Richter passed away in 1984 at the age of one hundred, but his museum remains open under the curatorship of his daughter, Helen Richter Kruppenbacher. She presides over an expanded institution that even houses collec-tions of beetles and seashells, along with a gift shop selling objets d'art made from real butterflies.

The Butterfly Museum, Wright Street, East Durham 12423, (518) 634–7759, is open during June, July, and August on Wednesday, Thursday, Saturday, and Sunday from 2:00 to 5:00 P.M.

In 1824 a young man named Zadock Pratt came to a settle-ment called Schoharie Kill to establish a tannery. He bought some land, surveyed it, and set up his factory. Over the next twenty years, more than 30,000 employees, using hides imported from South America, tanned a million sides of sole leather, which was shipped down the Hudson River to New York City. And in the meantime Mr. Pratt established Prattsville, one of the earliest planned communities in New York State.

Mr. Pratt went on to become a member of the U.S. Congress in 1836 and 1842. One of the bills he sponsored created the Smithsonian Institution, but one of the most enduring legacies he left behind was **Pratt Rock Park,** which he donated to the town in 1843. Carved into the park's cliffs are symbols of Mr. Pratt's life, including a huge bust of his son who was killed in the Civil War, a horse, a hemlock tree, an uplifted hand, his tannery, a wreath with the names of his children, and an unfinished tomb where Pratt was to be buried overlooking the village (he was buried in a conventional grave at the other end of town). There's also a gravesite with a stone bearing the names of his favorite dogs and horses.

While you're in Prattsville, take time to visit the **Pratt Museum** (518–299–3395), located in Zadock Pratt's restored homestead in the center of town. The museum is just a 0.5-mile from the rocks; it's open May through October, Wednesday through Sunday, 1:00 to 5:00 P.M. There is an admission fee.

Roxbury, New York, is where we again come into contact with the naturalist John Burroughs. He may have spent much of the last decades of his life at Slabsides, down on the Hudson, but it was here in Roxbury that he was born in 1837 and here where he spent the last ten summers of his life at Woodchuck Lodge. He was buried here, in a field adjacent to the lodge, on April 2, 1921. The gravesite and the nearby "Boyhood Rock" that he had cherished as a lad are now part of ◆**Burroughs Memorial State Historic Site.**

The Burroughs Memorial is unique among historic sites, in that its chief feature (apart from the grave and the rock) is simply a field, surrounded by forests and the rolling Catskill hills. This is as fine a memorial as one could possibly imagine for a man who once said about the Catskills, "Those hills comfort me as no other place in the world does—it is home there."

Burroughs Memorial State Historic Site, off Route 30 (take Hardscrabble Road to Burroughs Road), Roxbury 12474, (315) 492–1756, is open during daylight hours from April to November 1. Admission is free. Woodchuck Lodge is frequently open to visitors on weekends during the summer.

Many of John Burroughs's modern-day spiritual descendants use the term *appropriate technology* to refer to renewable, nonpolluting sources of energy. Over in the northwestern Catskills town of East Meredith, the ◆**Hanford Mills Museum** celebrates one of the oldest of these so-called alternative-energy sources, the power of running water harnessed to a wheel. Kortright Creek at East Meredith has been the site of waterpowered mills since the beginning of the nineteenth century, and the main building on the museum site today was built in 1846. In those days of clearing forests for farmland, lumbermilling was a big local industry, and a good many of the older wooden structures in the East Meredith area were built with stock milled here.

The old mill became the Hanford Mills in 1860, when David Josiah Hanford bought the operation. During the eighty-five years in which it owned the mill, the Hanford family expanded its output to include feedmilling and the manufacture of utilitarian woodenware for farms and small industries. The mill complex grew to incorporate more than ten buildings on 10 acres, all clustered around the millpond. Sold in 1945 to Joseph, Michael, and Frank Pizza, all longtime workers for the Hanfords, the mill continued in operation until 1967.

Contrary to what appropriate-technology buffs might prefer, waterpower was not always the exclusive source of energy at the Hanford Mills. Steam, internal combustion, and electric motors all had their day here—but in 1898, when the lights went on in East Meredith for the first time, the electricity came from a hydro plant installed at Hanford Mills.

Not long after its final closing in the 1960s, Hanford Mills reopened as a museum. What could be a more perfect setup? Much of the original nineteenth-century equipment was still in place and in good working order. Today's visitors can watch lumber being cut on a big circular saw and shaped with smaller tools, all powered by the waters of Kortright Creek. At the heart of the operation is a 10-by-12-foot waterwheel, doing what waterwheels have done for more than 2,000 years.

The Hanford Mills Museum, intersection of County Routes 10 and 12, East Meredith 13757, (607) 278–5744, is open May 1 to October 31, daily, 10:00 A.M. to 5:00 P.M. Admission is $4 for adults and $2 for children. Senior citizens receive a discount. Group rates are available. Winter ice-harvesting programs are presented during January and February. Call for information.

NEW YORK CITY AND LONG ISLAND

21

19

Long Island

17
18

7, 8

20

1–6

10

14 16

15

New York
City

9

11–13

10. Bowne House
11. Jacques Marchais Museum of
    Tibetan Art
12. Historic Richmondtown
13. Staten Island Institute of
    Arts and Sciences
14. African American
    Museum
15. Nautical Mile
16. Old Bethpage Village
    Restoration
17. Sands Point Preserve
18. Planting Fields
    Arboretum
19. Stony Brook
20. Bayard Cutting
    Arboretum
21. Shelter Island

1. National Museum of the
   American Indian
2. Lower East Side Tenement
   Museum
3. Museum of American Folk Art
4. *Intrepid* Sea-Air-Space Museum
5. Theodore Roosevelt Birthplace National Historic Site
6. Dyckman House
7. Poe Cottage
8. Wave Hill
9. Brooklyn Children's Museum

NEW YORK CITY AND LONG ISLAND

New York City needs no introduction—certainly not a cursory one of the length we're permitted here—except to note that this is where the most beaten of the state's paths converge. With one top-echelon attraction after another packed into the city, where do we find the lesser-known places of interest?

The answer is everywhere. One of the first things the traveler should realize about this city is that it is far more than a backdrop for the Statue of Liberty, the Metropolitan Museum of Art, Yankee Stadium, and their like. And natives often have to be reminded that New York isn't just a vast and cacophonous machine that reinvents itself daily. It is, in fact, a place with nearly 400 years of history, where Dutch farmers and quirky poets and future presidents have lived, and where people are concerned with Indian artifacts and Tibetan art and the minutiae of local history as well as with capital-C Culture.

As for Long Island, the main thing for people who don't live here to remember is that it's worth going to even if it isn't on the way to anything else. Starting near the city and heading east, we'll visit an assortment of historical sites and museums, along with places that remind us of the natural beauty and maritime flavor of Long Island before fast carpentry and fast food transformed so much of it into a vast suburb.

NEW YORK CITY

Of all the first-rank museums in the city of New York—institutions that can lay justified claim to being the most comprehensive of their kind—perhaps the least well known is the ◆ **National Museum of the American Indian.** Nowhere else can we learn so much about the indigenous peoples who first called home the West Indies, North, Central, and South America.

George Heye was an heir to an oil fortune who early in his life worked as a railroad construction engineer in the Southwest. In 1897 he bought the first of his Indian artifacts, a contemporary Navajo buckskin shirt, and from that point went on to develop a collecting mania that encompassed all things native from Alaska to Tierra del Fuego. He bought items that had just been made (including, it is said, the clothes off Indians' backs), and he

Beaded Buckskin Dress
National Museum of the American Indian

bought archaeological finds dating from long before the European discovery of America. Heye founded his museum in 1916, and it opened to the public six years later. At that stage the collector owned some four hundred thousand objects; today the museum has more than a million individual items.

Exhibits at the museum are arranged geographically, according to the regions inhabited by the major indigenous peoples of North America, the West Indies, Central America, and South America. Also, there are numerous items associated with individuals—Sitting Bull's war club, Crazy Horse's feather headdress, Geronimo's cane, among others. Much of the collection must be kept in storage, but the astounding variety of material that is on display should surely convince visitors that this is *the* museum of the peoples of the New World.

The National Museum of the American Indian, Smithsonian Institution, 3753 Broadway at 155th Street, New York City 10032, (212) 283–2420, is open Tuesday through Saturday, 10:00 A.M. to 5:00 P.M., and Sunday, 1:00 to 5:00 P.M. Admission is $3 for adults and $2 for students and senior citizens; members and children under 7 are admitted free. The museum is scheduled to move to a new location at the Alexander Hamilton U.S. Customs House at 1 Bowling Green Street by November 1994. Its new name will be the George Gustav Heye Center of the National Museum of the American Indian, Smithsonian Institution. Here the museum will be open daily. Admission fees will not change.

New York City is the home of the world's largest Jewish community, a fact that necessitates an extensive infrastructure for providing kosher food and drink. Part of the picture is a winery called **Schapiro's,** located not in the Finger Lakes but right downtown on Rivington Street. Schapiro's makes rich, heavy, sweet kosher wine, the traditional Passover drink made from Concord grapes—a product that, the firm boasts, you can almost "cut with a knife." The Schapiro list also includes sweet domestic standbys made from cherries and blackberries, along with tokay, sauterne, and white Concord.

The real revelations among the Schapiro offerings, though, are the imported Italian and French kosher wines. Did you know you could buy a kosher Valpolicella? How about a Sauvignon blanc, bottled at the chateau in Bordeaux—also kosher? There are even a couple of kosher champagnes, straight from Epernay.

Schapiro's sells all of these wines and more, but the fun of a visit to the company lies not only in picking from the list but also in taking an actual urban winery tour and seeing how Schapiro's own wines are made.

Schapiro's, 126 Rivington Street, New York City 10002; (212) 674–4404. Tours are given every Sunday, 11:00 am. to 4:00 P.M. Admission is free.

In the mid-1800s Lucas Glockner, a German-born tailor, bought a lot at 97 Orchard Street on the Lower East Side that measured 25 by 100 feet. The lot was originally intended for single-family townhouses, but Mr. Glockner erected a six-story tenement with apartments for twenty-two families as well as two storefronts in the basement. Each floor featured four three-room apartments with a total of 325 square feet. Only one of the three rooms had windows.

Because it was the convention in the area for landlords to offer a free month's rent at the beginning of a year's lease, frequent moves were customary. Although 1,100 people have been documented as living at 97 Orchard Street between 1863 and 1935, a more realistic estimate is that 10,000 people from more than twenty-five nations lived at 97 Orchard Street during its seventy-two-year residential service.

Ninety-seven Orchard Street is the first tenement to be preserved in America, and it is the site of the ◆**Lower East Side Tenement Museum,** whose mission is to "promote tolerance through the presentation and interpretation of the variety of urban immigrant experiences on Manhattan's Lower East Side, a gateway to America." The museum's "Hope and Dreams" exhibit is at 66 Allen Street. Tours for 97 Orchard Street leave from 90 Orchard Street, where visitors learn of the tenement's history through videos and displays.

Throughout the year the museum offers programs, including dramatic performances, walking tours, exhibitions, and lectures. Call to receive its calendar of events.

The Lower East Side Tenement Museum, 97 Orchard Street (between Broome and Delancey), New York City 10002, (212) 431–0233, is open Tuesday through Friday, 11:00 A.M. to 5:00 P.M., and Sunday, 11:00 A.M. to 6:00 P.M. Admission is free on weekdays; on Sundays the charge is $3 for adults and $1 for children ages 17 and under.

Harlem . . . a place rich in history, tradition, food, music, and bad press . . . where the majority of people go about their daily lives in peace, but tourists are usually too apprehensive to visit. An enterprising company called **Harlem Spirituals** now gives tours of uptown Manhattan, and visitors can enjoy all of the sights with peace of mind. The "Harlem on Sunday" tour includes a visit to a church service, complete with gospel music, and a stop at the historic high spots. If you opt for Sunday brunch, you'll end the morning with soul food and gospel music at the famous Cotton Club. Harlem Spirituals also offers weekday tours—which include stops at the Apollo Theater, souvenir shops, and the Addicts Rehabilitation Center to listen to the ARC Gospel Choir—and evening "Soul Food and Jazz" tours.

Harlem Spirituals, 1697 Broadway, #203, New York City 10019, (212) 757–0425, offers tours in English, French, German, Italian, and Spanish, as well as other languages, based on availability.

There's no question that Americans are an industrious lot—New York City itself is a perfect example. But the fabulous collection of paintings, drawings, sculpture, textiles, furniture, functional and decorative arts, photographs, and contemporary environmental works on display at the ◆**Museum of American Folk Art** is testament to the fact that man cannot live by bread alone—the soul too needs nurturing.

The museum, founded by a group of collectors in 1961, is devoted to preserving the country's rich folk heritage. The collection, dating from the middle eighteenth century to the present day, reflects the museum's increasingly broad definition of the field of folk art. The museum presents special exhibitions and events throughout the year and publishes the *Clarion,* the only publication in the country covering the growing field of American folk art.

The Museum of American Folk Art, Two Lincoln Square, New York City 10023, (212) 595–9533 (administrative offices: 61 West Sixty-second Street, New York 10023; 212–977–7170), is open Tuesday through Sunday, 11:30 A.M. to 7:30 P.M. Closed Monday. Admission is free.

It's fitting that a museum dedicated to preserving and presenting twentieth-century sea, air, and space history and technology be housed on an aircraft carrier. And it's appropriate that the USS *Intrepid,* a 40,000-ton, 900-foot-long battle-scarred veteran of thirty-seven years of service, was rescued from the scrap heap to serve yet again as the ◆*Intrepid* **Sea-Air-Space Museum.**

Designated a National Historic Landmark in 1985, she is the only World War II national battlefield located in New York Harbor. The major exhibition halls are in the carrier's vast hull and on its hangar deck. Most of the aircraft collection is located on the flight deck. Since the museum opened in 1982, several new additions have tied up alongside: the missile submarine *Growler,* the 1936 Coast Guard lightship *Nantucket,* and the destroyer *Edson.* And on board is the newest acquisition—a Lockheed A-12 Blackbird reconnaissance jet, the world's fastest aircraft.

Also in the museum's collection are numerous other aircraft; an armor exhibit, which includes U.S. Army and captured Iraqi tanks and guns; and an undersea frontier—a child's delight, with everything from live fish to treasures recovered from shipwrecks. There are also more than seven hours of movies, videos, and multimedia presentations.

The *Intrepid* Sea-Air-Space Museum, West Forty-sixth Street and Twelfth Avenue in the Hudson River, New York City 10036, (212) 245–2533, is open daily Memorial Day through Labor Day from 10:00 A.M. to 5:00 P.M.; hours Labor Day through Memorial Day are Wednesday through Sunday from 10:00 A.M. to 5:00 P.M. (closed Monday and Tuesday). Admission is $7 for adults, $6 for senior citizens and veterans, $4 for children ages 6 to 12, and free for uniformed members of the armed forces with a valid I.D.

Back in Buffalo, a couple of chapters ago, we saw where the most momentous turn in Theodore Roosevelt's life took place— the house where he was inaugurated president of the United States. Here in the city you can see where his life began, at the ❖ **Theodore Roosevelt Birthplace National Historic Site.** The building that stands here today is a faithful replica of the brownstone rowhouse in which TR was born on October 27, 1858. It was built following the ex-president's death in 1919, replacing a nondescript commercial building that had gone up only three years before, when the original Roosevelt home was torn down.

Open to the public since 1923, and a National Historic Site since 1963, the reconstructed Roosevelt home is furnished in much the same style—and with many of the same articles— familiar to the sickly lad who lived here for the first fourteen years of his life. The president's widow and his surviving sisters helped with the reconstruction, recalling room layouts, furniture placement, and even interior color schemes. The result is a careful study not only of the environment that produced the scholar and improbable athlete who would become a rancher, police commissioner, Rough Rider, New York governor, and president but also of the lifestyle of New York's more comfortable burghers in the middle of the last century. Finally, the "new" Roosevelt house stands in stubborn contrast to the modern buildings that surround it, reminding us of just how completely the neighborhoods of New York have thrown off one persona after another.

The Theodore Roosevelt Birthplace National Historic Site, 28 East Twentieth Street, New York City 10003, (212) 260–1616, is open Wednesday through Sunday, 9:00 A.M. to 5:00 P.M. Guided

Qui Plantavit Curabit

**The Roosevelt Arms
Theodore Roosevelt Birthplace**

tours are given until 3:30 P.M. Closed on federal holidays. Admission is $2 for adults; seniors over 62 and children under 17 are admitted free. There is no charge for educational groups, but reservations must be made at least two weeks in advance.

Theodore Roosevelt was the descendant of Claus Van Rosenvelt, who came to New Amsterdam from Holland in the 1640s. At about the same time, another Dutch emigrant, Jan Dyckman, found his way to the fledgling colony by way of the German province of Westphalia. He settled in the then far-out-of-the-way village of New Haarlem, up at the northern tip of Manhattan Island, from which a trip down to Peter Stuyvesant's community near the Battery must have seemed a major expedition. Dyckman's descendants were important landholders here for generations. One of them, William Dyckman (1725–87), built a house on what is now Broadway and 204th Street just two years before his death. It still stands and, by dint of sheer endurance, now has the honor of being the last eighteenth-century farmhouse on Manhattan Island.

The ◆**Dyckman House,** donated to the city in 1915 by the daughters of the last Dyckman to live there, is a classic gambrel-roofed Dutch Colonial structure. With two full floors and an attic

142

above a basement, it was substantial in its day—but remember, it was the main house of a sizable farm. In the fashion of the era, the winter kitchen was located in the basement, where the cooking fires would help to heat the house; here today are surviving examples of eighteenth-century cooking utensils as well as "modern" pieces from the 1800s. (The summer kitchen was kept out of the main building and occupied the small south wing. This portion of the Dyckman House is a survivor from an earlier structure that was destroyed during the revolution.)

Furnishings in the Dyckman House include numerous family-associated items dating to the eighteenth century. Another attraction for visitors is the small collection of American Revolution artifacts excavated on the site and in the vicinity of the one-time farm, which was used as a camp by the British and Hessians who held New York throughout much of the war. A hut, representative of bivouac accommodations of the era, has been reconstructed behind the house.

The Dyckman House, 4881 Broadway, New York City 10034, (212) 304-9422, is open Tuesday through Saturday, 11:00 A.M. to 4:00 P.M. Closed holidays. The suggested donation is $1.

And now, on to the U.S. mainland—to the only borough of the city of New York not located on an island. This is the Bronx, a place that ought to be recognized as more than the home of Yankee Stadium and the place you cross on Route 95 to get from New England to the George Washington Bridge. To get a handle on the story of this one-time suburban retreat that became one of New York's most densely populated residential districts, visit the **Museum of Bronx History.** The museum is housed in a building of a style and period not often encountered in a city that has torn down and rebuilt itself with as much abandon as has New York—a fieldstone house built in 1758, looking as if it would be more at home on a farm in Bucks County, Pennsylvania, than in the borough of endless rowhouses and apartment buildings.

The fieldstone house, built by early Bronx settler Isaac Varian, contains both permanent and changing exhibits chronicling the roles played by the Bronx and the Bronx people over the past three centuries. There's a lot to learn: For instance, the Bronx figured importantly in the American Revolution, particularly in the Battle of Pell's Point near present-day Pelham Bay Park. On October 12, 1776, 750 Continental troops under Col. John

143

Glover so harassed Sir Harry Clinton's British landing force that George Washington was given precious time in which to complete his retreat to White Plains. No, the history of the Bronx did not begin with Babe Ruth, Lou Gehrig, and the coining of the term *Bronx Bombers.*

The Museum of Bronx History, 3266 Bainbridge Avenue at 208th Street, Bronx 10467, (718) 881–8900, is open Saturday from 10:00 A.M. to 4:00 P.M., Sunday from 1:00 to 5:00 P.M., and weekdays from 9:00 A.M. to 5:00 P.M. by appointment. Admission is $2.

One chapter in Bronx history is an important part of American literary history as well. In 1846 a thirty-seven-year-old poet, short story writer, and critic named Edgar Allan Poe rented a small wooden cottage now known as the ◆ **Poe Cottage,** in Poe Park, East Kingsbridge Road and the Grand Concourse, not far from the campus of Fordham University (in Poe's day it was known as St. John's College). Part of the reason for his move was the fragile health of his wife; Fordham, Poe felt, was a more salubrious environment than the couple's former home of New York City. But Virginia Clemm Poe—who was also the writer's cousin—died of tuberculosis at the Bronx cottage early in 1847, leaving Poe in the state of despondency that accounted for his poem "Annabel Lee" and other melancholic verse.

Poe maintained his residence in the Bronx after his wife's death, drinking heavily and trying to keep up with his bills by delivering an occasional lecture. It was while returning from one of his lecture trips that he died in Baltimore in 1849.

Sometimes the world takes better care of dead poets' residences than it does the poets while they are alive, and such was the case with Edgar Allan Poe. The rapidly growing Bronx quickly enveloped the Poe Cottage during the latter half of the nineteenth century, but in 1902 the city dedicated a park in his honor across the street from the house. The house was moved to the park eleven years later and has been open as a museum since 1917.

The Edgar Allan Poe Cottage, Grand Concourse and East Kingsbridge Road, Bronx 10458, (718) 881–8900, is open Saturday, 10:00 A.M. to 4:00 P.M., and Sunday, 1:00 to 5:00 P.M. throughout the year. Admission is $2 for adults and free for children under 12.

Not all of the Bronx was gobbled up by developers in the decades following Poe's brief stay. There are, of course, the green expanses of the New York Botanical and Zoological Gardens, Van

Cortlandt Park, and Pelham Bay Park. But a visit to the borough should also include a stop at ◆ **Wave Hill,** a 28-acre preserve in the Riverdale neighborhood at the northwest corner of the Bronx. Wave Hill is not wilderness but a section of the borough that remained in its natural state until the middle of the last century, when it was first acquired as a country estate. Today it is the only one of the great Hudson River estates preserved for public use within the city limits.

In 1836 New York lawyer William Morris bought 15 acres of riverbank real estate in the Wave Hill area and built Wave Hill House, one of the two mansions that today grace the property, as a summer retreat. Thirty years later the Morris tract was acquired by publisher William Appleton. Appleton remodeled the house and began developing the gardens and conservatories for which the property would become famous. The gardens were brought to their apogee, however, by financier George Perkins, who bought the estate in 1893 and increased its size to 80 acres, with a scattering of six fine houses, including not only Wave Hill but also **Glyndor,** which had been built by Oliver Harriman. (Burned in 1927, Glyndor was rebuilt by Perkins's widow. "Glyndor II," as it is known, is still a part of the Wave Hill property.) Perkins's gardener was the talented Albert Millard. Under his direction plantings on the estate were expanded to include eight additional greenhouses and exotic Oriental trees.

The attractions of Wave Hill for today's visitor include art exhibits, concert series, outdoor dance performances, and special events. But the essential reason for a trip to the old estate remains its lovely grounds, some manicured and some an approximation of the wild state of this stretch of Bronx shoreline. There are 350 varieties of trees and shrubs, plus the wild and cultivated flowers planted in three greenhouses, in formal and informal gardens, and along the pathways of the estate. A 10-acre section of woods has been restored as a native Bronx forest environment, complete with elderberries, witch hazel, and native grasses.

Wave Hill, 249th Street and Independence Avenue, Bronx (mailing address: 675 West 252nd Street, Bronx 10471), (718) 549–3200, is open daily, 9:00 A.M. to 4:30 P.M.; closed Christmas and New Year's Day. Admission is free weekdays; on Saturdays and Sundays it is $4 for adults, $2 for seniors and students, and free for children 6 and under. Tours are given each Sunday.

145

The kids have been great. They've listened to you quote stanzas from "The Raven" and heard about Teddy Roosevelt's charge up San Juan Hill. So now head over to the ❖ **Brooklyn Children's Museum.** Founded in 1899, it was the first museum in the world designed expressly for children. It will give you a chance to stop worrying about them touching everything—here the philosophy is "touch and learn."

The museum is now housed in a unique, 35,000-square-foot underground structure and features a turn-of-the-century kiosk entrance and a "stream" running the length of the "people tube," a huge drainage pipe that connects four levels of exhibit space. According to the museum's brochure, "exhibits combine 'hands-on' components and objects to aid in the exploration of natural science, culture and history"—which translates to "learn and have fun at the same time."

The Brooklyn Children's Museum, 145 Brooklyn Avenue, Brooklyn 11213, (718) 735–4400, is open Wednesday through Friday from 2:00 to 5:00 P.M. and Saturday, Sunday, and most school holidays from noon to 5:00 P.M.; closed Monday and Tuesday. There is a suggested contribution of $3 per visitor.

The borough of Queens is New York's most residential neighborhood—or rather, collection of neighborhoods, each retaining its own distinctive character. One such neighborhood is Flushing, best known to many non-native New Yorkers as the site of the 1939 and 1964 World's Fairs. The history of this district goes back well over 300 years, as a visit to the ❖ **Bowne House** will demonstrate.

John Bowne built the house that today bears his name in 1661. To get some idea of what the future outlying boroughs of New York were like in those days, consider that two years after the Bowne House was built, the town meeting of nearby Jamaica offered a bounty of seven bushels of corn for every wolf shot or otherwise done away with. But wolves weren't the only threat John Bowne faced. A Quaker, he openly challenged Governor Peter Stuyvesant's edict banning that religion by holding meetings of the Society of Friends in his kitchen. He was arrested and sent back to Europe in 1662 but came back to New York two years later, after having been exonerated by the Dutch West India Company, managers of the New Amsterdam colony.

Now the oldest house in Queens, the Bowne House reflects not only the Dutch/English Colonial style in which it was originally built but also all of the vernacular styles with which it was modified over the years. The original three-room structure was expanded to include a parlor in 1680; the living room was added in 1696 and later paneled in the Georgian style. Extra space upstairs and a first-floor rear room were created early in the nineteenth century by a raising of the roof.

Indoors the Bowne House displays styles of furnishing and portrait painting as they developed over the first two centuries of its existence. Everything here belonged to the Bownes, making this property a unique documentation of one family's experience in New York virtually from the time of its founding to the beginning of the modern era.

The Bowne House, 37-01 Bowne Street, Flushing 11354, (718) 359–0528, is open Tuesday, Saturday, and Sunday, 2:30 to 4:30 P.M.; closed major holidays and mid-December to mid-January. Admission is $2 for adults and $1 for children. Groups welcome by appointment.

A seventeenth-century Quaker going to a clandestine meeting at the Bowne House might seem to have little in common with a twentieth-century Tibetan Buddhist, but the two share a bond of persecution. One of the uglier aspects of the Maoist period in China was the annexation of Tibet and the suppression of its ancient culture and religion. Despite some recent liberalization on the part of the Chinese occupiers of Tibet, it is still an extremely difficult place to visit; and ironically, those Westerners interested in Tibetan art and religious artifacts have learned to rely on foreign rather than native Tibetan collections. One such collection is the ◆**Jacques Marchais Museum of Tibetan Art** on Staten Island. The museum houses more than a thousand examples of Tibetan religious art—paintings, carved and cast statues, altars, and even musical instruments—each of which was created to aid in the meditation that is such an important part of Buddhism, especially as practiced in Tibet.

And who was Jacques Marchais? "He" was a woman named Jacqueline Coblentz Klauber who operated a Manhattan art gallery under the masculine French pseudonym. Klauber/Marchais had a lifelong interest in things Tibetan, nurtured in childhood when she would play with Tibetan figures her great-grandfather had

Baldwin

Crowned Buddha
Jacques Marchais Museum of Tibetan Art

brought back from the Orient. She never traveled to Tibet, but she carefully added to her collection until her death in 1947.

With its terraced gardens, lily pond, and air of detachment and serenity, the Marchais Museum is indeed an appropriate setting for the religious objects that make up the collection, representing centuries of Tibetan culture.

The Jacques Marchais Museum of Tibetan Art, 338 Lighthouse Avenue, Staten Island 10306, (718) 987–3478 or 987–3500, is open 1:00 to 5:00 P.M. Wednesday through Sunday, from mid-April through mid-November; December through March, by appointment. Closed Memorial Day, July 4, Labor Day, Thanksgiving, and the Friday following Thanksgiving Day. Admission is $3 for adults, $2 for senior citizens, and $1 for children.

Within walking distance of the Marchais Museum is a collection of buildings representative of cultural continuity rather than upheaval and transplanting. ◈ **Historic Richmondtown** is a collection of twenty-seven buildings, fourteen of them restored and open to the public, that reminds us that Staten Island has a richer history than might be suggested by the tract houses and refineries that characterize the present-day borough of Richmond.

Richmondtown seems like a country village far from the bustle of Manhattan, and with good reason—that's what it was, in the seventeenth and eighteenth centuries when these houses and community buildings were built. Among them are the "Voorlezer's [Teacher's] House," a Dutch-era one-room school; an old county courthouse; a general store; and a farmhouse. Many of the buildings are staffed by craftspeople working with period equipment. White clapboard farmhouses dot the property's 100 acres, and a central museum houses exhibits of Staten Island–made products that reveal the history and diversity of New York's least populous borough. There are special events through the year, and nineteenth-century dinners are served during the summer.

Historic Richmondtown, 441 Clark Avenue, Staten Island 10306, (718) 351–1611, is open Wednesday through Sunday, 1:00 to 5:00 P.M. Closed weekends in January, February, and March. Hours are extended in July and August. Admission is $4 for adults and $2.50 for students, senior citizens, and children 6 to 18.

The oldest cultural institution on Staten Island is the ◈ **Staten Island Institute of Arts and Sciences,** founded in 1881 and headquartered in the small community of St. George just 2 blocks from the Staten Island Ferry Terminal. The institute's collection has been described as "eclectic"—and eclectic it is. Exhibits focus on the art, natural science, and cultural history of Staten Island and its people, drawing from the institute's collections of more than two million artifacts and specimens.

The art collection includes many fine works from ancient to contemporary periods, including works by Staten Island artists such as Jasper Cropsey, Guy Pene duBois, and Cecil Bell. Also included are pieces by internationally acclaimed talents such as Marc Chagall, Reginald Marsh, and Robert Henri, as well as decorative arts, furniture, clothing, and more. The natural history collections include 500,000 insects, 25,000 plant specimens, and geologic, shell, and archaeological specimens. The archives and library comprise the largest holdings of Staten Island history and science anywhere. Public programs for all ages include weekly "Lunch & Learn" buffets.

The Staten Island Institute of Arts and Sciences, 75 Stuyvesant Place, Staten Island 10301, (718) 727–1135, is open Monday through Saturday, 9:00 A.M. to 5:00 P.M., and Sunday, 1:00 to 5:00 P.M. Suggested admission is $2.50 for adults and $1.50 for students and senior citizens. Parking behind the institute is available. Special tours and programs, including gallery tours, guided ferry rides, St. George walking tours, and formal classroom programs, are available to groups.

The best bargain in New York City is a 50-cent, round-trip, 5-mile ride aboard the Staten Island Ferry and then a visit to the **Staten Island Ferry Collection of the Staten Island Institute of Arts and Sciences** at St. George Terminal, just a short distance from the institute.

The ride aboard the ferry offers a complete view of the harbor, including the Brooklyn Bridge, Manhattan skyline, Statue of Liberty, Ellis Island, Governors Island, Robin's Reef Lighthouse, and Verrazano-Narrows Bridge. The Staten Island Ferry Collection's exhibition explores the history of the ferry line and New York Harbor using striking displays of artifacts and photographs.

The Staten Island Ferry Collection of the Staten Island Institute of Arts and Sciences, St. George Terminal, Staten Island 10301, (718) 727–1135, is open Monday through Friday, 10:00 A.M. to 3:00 P.M.; Saturday, 10:00 A.M. to 4:00 P.M.; and Sunday, 11:00 A.M. to 4:00 P.M. Admission is $1 for adults and 25 cents for children 12 and under.

LONG ISLAND

East of New York City, beyond the borders of the boroughs of Brooklyn and Queens, Long Island stretches from the populous cities and towns of Nassau County to the beaches and New England–style villages of Suffolk County. Beginning in the Nassau County city of Hempstead, our first stop is the ◆**African American Museum.**

Founded in 1970 under the auspices of the Nassau County Department of Recreation and Parks in response to growing awareness of the contributions of blacks on Long Island, the Black History Exhibit Center recently changed its name to the African American Museum and altered its emphasis to include interpretive exhibits of traditional and contemporary native African culture as well as local American black history and lore.

The black experience in New York State is by no means concentrated in New York City; nor is it a phenomenon largely associated with twentieth-century migrations from the South. A hundred years ago and more, blacks were farming, whaling, and working at crafts and small businesses on Long Island. Their ancestry, in many cases, dated back to the seventeenth- and eighteenth-century days when slavery—though not as widespread as it would become in the South—was still practiced in New York and the New England states.

The African American Museum tells the story of Long Island's blacks through displays of photographs and artifacts, lectures, workshops, and performing arts. Local artistic talent is especially promoted. African-oriented exhibits and special programs have included shows devoted to West African crafts, art from Sierra Leone, African toys, and black artistic expression in South Africa.

The African American Museum, 110 North Franklin Street, Hempstead 11550, (516) 572–0730, is open Thursday through Saturday, 10:00 A.M. to 4:00 P.M., and Sunday, 1:00 to 4:00 P.M. Admission is free.

Another Hempstead attraction is not really in Hempstead but in the south-shore village of Lawrence, just across the New York City limits from Far Rockaway, Queens. This is **Rock Hall Museum,** a 1767 mansion built by Tory merchant Josiah Martin.

Rock Hall represents the high-water mark of late Georgian architecture in this part of the country, particularly in its interior detailing. The paneling and mantels, as well as much of the eighteenth- and early nineteenth-century furniture and the replica of a colonial kitchen (the original kitchen was in an outbuilding), came down virtually unchanged to our own time. Josiah Martin's family, having come through the revolution none the worse for being on the wrong side, lived here until 1823. The following year Thomas Hewlett bought Rock Hall; his family lived in the mansion for more than a century after his death in 1841. In 1948 the Hewletts gave the place to the town of Hempstead—presumably then a larger municipal entity—for use as a museum.

151

Rock Hall Museum, 199 Broadway, Lawrence 11559, (516) 239–1157, is open April 1 through November 30 on Monday and on Wednesday through Saturday, 10:00 A.M. to 4:00 P.M.; on Sunday hours are noon to 4:00 P.M. Closed Tuesday. Admission is free.

With 8.5 miles of waterfront, Freeport calls itself "The Boating and Fishing Capital of the East." Woodcleft Avenue, informally known as ◆Nautical Mile, is rumored to have once been a haven for bootleggers, pirates, and other scoundrels. Today it is a mecca for sightseers, browsers, and seafood lovers. Restaurants, pubs, fish markets, and gift shops line the avenue, and one of the Island's largest charter/sport fishing fleets sails out of the harbor daily in season.

Since 1977, Long Island bargain hunters have headed every Wednesday and Sunday for the **Roosevelt Raceway Flea Market** in Westbury. The flea market is held indoors during the winter. On warm summer days between one and two thousand vendors set up indoor and outdoor tables. Roosevelt Raceway Flea Market, Westbury, Long Island 11590, (516) 222–1530, charges an admission fee of $2 per carload; $1 for walk-ins.

On Long Island's south shore in Seaford is a museum and preserve dedicated to life on the island as it was lived even before the era of farm and village life. The **Tackapausha Museum and Preserve** is an 80-acre introduction to the ecology and natural history of the Northeast's coastal woodlands as they existed before human intervention. Well, at least before European intervention. Tackapausha is named after a sachem (chief) of Long Island's native Massapequa Indians, a group that by and large managed to live on this land without greatly affecting its wildlife, its plant communities, or the balance of natural forces.

The Tackapausha Museum is a small facility designed to serve as an introduction to the plants and animal life of the preserve itself. Exhibits explain the relationship between habitat groups, the differences between diurnal and nocturnal animals, and the changes in life patterns brought about by the different seasons. There is also a small collection of native animals, housed in as natural a setting as possible.

The preserve itself is a lovely piece of land, incorporating a variety of ecosystems. A self-guiding trail (pick up the interpretive map at the museum) takes visitors through the different environments.

Quilting in the Noon Inn
Old Bethpage Village Restoration

The Tackapausha Museum and Preserve, Washington Avenue, Seaford 11783, (516) 571–7443, is open Tuesday through Saturday, 10:00 A.M. to 4:00 P.M., and Sunday, 1:00 to 4:00 P.M. Admission is $1 for adults, 50 cents for children 5 or older, and free for children under 5.

At our next stop we find plentiful evidence of the relentless trend toward suburbanization that has characterized this place during the past forty years. But we also find an institution that has set as its goal the preservation of as much as possible of the old, rural Long Island way of life. ◆**Old Bethpage Village Restoration** is a re-creation of the world as it was long before there was a Levittown or Long Island Expressway. In fact—at least as far as its buildings are concerned—it is the architectural equivalent of a wildlife preserve. Starting in the middle 1960s, the

153

curators of the village (it's managed by the Nassau County Department of Recreation and Parks) began moving threatened colonial and early nineteenth-century structures here, where they could be set up in a close approximation of a Long Island village of the Civil War era. There are now nearly fifty buildings on the site, all of them having been chosen to represent typical domestic, commercial, and agricultural structures of the era.

All of those buildings without people and activity would make for a rather dry museum, so Old Bethpage Village has been staffed with working artisans and craftspeople. There's even an Old Bethpage Village militia, which will presumably come in handy if the place is ever attacked by a contingent from the Genesee Country Village or the Farmers' Museum at Cooperstown.

One engaging feature of life at Old Bethpage Village is the full calendar of seasonal events, all of them suggestive of the things people used to do at different times of the year back when there *were* different times of year, other than in terms of the weather.

Old Bethpage Village Restoration, Round Swamp Road, Old Bethpage 11804, (516) 572–8400 (recorded message) or 572–8401, is open Wednesday through Sunday from 10:00 A.M. to 4:00 P.M. Closed Mondays and Tuesdays. Admission is $5 for adults and $3 for children and senior citizens. Closed holidays except Memorial Day, July 4, Labor Day, and Columbus Day, when the restoration is closed the day after. Call for information on the holiday candlelight evenings.

The **Gold Coast,** up on the north shore of Long Island, was created during the Roaring Twenties by families such as the Vanderbilts, the Chryslers, the Phippses, the Woolworths, and the Guggenheims, who built great mansions there.

For information on which ones are open to the public for tours call the **Long Island Convention and Visitors Bureau,** (800) 441–4601.

◆**Sands Point Preserve** overlooking Long Island Sound has something for both mansion and nature lovers. A large portion of the 209-acre property was owned by railroad heir Howard Gould at the turn of the century. He built the Tudor-inspired **Hempstead House** and **Castlegould,** the enormous turreted stable and carriage house that now serve as a visitor center. In 1917 the Daniel Guggenheim family purchased the estate, and in 1923 Harry Guggenheim, Daniel's son, built the Norman mansion **Falaise** (the French word for cliff) on his share of the family property.

Today the property is owned by the Nassau County Department of Recreation and Parks, which preserves it not only as a focus of historical interest but also for the preservation and public enjoyment of its natural surroundings. There are six marked nature trails; two of them are self-guiding, and one follows the shoreline. In addition to numerous geological phenomena, such as glacial erratics (large granite boulders dropped from the ice during the last continental glaciation about 20,000 years ago), there is a wide range of plant and bird life within the preserve. Kids will enjoy following the special Dinosaur Trail, with its replicas of real fossilized dinosaur tracks. Pick up trail maps at the visitor center in Castlegould.

Sands Point Preserve, Middleneck Road, Port Washington 11050, (516) 888–1612, is open year-round, Tuesday through Sunday, from 10:00 A.M. until 5:00 P.M. Falaise is open for guided tours from May through October, call for times. There is a charge for admission to the preserve and a separate charge for the tour of Falaise.

Another Gold Coast mansion, ◆**Planting Fields Arboretum** is the legacy of William Robertson Coe, a British-born insurance magnate who purchased this property in 1913. Coe immediately set about making his 409-acre estate into as complete a farm-garden-arboretum as possible. He began building greenhouses in 1914 (Coe Hall, the great house on the property, did not go up until 1919–21) and imported his camellia collection in 1917. The camellias couldn't make it through a Long Island winter, so a special greenhouse was built for them. Coe set up a working dairy and kept pigs and chickens as well. (Milk and produce from Planting Fields were donated to the needy during the Great Depression.)

But it was trees and shrubs that most commanded Coe's attention, and they were the subject of some of his greatest extravagances. The copper beech on the north lawn, for instance, was moved here from Massachusetts by barge and a team of seventy-two horses when it was already 60 feet high. Working with master landscape gardeners such as A. Robeson Sargent, and James Dawson of Olmsted Brothers, Coe created grand allees of trees designed to frame the views from the house, and he established rambling azalea walks. As late as the 1950s, in the last years of his life, Coe planted the rhododendron park, which remains one of the outstanding features of Planting Fields.

155

There are concerts in the Haybarn (write for a schedule), and from April through September visitors can tour Coe Hall Monday through Friday and Sunday, 12:30 to 3:30 P.M. The fee is $2 for adults and $1 for seniors and children ages 12 and over.

Planting Fields Arboretum, Box 58 (off Mill River Road), Oyster Bay 11771, (516) 922–9200, is open daily, 9:00 A.M. to 5:00 P.M. There is a $3 entry charge per car; from Labor Day through mid-April, it is charged on Saturdays, Sundays, and holidays only.

Those who want a taste of what dining in a Gold Coast mansion was like should visit **Spencer's,** a restaurant in the mansion that Andrew W. Mellon purchased for his daughter. The town of Oyster Bay now owns the 120-acre estate, **Woodlands,** and leases the mansion to the restaurant.

The menu at Spencer's is inspired by Italian cuisine, and the prices are fairly moderate. Dinner specialties include *Paglio e Fieno* (hay and straw), white and green pasta in a cream sauce, tossed with peas, ham, and Parmesan cheese; mixed grill of filet mignon, tenderloin pork chop, and fresh sausage (at $20.95, the most expensive entrée on the menu); and Veal Milanese.

Sunday brunch at Spencer's is truly a Roaring Twenties affair. The $13.95 fixed price includes unlimited eye-openers such as Bloody Marys, mimosas, and champagne, as well as a large selection of entrées, including coquilles St. Jacques, croque madame, and eggs Benedict. Sitting on the patio overlooking the Sound and sipping a mimosa, you might almost expect to see the Great Gatsby sitting at the next table.

Spencer's, in the mansion at the Town of Oyster Bay Golf Course, South Woods Road, Woodbury 11797, (516) 364–3973, is open for lunch Tuesday through Friday, noon until 3:00 P.M.; for dinner, Tuesday through Thursday, 5:00 to 10:00 P.M., and Friday and Saturday, 5:00 to 11:00 P.M. Sunday brunch is served from noon to 3:00 P.M., and Sunday dinner from 3:30 to 8:30 P.M. Reservations are requested. No sneakers, shorts, or tank tops are permitted. Jackets are appreciated at dinner.

> Tis advertised in Boston, New York and Buffalo,
> Five hundred brave Americans a-whaling for to go,
> Singing "Blow, ye winds in the morning,
> Blow ye winds heigh-o,
> Heave away, haul away, and blow, winds, blow."

So goes the old chantey.

Whaling Museum

But where would these brave whalers ship out from, once they had answered the call? Most often they would go down to the sea at New Bedford or Nantucket; if they began their hard voyages on Long Island, most likely their home port would be Sag Harbor. But there were also smaller whaling ports on Long Island, such as Cold Spring Harbor. Here today the **Whaling Museum** celebrates the skills and adventures of the town's own whalers as well as those of other men who worked in this arduous industry from colonial times through the nineteenth century.

The Whaling Museum houses a large collection of the implements used in the whale "fishery," as it was known. Here are harpoons, lances, and the tools used in separating blubber from whale carcasses. A permanent exhibit, "Mark Well the Whale," details the history and impact of whaling on the locality. The museum features the state's only fully equipped nineteenth-century whaleboat with original gear; an extensive collection of the whaler's art of scrimshaw; and "The Wonder of Whales" conservation gallery for children.

The Whaling Museum, Box 25, Cold Spring Harbor 11724, (516) 367–3418, is open daily from Memorial Day through Labor Day; closed Monday during the rest of the year. Hours are 11:00 A.M. to 5:00 P.M. Admission is $2 for adults, $1.50 for senior citizens, $1 for children 6 and older, and free for children 5 and under.

Several decades before the whaling industry at Cold Spring Harbor hit its stride, there was born in the nearby town of Huntington a boy who would become a printer, newspaperman, schoolteacher, Civil War nurse, Washington bureaucrat, and one of the greatest poets America has produced. Walt Whitman (1819–92) first saw daylight in a Huntington farmhouse built about 1816, which is today preserved as the **Walt Whitman Birthplace.**

Although Whitman's ancestors had lived in the area around Huntington since the middle seventeenth century, the boy moved to Brooklyn with his family when he was only four years old. He came back after his apprenticeship as a journalist, though, and founded the *Long Islander,* a weekly newspaper that survives to this day. He also taught school in Huntington.

The house in which Walt Whitman was born is atypical (in interior architectural detail) of most farmhouses of the early nineteenth century, but it might have had little hope of surviving into the twenty-first had not one of its first inhabitants gone on to become the "Good Grey Poet." It has been completely restored and is now a New York State Historic Site, administered by the Walt Whitman Birthplace Association.

The Walt Whitman Birthplace, 246 Old Walt Whitman Road, Huntington Station 11746, (516) 427–5240, is open Wednesday through Friday, 1:00 to 4:00 P.M.; Saturday and Sunday, 10:00 A.M. to 4:00 P.M. Admission is free.

It was Whitman's contemporary Henry Wadsworth Longfellow who wrote, "Under the spreading chestnut tree / The village smithy stands." Just a short hop east of Huntington, in Northport, stands an institution that either Whitman or Longfellow would easily recognize—a blacksmith shop. The **Village Blacksmith** is a family enterprise, launched in 1977 by Bernard and Ann Reichert and their sons, James and William. Not many families start up blacksmith shops anymore, but the Reicherts did it up right. They purchased an 1830 farmhouse that had served as a gas station, installed a forge, and set up shop selling handcrafted ironware made on the premises as well as items such as cast-iron and pewter reproductions. The output of the Reichert forge includes fireplace tools, trivets, chandeliers, sconces, hooks—just about every sort of useful wrought ironware, some of it commissioned by the smithy's clientele as custom work.

The Village Blacksmith, 141 Main Street, Northport 11768, (516) 757–3620, is open Monday through Saturday from 10:00 A.M. to 5:30 P.M.; Sunday, 11:00 A.M. to 5:00 P.M.

Don't miss a visit to the National Landmark **St. James General Store,** 516 Moriches Road, St. James, (516) 862–8333. In business since 1857, it's the oldest operating general store in the country and looks just as it did in 1890. More than four thousand nineteenth-century-style items, including handmade quilts, salt glaze pottery, hand-carved decoys, penny candy, exotic teas, and bonnets, fill the store's venerable shelves. The store is open daily from 10:00 A.M. to 6:00 P.M.

The village of ◆**Stony Brook,** on Long Island Sound, has it all: a scenic location, a fascinating history, great food and lodgings, museums, and terrific shopping. And it owes its present-day success primarily to one man, Ward Melville, whose vision helped the rural village to successfully metamorphose into a suburban center while still retaining its historic integrity. His plan, unveiled to the community in 1939, called for relocating businesses and homes so as to open the view to the harbor. The shops were moved to a "shopping center" at the head of the village green, and today more than forty of the trendiest shops on Long Island are housed at the **Stony Brook Village Center.** Up the road, the **Three Village Garden Club Exchange** features two floors of antiques and collectibles.

Stony Brook's **Three Village Inn,** built in 1751, was until 1867 the home of Captain Jonas Smith, Long Island's first millionaire/sea captain. Today it's a charming inn and restaurant, featuring homemade breads and deserts and house specialties such as cold plum soup, pan-roasted chicken breast stuffed with ham and Monterey Jack cheese, baked lobster pie, and, every

Sunday, a "Thanksgiving" turkey dinner with all the trimmings. To make a room or meal reservation (lunch, dinner, and Sunday brunch), call (516) 751–0555.

Within walking distance of the inn, on Route 25A, is Stony Brook's museum complex housing the **Margaret Melville Blackwell History Museum,** featuring American decor in miniature in a gallery of fifteen period rooms and one of the country's finest collections of antique decoys; the **Dorothy and Ward Melville Carriage House,** with its collection of eighty horse-drawn carriages; and the **Art Museum,** exhibiting American art from the eighteenth century to the present, as well as collected works of genre painter William Sidney Mount (1807–1868). There are also a **1794 barn,** an **1867 carriage shed,** an **1875 blacksmith shop,** and an **1877 one-room schoolhouse.** The museums are open year-round, Wednesday through Saturday, Monday, and holidays, 10 A.M. to 5:00 P.M.; and Sunday, noon to 5:00 P.M. Closed Thanksgiving, December 24 and 25, and New Year's Day. Admission is $6 for adults; $4 for seniors and students; $3 for children ages 6–12. There's also a family rate of $15 for a group for four with a maximum of two adults. For information call (516) 751–0066.

A "must see" before leaving town is the working **Gristmill** on Harbor Road, built circa 1751 and renovated through the efforts of Mr. Melville in 1947. It's open Wednesday through Friday, 11:00 A.M. to 4:30 P.M., and Saturday and Sunday, noon to 4:30 P.M. Admission is $1 for adults; children under 12, 50 cents. For information, call (516) 751–2244.

Like Planting Fields in Oyster Bay, the south shore's ◆**Bayard Cutting Arboretum** is another rich man's estate that has become a mecca for those who enjoy majestic trees and beautiful gardens. The arboretum, which is virtually adjacent to the state-managed Connetquot River Park, was once the property of one of New York City's ablest financial operators. William Bayard Cutting (1850–1912) was a lawyer, railroad director and president, banker, insurance executive, and philanthropist, noted for having built the first block of Manhattan tenements to feature indoor plumbing.

In his leisure time (whenever that might have been), Cutting enjoyed himself by improving his Long Island retreat. He built the sixty-eight-room Tudor mansion that stands on the arboretum grounds in 1886, with a few decorative touches by his friend

Louis Comfort Tiffany. (Visitors can enter the mansion, the former breakfast room of which houses a well-maintained collection of mounted birds.) When it came to landscaping, Cutting placed a good deal of trust in another friend, the great Harvard botanist and silviculturist Charles Sprague Sargent. Together with none other than Frederick Law Olmstead, Sargent was responsible for much of the appearance of the Cutting estate and, subsequently, the arboretum.

The Bayard Cutting Arboretum is an especially pleasant place for a quiet stroll, even for those not well versed in tree species. Azaleas and rhododendrons grow here in profusion. The streams and pond, with their ducks and geese and graceful little footbridges, are reason enough to spend an afternoon at the Cutting.

The Bayard Cutting Arboretum, Route 27A, Oakdale 11769, (516) 581–1002, is open Wednesday through Sunday, 10:00 A.M. to 5:00 P.M. (4:00 P.M. when Eastern Standard Time is in effect). Admission is $3 per car; free from November through March.

One of Long Island's best off-the-beaten path tourist attractions is free—wild deer watching at **Heckscher State Park** in East Islip. Every day at 3 P.M. between Thanksgiving and Easter the park rangers dump pails of feed on the grass alongside Parking Field 1 for the deer in the 1,657-acre park. You can sit quietly in your car and watch as they come out for dinner.

Within a few miles of the Bayard Cutting Arboretum, on the Great South Bay that divides the barrier beach of Fire Island from the Long Island mainland, is the village of West Sayville, with its **Long Island Maritime Museum.** The whalers of Cold Spring Harbor were by no means the only brave Long Islanders to go down to the sea in ships to pursue their quarry; here in West Sayville, men went out into dangerous waters to harvest the more prosaic but nonetheless important oyster. The maritime museum, in fact, includes a vintage 1907 restored oyster house and has among its holdings the largest collection of small craft on Long Island. There is also a restored boat-builder's shop, illustrative of the skill and care that went into the buildings of these essential commercial vessels. Other exhibits concentrate upon the tools of oystermen over the years.

It isn't all oysters at the Long Island Maritime Museum. Displays of yachting and racing memorabilia, model boats, and artifacts related to the lifesaving service of the nineteenth century round out the museum's collection. Duck and other shorebird decoys, an integral part of American folk art in shoreline communities well into this century, are also on exhibit. The Bayman's Cottage depict the style of living at the turn of the century.

Long Island Maritime Museum, Route 27A, West Sayville 11796, (516) 854–4974, is open Wednesday through Saturday, 10:00 A.M. to 3:00 P.M.; Sunday, noon to 4:00 P.M. Admission is free, but donations are appreciated.

If you're looking for peace and quiet, beautiful beaches, or simply a taste of island life, take a short ferry ride to ◆ **Shelter Island,** cradled between the North and South forks of Long Island. The car ferries leave from Greenport on the North Fork and North Haven on the South Shore. The Nature Conservancy owns nearly one-third of the 8,000-acre island, assuring that this portion, at least, will remain unspoiled. There are four trails on the Conservancy's **Mashomack Preserve** for nature study and bird-watching, varying in length from 1.5 miles to 11 miles, and a barrier-free Braille trail for the visually impaired. In the village, you can rent bicycles at **Piccozzi's Bike Shop** (516–749–0045), sip a frozen drink on the waterfront patio at **Alfred's Place, Ltd.** (516–749–3355), grab a bite at **The Cook Restaurant** (516–749–2005), have a lovely meal at the Victorian **Chequit Inn** (516–749–0018), or stop in at one of the other restaurants. By now you'll have fallen in love with the island and vowed never to leave. There are plenty of places to put up. The Chequit Inn also has guest rooms, as do a number of other places, including the **Beech Tree House** (516–749–4252), which has suites with full kitchens, and **Shelter Island Resort,** overlooking Shelter Island Sound (516–749–2001). For more information contact the Shelter Island Chamber of Commerce, Box 598, Shelter Island 11964, (516) 749–0399.

INDEX